My Father's Glory
and
My Mother's Castle

MEMORIES OF CHILDHOOD

by Marcel Pagnol

Translated by Rita Barisse

With a Foreword by Alice Waters

NORTH POINT PRESS
San Francisco

Library of Congress
Catalogue Card Number: 86-60989
ISBN: 0-86547-257-2
THIRD PRINTING
Cover illustration: Wolfgang Lederer
Cover design: David Bullen

TO THE MEMORY OF
THOSE I LOVED

M. P.

FOREWORD

FIFTEEN years ago, when I was making plans to open a café and restaurant in Berkeley, my friend Tom Luddy took me to see a Marcel Pagnol retrospective at the old Surf Theater in San Francisco. We went every night and saw about half the movies Pagnol made during his long career: *The Baker's Wife* and *Harvest*, taken from novels by Jean Giono, and Pagnol's own Marseille trilogy—*Marius*, *Fanny*, and *César*. Every one of these movies about life in the south of France fifty years ago radiated wit, love for people, and respect for the earth. Every movie made me cry.

My partners and I decided to name our new restaurant after the widower Panisse, a compassionate, placid, and slightly ridiculous marine outfitter in the Marseille trilogy, so as to evoke the sunny good feelings of another world that contained so much that was incomplete or missing in our own—the simple wholesome good food of Provence, the atmosphere of tolerant camaraderie and great lifelong friendships, and a respect for both the old folks and their pleasures and for the young and their passions. Four years later, when our partnership incorporated itself, we immodestly took the name Pagnol et Cie., Inc., to reaffirm our desire of re-creating an ideal reality where life and work were inseparable and the daily pace left you time for the afternoon anisette or the restorative game of pétanque, and where eating together nourished the spirit as well as the body—since the food was raised, harvested, hunted, fished, and gathered by people sustaining and sustained by each other and by the earth itself.

Pagnol lived the life of his movies and books. The book you

are holding contains two volumes of his memoirs about his earliest years. More than just the reminiscences of a happy childhood, these pages resonate with the inspirational qualities of all Pagnol's work: good humor, love of nature, sensuality, and strong feeling for family and tradition.

Here is a little recipe inspired by these first memoirs:

Grilled Quail with Wild Herbs and Olive Toasts

Marinate the quail with olive oil, a little sweet wine from Provence, fresh thyme, rosemary, and sage for several hours. Salt and pepper the quail. Grill them over fairly hot wood embers about 4–5 minutes on the skin side, until nicely browned. Turn over and cook a few more minutes. While they sit, toast thin slices of bread over the coals and spread them with a paste of olives crushed with garlic and made smooth with olive oil. Serve with a salad of bitter greens and a bottle of Bandol.

Alice Waters

PREFACE

THIS is the first time—not counting a few modest essays—that I write in prose.

For, to my mind, there are three very different kinds of literary expression: poetry, which is sung: plays, which are spoken; and prose, which is written.

What frightens me is not so much the choice of words or turns of phrases nor the grammatical subtleties—these are within everybody's reach, after all—but rather the novelist's position, and the even more risky one of the writer of memoirs.

★

The language of the stage is heard as sounds coming from an actor's lips: it must seem improvised, and each line must be immediately understood, for once uttered it is gone. On the other hand, it cannot be a model of literary style, for it is not the language of a writer, but of a stage character.

★

The dramatist's style lies in his choice of characters, in the feelings he gives them, in the development of the plot. His personal position is a modest one: he must hold his tongue! As soon as he wants to make his own voice heard, the dramatic movement stops. He mustn't leave his place in the wings; his opinions, when expressed by himself, are of no concern to us. His actors speak to us for him, and they impose his thoughts and emotions on us by making us believe they are ours.

★

The writer's position is no doubt more difficult.

It is no longer Raimu, the famous actor, speaking, but I myself. I shall expose myself entirely just by the way I write, and if I am not sincere—that is to say, without any shame—I shall have wasted my time and spoilt good paper.

So I must walk out of the wings and sit down in front of the reader, who will gaze at me fixedly for two or three hours. This is a most upsetting thought, and one that paralysed me for a long time.

However, I have considered the other side of the problem.

The theatre-goer wears collar and tie and the anonymous suit that the English have foisted on us.

He is not at home; he has even paid quite a lot to come and hear me. Moreover, he is not alone, but observes his neighbours who, in turn, observe him. That's why he is interested not only in the parts played by my actors, but also in his own role: for he himself acts the character of an intelligent and distinguished playgoer.

He always shows his feelings: he often laughs, or applauds, and the author in the wings is filled with pleasure. But at other times he coughs, blows his nose, mutters, boos, walks out. The author no longer dares look anyone in the face, he listens appalled to the invariably ingenious explanations thought up by his friends: no late supper at a night-club for him tonight!

The reader—I mean the genuine reader—is almost always his friend.

He has chosen the book, has carried it away under his arm, has invited it into his home.

He reads it all alone, and won't stand anyone else reading over his shoulder. He is probably in his dressing-gown or in pyjamas, a pipe in his hand: his good faith is complete.

This does not mean that he will like the book. He may perhaps shrug his shoulders on reaching page 30, and grumble bad-temperedly: 'I wonder why people bother to print such rubbish!'

But the author won't be there, he'll never know it. And if his book fails to sell, his publisher and accomplice will sometimes camouflage the catastrophe by printing '15th thousand' on the jackets of the third and ultimate thousand.

Thus, while the great success of a book has as much merit as that of a play, the prose-writer's 'flop' is not so cruel.

These are the—not very honourable, but reassuring—considerations that have persuaded me to publish this book. It has few pretensions, anyhow. It is merely a testimony of a bygone age and a little song of filial piety which in our day, perhaps, may pass for a great novelty.

MARCEL PAGNOL.

PART ONE

My Father's Glory

CHAPTER ONE

I WAS born in the town of Aubagne, beneath the goat-crowned Garlaban, in the days of the last goat-herds.

Garlaban is a huge tower of blue rock, standing on the edge of the *Plan de l'Aigle*, the Eagle Plateau, an immense, rocky table-land which dominates the green valley of the Huveaune.

The tower is slightly broader than it is tall; but as it rises from the rock at some two thousand feet, it rears up high into the sky of Provence and, at times, a white July cloud comes and rests on it for a moment.

Thus it is not a mountain, but it is more than a hill: it is Garlaban, where Marius's look-out men, on seeing in the dead of night a glow of fire on Sainte-Victoire, lit a bonfire of brushwood: the red bird, flitting from hill to hill through the June night, alighted at last on the rock of the Capitol, bringing Rome the news that her legions in Gaul had slaughtered Teutobocchus' hundred thousand barbarians in the plain of Aix.

*

My father was the fifth child of a stone-cutter of Valréas, near Orange.

The family had been settled there for several centuries. Where did they come from? From Spain no doubt, for I found in the records at the town hall names like Lespagnol and, later, Spagnol.

What's more, they were armourers from father to son, tempering swords in the waters of the Ouvèze—which is, as everyone knows, a nobly Spanish pursuit.

However, as the need for courage has always been in an inverse

15

ratio to the distance that separates the combatants, blunderbusses and pistols soon replaced bilboes and rapiers; that was the time when my forefathers became artificers, that is to say, they manufactured gunpowder, cartridges and rockets.

One of them, a great-grand-uncle of mine, one day was blown out of his shop through a closed window, in a glory of showering sparks, surrounded by Catherine wheels, and riding on a sheaf of Roman candles.

He did not die of it, but his beard never grew again on his left cheek. That is why, to the end of his days, he was called '*Lou Rousti*', which means 'The Roasted One'.

It may have been on account of this spectacular accident that the succeeding generation—without giving up either cartridges or rockets—decided not to fill them with gunpowder any more, and they became cardboard makers, which is what they still are today.

Now this is a fine example of Latin wisdom: they first eschewed steel—a heavy, hard, cutting substance; then gunpowder which is the enemy of cigarettes; and they devoted their labours to cardboard—a light, compliant commodity, soft to the touch and, at any rate, non-explosive.

My grandfather, however, not being the eldest son, did not inherit the cardboard factory, and he became—I don't know why—a stone-cutter. So he journeyed round France, as craftsmen did, and eventually set up business at Valréas, and later at Marseilles.

He was small, but broad-shouldered and sturdy.

When I knew him, he wore long white locks which reached down to his collar, and a fine curly beard.

He had delicate but clean-cut features, and his black eyes glowed like ripe olives.

His authority over his children had been awe-inspiring, his decisions beyond appeal. But his grandchildren could twist his beard into plaits and push beans into the hollows of his ears.

At times, he would gravely talk to me about his craft, or rather his art, for he was a master bondman.

He held stone-masons in low esteem: 'The walls *we* put up', he'd say, 'are of bonded stones, that is stones that are neatly fitted by means of tenons and mortices, joggles, dove-tails, scarf-joints. . . . Of course, we'd also run lead into the grooves to prevent the stones slipping. But that was sunk inside the two blocks and didn't show! Whereas the masons take the stones as they come and just bung up the holes with mortar. . . . A smotherer of stones, that's what a mason is—he hides them because he doesn't know how to cut 'em.'

Whenever he had a day of leisure—that is, five or six times a year—he would take the whole family on a picnic some fifty yards from the Pont du Gard—the famous bridge over the river Gard.

While my grandmother was getting the meal ready and the children were splashing about in the river, he would climb onto the double platforms of this monument, take measurements, examine the joints, make surveys of cross-sections, fondle the stones.

After lunch, he would sit down in the grass in front of the family seated in a semi-circle, facing that ancient Roman master-piece, and gaze at it till nightfall.

And that's the reason why, thirty years after, his sons and daughters, at the mere mention of the Pont du Gard, would raise their eyes to heaven and utter long groans.

I have a precious paperweight on my writing-table. It is an oblong, iron cube, with an oval hole cut in its centre. On each of its extremities, the battered metal is almost funnelled out. This is grandfather André's hammer which, for fifty years, kept hitting the hard heads of steel chisels.

*

This skilful man had received only the most rudimentary schooling. He could read and sign his name, but nothing more. This mortified him all his life, and he eventually came to believe that learning was the Sovereign Good and imagined that the most learned people of all were those who taught others. He therefore bled himself white to establish his six children in the teaching profession, and so it came about that my father, at the age of twenty, graduated from the teachers' training college at Aix-en-Provence and became a public schoolmaster.

CHAPTER TWO

THE primary Normal Schools—teachers' training colleges
—in those days used to be real seminaries, where the study
of theology, however, was replaced by classes in anti-
clericalism.

The students were taught that the Church had never been anything but an instrument of oppression, and that it was the priest's
task and purpose in life to blindfold the people with the black
bandage of ignorance, while lulling them with fables of hell and
paradise.

The artfulness of the *curés* was proved, moreover, by their use
of Latin, a mysterious tongue which had the insidious power of
magic formulae in the eyes of the benighted faithful.

The Papacy was worthily represented by the two Borgias, and
the kings got off no better than the popes: those lewd tyrants
busied themselves exclusively with their paramours, when they
were not having a game of cup-and-ball; and in the meantime
their minions would collect crushing taxes that came to as much as
TEN percent of the national income.

This means that the history lessons had been smartly doctored in
favour of Republican truth.

I am not holding it against the Republic: no history text-book
in the world has ever been anything but a propaganda pamphlet
in the service of governments.

The newly-fledged Normal School graduates were thus convinced that the Great Revolution had been an idyllic period, the
Golden Age of generosity, and of fraternity carried to the point
of tenderness—in short, an explosion of loving-kindness.

I don't know how it was explained to them—without attracting their attention—that those secular angels, after committing some twenty thousand murders followed by thefts, had guillotined each other out of existence.

On the other hand, it is true that my village *curé*, who was most intelligent and a man of dauntless charity, considered the Holy Inquisition as a kind of Family Council: he said that if the prelates had burnt so many Jews and scientists, they had done so with tears in their eyes and only in order to assure them of a place in Paradise.

Such is the weakness of our reasoning faculty: more often than not, it only serves to justify our beliefs.

*

The curriculum of the Normal School students was not, however, confined to anti-clericalism and laicized history. There was a third enemy of the people, and one which was not at all a thing of the past: and that was Alcohol.

Zola's *The Dram-Shop* dates from that period, as do the frightful pictures that used to cover the schoolroom walls. They showed rusty-red livers so utterly unrecognizable (because of their green swellings and violet constrictions, which gave them the shape of Jerusalem artichokes) that the artist had to paint, beside them, the appetizing liver of a good citizen: its harmonious bulk and wholesome red colour enabled the spectator to appreciate the seriousness of the neighbouring catastrophe. The Normal School students, pursued as they were right into their dormitories by this appalling organ (not to mention a pancreas shaped like an Archimedean screw, and a hernia-sporting aorta), were thus driven gradually into a state of terror. At the sight of a glass of wine, they'd purse their lips with disgust. The café terraces at the pre-prandial hour of the *apéritif* seemed to them a kind of suicides' graveyard. A friend of my father's, drunk on filtered water, one day knocked over the café tables, like the lay Polyeuctus he was. But what they loathed most fiercely were the 'digestive' liqueurs —Bénédictines and Chartreuses—concocted 'by Royal Privilege', which combined, in one baneful Trinity, the Church, Alcohol and Royalty.

Apart from the fight against these three scourges, their programme of studies was extremely wide and admirably conceived to turn them into teachers of the common people whom they understood so well, for almost all of them were the sons of peasants or workers.

They were given an all round education in general knowledge, more broad than deep no doubt, but which was quite a novelty; and as they had always seen their fathers work twelve hours a day—in the field, the fishing-boat or on the scaffolding—they congratulated themselves on their happy lot, because they could go out on Sundays and, three times a year, had holidays which they could spend at home.

On those occasions, the fathers and grandfathers, and sometimes even the neighbours—who had never studied except with their hands—would come and put questions to them, submit small abstract problems, the key to which nobody in the village had ever found. They would answer, the elders would listen, gravely nodding their heads. . . . And that's why, for three solid years, they lapped up knowledge like a precious nourishment of which their forebears had been deprived; that's why, during breaks between lessons, the Director would make the rounds of the classrooms to drive out some over-zealous students and condemn them to playing games.

At the end of the training course, they had to sit for the Higher Certificate, the results of which proved that the class had come to maturity.

Then, by a sort of dehiscence, the good seeds would be squirted to the four corners of the *département*, to battle against ignorance, glorify the Republic, and keep their hats on when religious processions passed.

After several years of this lay apostleship in the snows of forgotten hamlets, the young schoolmaster would slide halfway down the mountainside to the villages where he'd marry, *en passant*, a local school-teacher or postmistress. He'd stop at several such villages, with their still sloping streets, and each stop was punctuated by the birth of a child. By the time the third or fourth was born, he had reached the sub-prefecture down in the plain, after which he would at last effect his entrance into the county capital, with his skin by now loosely sagging under a halo of grey hair. Here he would take charge of a school of eight or ten classes and himself teach the upper forms, sometimes even a Senior Class.

The day would come when a solemn ceremony celebrated his being awarded the *palmes académiques**. Another three years, and he could retire, i.e. the regulations pensioned him off by force. He would smile happily and say: 'At last I'll be able to grow my own cabbages!'

Whereupon he would lie down, and die.

I have known a great many of these schoolmasters of the old days.

They had utter faith in the beauty of their mission, a radiant confidence in the future of the human race. They despised money and luxury, refused a chance of promotion so that someone else might benefit, or else to carry through a task they had set themselves in some God-forsaken hole.

A very old friend of my father's, who had graduated from training college at the top of his class, was able because of this feat to start his career in a district of Marseilles: a squalid slum peopled with down-and-outs, where no outsider dared to set foot after dark. He stayed there from the day he began until his retirement, forty years in the same class-room, forty years in the same chair.

My father asked him one night:

'Haven't you ever had any ambitions?'

and he replied:

'Why, yes! Of course I have! And I do think I've succeeded nicely. Just imagine, my predecessor, in the course of twenty

* Insignia of a distinction granted by the French Ministry of Education.

years, saw ten of his pupils guillotined, whereas I, in forty, have only had two—and another who had a last-minute reprieve. Oh yes, it was well worth while staying on.'

★

For the remarkable thing was that these rabid anti-clericals had the souls of missionaries. To frustrate *Monsieur le Curé* (whose virtue was supposed to be a sham) they themselves lived like saints, and their morals were as inflexible as those of the early Puritans. The School Inspector was their bishop, the *Recteur d'Académie* their archbishop, and their pope was the Minister: to him you wrote only on special notepaper, and in ritual formulas.

'Like the parsons,' my father used to say, 'we work for the life to come. Only our concern is with other people's—down here.'

CHAPTER THREE

BECAUSE my father, too, did very well in his finals, he was not 'exiled' too far away from Marseilles, and he landed at Aubagne.

This was a town of ten thousand inhabitants, perched on the hills of the Huveaune valley, and through it passed the dusty road that led from Marseilles to Toulon.

Here people baked tiles, bricks and earthenware jugs, stuffed black-puddings and chitterlings, and tanned hides which, after seven years in the bark-pit, never wore out. They also manufactured colourful '*santons*', which are small clay figures for Nativity crib scenes.

My father, whose first name was Joseph, was a swarthy young man in those days, of less than medium height, though not exactly small. He had a biggish nose, but it was perfectly straight and advantageously shortened by his moustache and his spectacles, which had oval lenses set in narrow steel rims. His voice was deep and pleasant, and his blue-black hair fell into natural waves on rainy days.

One day he met a little, dark-haired seamstress, called Augustine, and he found her so pretty he promptly married her.

I never knew how they had met: it wasn't the sort of thing one talked about at home. Nor did it ever occur to me to question them on the subject, for their youth and childhood were beyond my imaginings. My father's age was twenty-five years more than mine, and nothing could ever alter that.

They were my father and mother, from time immemorial and for evermore.

23

All I know is that Augustine was dazzled by the serious-looking young man who was so good at playing bowls and who invariably earned fifty-four francs a month.

So she gave up sewing for others and settled in a flat that was all the more pleasant for being rent-free.

In the months that preceded my birth, my mother, who was only nineteen—and she remained nineteen all her life—grew increasingly worried and declared with a sob that her baby would never be born because she 'felt she didn't know how to go about it'.

My father tried to reason with her. Whereupon she would say furiously: 'And when I think all this is *your* doing!'

And she would burst into tears.

When the intruder began to stir, she had attacks of giggles in between bouts of sobbing.

Frightened by such unreasonable conduct, my father called in his elder sister. It was she who had brought him up. She was—naturally—a headmistress, of a school at La Ciotat, and a spinster.

His sister was perfectly delighted and decided that my mother should be moved immediately to her home on the shores of the Mediterranean: which was done that very evening.

I have been told that Joseph was charmed by this idea, and that he turned his freedom to account by dallying with the baker's wife while straightening out her accounts. But this is an unpleasant suggestion, which I have never credited.

In the meantime, the expectant mother was strolling along the beach under the gentle January sun, watching the distant sails of the fishing-boats as they put out at three o'clock towards the setting sun. Then, seated near the hearth, where the logs of olive-wood burnt with a hissing blue flame, she would knit the layette for her kicking progeny while Aunt Marie hemmed the babies' napkins and sang in her clear and pretty voice:

> *Sur le brick léger que le flot balance*
> *Quand la nuit étend son grand voile noir . . .*

24

She was now feeling reassured, all the more so since her dear Joseph came down every Saturday on the baker's bike. He brought almond biscuits, frangipane tarts and a small bag of white flour for making pancakes or fritters.

She had become rosy-cheeked, and everything promised to go splendidly when, in the small hours of February 28, she was wakened by some pains.

She promptly called Aunt Marie who decreed that this meant nothing, since the doctor had announced the birth of a little girl for the end of March; she then lit the fire to brew herb-tea. But the patient declared that the doctors didn't understand anything and that she wanted to go back to Aubagne at once.

'The child must be born at home! Joseph must be there to hold my hand! Marie, Marie, do let's go quickly! I'm sure he wants to get out!'

The gentle Marie tried to soothe her with linden-tea and words. Strainer in hand, she promised that should Augustine's forecast prove correct, she would go and tell the fishmonger who left for Aubagne every morning at eight, so that Joseph could dash over on his pedal machine as fast as the wind.

But Augustine pushed the flowered cup away and wrung her hands, weeping big tears.

So Aunt Marie went and knocked at the shutters of a neighbour who owned a little horse and trap. People were neighbourly in those blessed days, and help was yours for the asking.

The man harnessed his horse, Aunt Marie wrapped Augustine up in shawls, and off we went at an easy trot, while on the crest of the hills the upper half of a big red sun was peering at us through the pine-trees.

But when we had got as far as Bédoule, which is just about half-way, the labour pains started again, and this time it was my Aunt's turn to get panicky. She hugged my muffled-up mother in her arms and gave her advice:

'Augustine,' she said, 'hold yourself in!' For she was a virgin.

But Augustine, very pale, opened wide a pair of big black goggling eyes, and sweated as she groaned.

Happily we had reached the pass, and the road was descending towards Aubagne. The neighbour released the brake (which was called the 'mechanism' in those days) and whipped the little horse, which merely had to let itself be pushed along by the weight of the carriage. We arrived in the nick of time, and Madame Négrel, the midwife, came in a hurry to deliver my mother, who could at last dig her nails into Joseph's powerful arm.

*

This is not a very surprising story; but wait a minute: it's going to be.

At the beginning of the 18th century, there lived at Aubagne a very rich and very ancient family of merchants, called Barthélémy. Their merits were so outstanding that the king eventually raised them to the nobility.

Now, in the night between January 19 and 20, in 1716, Madame Barthélémy, who was very young, who lived at Aubagne, and whose husband's name was Joseph, 'felt the first labour-pains'. She mounted 'precipitously' into a carriage in order to be with her mother in their family mansion, which was the finest house in Cassis.

Cassis was a small fishing-port, only a mile from La Ciotat, and for three-quarters of the journey the same road leads to Aubagne. Madame Barthélémy thus travelled through the same gorges, then over the Col de la Bédoule, groaning under her blankets. . . . She arrived at Cassis, 'swooning with pain, and while she was being put to bed she gave birth to a little boy'.

This child of Aubagne was to become the Abbé Barthélémy, the illustrious author of the '*Voyage du jeune Anacharsis en Grèce*'. He was elected to the *Académie Française* on March 5, 1789, to occupy the twenty-fifth chair: the very chair which it has been my honour to occupy since March 5, 1946.

One might draw a singular conclusion from this double anecdote: namely, that one of the means of entering some day into the Illustrious Company is to be the son of a Joseph and to try and start being born, on an early winter morning, in a doubly groaning shandrydan on the Bédoule road.

CHAPTER FOUR

M Y memories of Aubagne are few, because I lived there
for only three years.

The first sight I recall is a very lofty fountain, under
the plane-trees along the *Cours*, just in front of our house. This is
the monument which his countrymen erected in honour of our
Abbé Barthélémy. He was believed to have been a Radical, on
account of his *Voyage du jeune Anacharsis*: few people had read the
book, and many referred to it in perfectly good faith as 'The
Young Anarchist'. Naturally, I knew nothing of it at the time,
but I would listen enchanted to the little song of the fountain, as
it chirped in chorus with the sparrows.

The next thing I see is a ceiling falling towards me with dizzy
speed, while my horrified mother shouts: 'Henri! Stop being
stupid! Henri, I forbid you. . . .'

For Uncle Henri, my mother's brother, is flinging me into
the air and catching me in flight. I howl with terror, but when
my mother takes me back into her arms, I shout: 'Again!
Again!'

My uncle Henri was thirty, had a handsome brown beard, and
was a steam-engine mechanic. He worked at making steam-
engines in the *Ateliers des Forges et Chantiers*, as his father had done,
my maternal grandfather whom I never knew.

The latter was born at Coutances towards 1845, and his name
was Guillaume Lansot. A Norman of pure stock, he had reached
Marseilles in the course of his travels through France as a journey-
man. My Marseillaise grandmother took his fancy, and so he
stayed on.

He had three children by the time he was only twenty-four, and my mother was the baby of the family.

As he was skilled at his craft and the sea did not frighten him, he was sent out to Rio de Janeiro one day to repair a steamship whose engine had broken down. He arrived in that still uncivilized land without inoculations of any kind. He saw people dying of yellow fever, and, like a fool, he did the same. . . .

His children didn't have time to get to know him, and my grandmother, who had been married to him for only four years, could not tell us much, except that he was very tall, had sea-blue eyes, very white teeth, sandy almost ginger hair, and that, like a child, he would laugh at anything.

I have not even a photograph of him. Sometimes at night, in the country, sitting by the fireside, I conjure him up, but he does not come. I suppose he is still in the Americas. So as I gaze, all alone, at the dancing flames, I dream of my twenty-four-year-old grandfather, who died unspectacled, with all his teeth, under a thick golden mop of hair, and I marvel at being such an elderly grandson of that tall young man from Coutances.

Another memory of Aubagne is the bowling match under the planes on the *Cours*. My father, surrounded by other giants, would make enormous bounds and hurl a lump of iron unimaginable lengths. Sometimes there would be tremendous applause, then the giants would invariably begin to squabble over a piece of string which they tore from one another's hands, but they never came to blows.

CHAPTER FIVE

FROM Aubagne we moved to Saint-Loup, which was a fairly big village on the outskirts of Marseilles. Facing the school was the municipal slaughter-house: just a kind of shed where two enormous butchers operated in full view.

While my mother was attending to her small household, I would climb onto a chair in front of the dining-room window, and watch the murder of the pigs and oxen with the liveliest interest. I believe man is cruel by nature: children and savages prove it every day.

When the unfortunate ox was struck between his horns by the pole-axe and slumped to his knees, I simply admired the butcher's strength and man's victory over the beast. The slaughter of the pigs would make me laugh till I cried, because they were pulled by the ears and uttered strident squeals. But the most interesting spectacle was the murder of a sheep.

The butcher would elegantly slit its throat while he continued to chat with his assistant, without paying the least attention to what he was doing. When he had slaughtered three or four, he would place the corpses, legs up, on a sort of cradle. Then, with a pair of bellows, he would blow them up most prodigiously, in order to detach the skin from the flesh. I thought he was trying to turn them into balloons and hoped to see them fly away. But my mother, who always turned up at the most exciting moment, made me come down from my observatory, and while cutting up chunks of meat for the family *pot-au-feu*, she would hold forth, quite incomprehensibly, on the gentleness of the poor ox, the sweet nature of the curly little sheep, and the butcher's villainy.

When she went out shopping, she would deposit me in my father's class-room, where he was teaching youngsters of six or seven to read. I would sit in the front row, on my best behaviour, and admire the paternal omnipotence. In his hand was a bamboo cane: he used it to point out the letters and words he had written on the blackboard and, sometimes, to tap the fingers of a day-dreaming dunce.

One morning, my mother left me in my usual place and went out without a word, while he wrote on the blackboard in big beautiful letters: 'The mother punished her little boy who had been naughty.'

As he was rounding off an admirable full-stop, I shouted: 'No! It isn't true!'

My father spun round, stared at me in amazement and cried: 'What did you say?'

'Mama didn't punish me! You didn't write down the truth!'

He came up to me;

'Who said anything about your being punished?'

'It's written there.'

Surprise left him speechless for a moment.

'Well! Well!' he said at last. 'Can you read?'

'Yes.'

'Well! Well! . . .' he said again.

He pointed the tip of his bamboo stick at the blackboard.

'All right, read.'

I read the sentence out aloud.

He then picked up a primer and I read out several pages, without any difficulty. . . .

I believe he experienced that day one of the happiest and proudest moments of his life.

When my mother came to fetch me, she found me surrounded by four school-teachers: they had sent their own pupils out into the yard and were listening to me slowly spelling out the tale of Tom Thumb. . . . But instead of admiring my exploit, she grew pale, dropped her parcels, snapped the book shut and carried me off in her arms, muttering: 'Oh Lord! Oh Lord! . . .'

At the door, the caretaker, an old Corsican woman, was crossing herself. I learnt later that it was she who had gone to fetch my mother, assuring her that 'those gentlemen' were 'bursting my brain'.

At dinner, my father affirmed that these were just ridiculous superstitions: I had not exerted myself in any way, I had learnt to read as a parrot learns to talk, and he had not even been aware of it. My mother was not convinced, and from time to time she would place her cool hand on my brow and ask: 'You haven't got a headache?'

No, I had no headache, but until the age of six, I was no longer allowed to enter a classroom or open a book, for fear of a cerebral explosion. She was only reassured two years later, when, at the end of my first term, my school-mistress told her that I was gifted with an astonishing memory but that my mental maturity was that of a babe in arms.

CHAPTER SIX

FROM Saint-Loup my father shot ahead like a comet, for he skipped the suburbs in one bound and was appointed straight away—to his great surprise—as a regular teacher at the school in the Chemin des Chartreux, the biggest elementary school in Marseilles.

The school was run by a non-teaching head who ranked as a sort of supervisor. He could visit the *Inspecteur d'Académie** without being summoned, he sat on the board of examiners for the lower certificate and, sometimes, even for the higher one!

The caretaker moreover had told my delighted father in front of me that the twelve school-teachers of the Chemin des Chartreux were 'the élite of the profession' and that, after four or five years there, those who wished could immediately get a headmaster's post, often right in Marseilles.

This authoritative statement by the Chartreux school caretaker was often quoted in the family, and my mother—basking in this reflected glory—repeated it to Mme Mercier and Mlle Guimard, though she took pains to add that perhaps the caretaker was exaggerating: but she didn't look as if she really thought so for a moment.

She was still pale and delicate, but happy with her Joseph, her two boys, and her brand-new sewing machine.

This marvellous modern invention enabled me to help her with her work. Kneeling against her skirt under the small table, I would rock the big treadle with my hands, stopping dead at the word of command.

* Departmental inspector of secondary schools.

My brother Paul was a little fellow of three, white-skinned, round-cheeked, with large eyes of a very pale blue, and the golden curls of the grandfather we never knew. He was a thoughtful child, who never cried but played alone under a table, with a cork or a hair-curler. His greed, however, was astounding and, now and then, a lightning drama would flare up: he would suddenly be seen stumbling forward, with outflung arms and purple face: he was on the verge of choking to death.

My frantic mother would pat his back, push her finger down his throat, and hold him up by his heels and shake him, as Achilles' mother did.

Then, with a terrible death rattle, he'd expel a big black olive, a peach-stone, or a long strip of bacon-rind.

After which he would resume his lonely games, squatting on his haunches like a fat frog.

Joseph had become magnificent. He had a new navy blue suit, worthy of the Chartreux school. His spectacles, once steel-rimmed, now gleamed in a golden frame, and their lenses had become round. Finally, he wore an artist's tie, a black corded ribbon with two dangling ends. But this conceit was justified by the fact that he had gone into partnership with his colleague Arnaud to reproduce wall-maps, on their free Thursdays and Sunday mornings, for which the publisher, Vidal-Lablache, paid up to one hundred francs apiece. In the family budget, Vidal-Lablache figured at twenty-five francs per month, and this double-barrelled name was doubly blessed.

CHAPTER SEVEN

I WAS now almost six, and attending Mlle Guimard's kindergarten at school.

Mlle Guimard was very tall, she had a pretty little brown moustache, and when she spoke, her nose wriggled. Yet I thought her ugly because she was as yellow as a lemon, and had big protruding eyes.

She patiently taught my little classmates their ABC but paid no attention to me, because I could read fluently already: this she considered a deliberate discourtesy on my father's part. To get her own back, during singing lessons she would say in front of the whole class that I was singing out of tune and that I had better keep silent, which I gladly did.

So while all the youngsters were shouting themselves hoarse as they followed her baton, I remained dumb, peaceful and smiling. With closed eyes, I was telling myself stories and wandering along the pond in Borély Park, which is a lovely park at the far end of the Prado in Marseilles.

On Thursdays and Sundays, Aunt Rose, who was my mother's elder sister and just as pretty, came to lunch with us, and afterwards she took me by tram to that enchanted place.

There one could find avenues shaded by age-old plane-trees, wild shrubberies, lawns that invited you to roll in the grass, park keepers who forbade you to do so, and ponds with whole fleets of ducks.

One also found there, in those days, a certain number of people learning to master bicycles. With fixed gaze and clenched jaws, they would suddenly bolt away from their teacher, shoot across the avenue, vanish into a thicket, and reappear with their machines round their necks. The sight was not uninteresting, and made me roar with laughter. But my aunt never left me for long in this danger zone; she would drag me, with my head screwed back to front, towards some quiet corner by the pond.

We would sit down on a bench, always the same one, with its back to a clump of laurel-bushes between two plane-trees. She would extract some knitting from her bag and I would tackle the chores of childhood.

My principal occupation was to feed bread to the ducks. Those silly birds knew me well. As soon as I showed them a crust of bread, the flotilla would come strenuously paddling towards me, and my distribution would start.

When my aunt was not looking, and while still cooing honeyed words at them, I would also pelt them with pebbles, firmly determined to make a kill. This hope, though always disappointed, was the main charm of these outings, and I would tremble with hopeful anticipation as I sat in the creaking Prado tram.

But one fine Sunday, I was unpleasantly surprised to find a gentleman sitting on Our Bench. His face was old rose in colour, he had a thick brown moustache, bushy, russet-brown eyebrows, and his large blue eyes were slightly bulging; a few silver threads showed at his temples. As, moreover, he was reading a newspaper, I promptly classed him among the old people.

My aunt tried to tug me away to some other resting-place, but I protested: this was *our* bench, and it was up to the gentleman to go away.

He was tactful and polite. Without a word, he slid to the end of the bench, pulling towards him his bowler-hat; on it lay a pair of leather gloves, an incontrovertible sign of wealth and breeding.

My aunt settled down at the other end, took out her knitting, and I ran to the edge of the pond with my little bag of crusts.

35

I first selected a very nice pebble, as big as a five franc piece, rather flat and wonderfully sharp. Unfortunately, a park-keeper was looking: so I hid it in my pocket and started to dole out the crumbs with such sweet and friendly words that I was soon facing a whole squadron drawn up in a semi-circle.

The keeper—a blasé fellow—did not seem to take much interest in this scene. He simply turned his back and walked away with measured strides. I immediately grasped my pebble and had the—rather alarming—joy of hitting the old father drake right on the head. But instead of capsizing and sinking on the spot, as I had fondly hoped, the tough old bird simply tacked about and fled, head over webbed heels, loudly screeching with indignation. Ten yards from the bank he stopped and turned towards me again; upright in the water and beating his wings, he hurled at me all the insults he knew, supported by the heart-rending squawks of his whole family.

The park-keeper was not very far away, and I raced to my aunt for protection.

She had seen nothing, heard nothing, she was not knitting: she was in conversation with the gentleman on the bench.

'Oh, what a charming little boy!' he said. 'How old are you?'

'Six.'

'Why, he looks seven!' the gentleman said. Then he complimented me on looking so well and declared I had really beautiful eyes.

My aunt hastened to say that I was not her son, but her sister's, and added that she was unmarried. Whereupon the friendly old codger gave me two *sous* to buy myself some *'oublies'* from the man who sold sweets at the bottom of the avenue.

I was left much freer than usual. I used my freedom to go to watch the cyclists. Standing on a bench—out of prudence—I was the interested spectator of some inexplicable downfalls.

The most frankly comical disaster befell an old fogey of at least forty: with the most amusing grimaces, he wrenched the handlebars off the machine and suddenly toppled over sideways, still frantically clutching the rubber grips. He was helped up,

36

covered with dust, his trousers torn at the knees, and quite as indignant as the old drake. I was hoping for a grown-up fight, when my aunt and the gentleman from the bench arrived and pulled me away from the vociferous group, for it was time to go home.

The gentleman boarded the tram with us, he even paid our fares, despite the vehement protests of my aunt who, to my great surprise, blushed crimson. Only much later did I understand that she had thought herself a proper courtesan, because a strange gentleman had paid three *sous* for us.

We left him at the terminus, and he waved his bowler-hat at us most cordially.

When we reached our door-step, my aunt warned me, in a whisper, never to mention this encounter to anyone. She informed me that the gentleman was the owner of Borély Park and that, if we so much as mentioned his name, he would certainly hear of it and then forbid us to go there again. When I asked her why, she said it was a 'secret'. I was delighted to know, if not a secret, at least the existence of one. I promised, and I kept my word.

Our walks in the park became more and more frequent, and the amiable 'owner' was always waiting for us on our bench. But it was rather difficult to recognize him from a distance, for he never wore the same suit twice. Now it was a light coat with a blue waistcoat, now a hunting jacket with a knitted waistcoat; I even saw him in a morning-coat.

My aunt Rose, for her part, was nowadays wearing a feather boa and a little muslin toque surmounted by a blue bird with spread wings, which looked as if it were hatching her chignon.

She would borrow my mother's sunshade, or her gloves, or her bag. She would laugh, and blush, and she became prettier every day.

No sooner had we arrived than the 'park-owner' would hand me over to the donkey-man. I'd ride on the donkeys for hours, then pass on to the omnibus pulled by four goats, then have a go on the toboggan. I knew these lavish gestures did not cost him any-

thing since all the park belonged to him, but I was still very grateful, and proud to have such a rich friend and one who gave me
proof of such perfect love.

Six months later, while playing hide-and-seek with my brother
Paul, I locked myself up in the bottom part of the sideboard,
having pushed the plates out of the way. While Paul was looking
for me in my room and I was holding my breath, my father,
my mother and my aunt came into the dining-room. My
mother was saying:

'All the same, thirty-seven, that's pretty old!'

'Fiddlesticks!' my father said. 'I'll be thirty at the end of the
year, and I consider myself a young man still. Thirty-seven is the
prime of life. Besides, Rose isn't eighteen herself!'

'I'm twenty-six,' said Aunt Rose. 'And moreover I like him.'

'What does he do at the *Préfecture*?'

'He's a deputy chief clerk. He earns two hundred and twenty
francs a month.'

'Aha!' said my father.

'And he has some small annuities from his family.'

'Oho!' said my father.

'He told me that we could count on three hundred and fifty
francs a month.'

I heard a long whistle, then my father added:

'Well, my dear Rose, I congratulate you! Now don't tell me
he's handsome too?'

'No,' said my mother. 'Handsome, that one can't say.'

At that point I suddenly pushed the sideboard door open, leapt
on to the floor and shouted:

'Yes, he is! He's superb!'

And I rushed into the kitchen, locking the door behind me.

★

The upshot of it all was that the 'park-owner' appeared at home
one day, accompanied by Aunt Rose.

He was smiling broadly, under the curly brim of a shining black
bowler-hat. Aunt Rose was entirely rosy, dressed in rose-pink

from head to toe, and her lovely eyes shone behind a blue veil fastened to the brim of her boater.

They had both come back from a short trip, and there was a lot of kissing: yes, the 'park-owner', under our startled eyes, kissed my mother, then my father!

Then he lifted me up by the armpits, looked at me for a moment and said: 'Now you must call me Uncle Jules, for I'm Aunt Rose's husband.'

CHAPTER EIGHT

THE most astonishing thing was that he was not called Jules at all. His real Christian name was Thomas. But my dear aunt having heard it said that country-people called their chamber-pots Thomas, had decided to call him Jules—which is, in fact, an even more usual name for the same utensil. The innocent creature, not having done military service, was unaware of this, and nobody dared to tell her, not even Thomas-Jules, who loved her too much to contradict her, especially when he was right!

Uncle Jules was born among the vines in the golden province of Roussillon, where rolling wine barrels is an extremely common pursuit. He had left the vineyards in his brothers' care and had become the intellectual of the family, for he had read law: but he had remained a Catalan, and his tongue rolled over the 'r's' as a brook rolls over gravel.

I used to mimic him to make my brother Paul laugh, for to our mind the Provençal accent was the only true French accent, since it was our father's and he was an examiner for School Certificate. So Uncle Jules' 'r's' seemed to us the outward sign of a hidden infirmity.

My father and he were great friends, although Uncle Jules, the older and richer of the two, sometimes assumed a protective air.

Now and then he would protest against the excessive length of the school holidays.

'I grant you,' he would say, 'that children need a long rest. But during that time teachers might be employed in other things!'

'Why, certainly!' my father would retort ironically. 'They

might, for instance, spend their two months replacing the civil servants of the *Préfecture*, who are worn out by their long siestas, their backsides sore from sitting on leather cushions!'

But these friendly skirmishes stopped there, and the most important subject was never broached, except by discreet hints: Uncle Jules went to Mass!

When my father learnt—from my mother, to whom Aunt Rose had confided it—that he received Holy Communion twice a month, he was positively staggered, and declared that 'it was the limit'. My mother then implored him to accept this state of affairs and to forego, in my uncle's presence, his little repertory of jokes about priests and, in particular, a certain ribald ditty about the venerable Father Dupanloup.

'Do you think it would really vex him?'

'I'm sure he'd never set foot in this house again, and he'd forbid my sister to see me.'

My father sadly shook his head, then exclaimed with sudden fury:

'There you are! There you have the intolerance of those fanatics! Do I prevent him from going to eat his God every Sunday? Do I forbid you to see your sister, because she's married to a man who believes that the Creator of the Universe descends in person every Sunday into a hundred thousand goblets? Well, I want to show him my broad-mindedness. I'll ridicule him by my liberalism. No, I won't mention the Inquisition before him, nor the Calas affair, nor John Hus, nor any of the others whom the Church sent to the stake. I won't refer to the Borgia popes, or the Popess Joan! And even if he tries to preach to me the puerile conceits of a religion as childish as my grandmother's fairy tales, I'll reply *politely* and shall be content to chuckle quietly into my beard!'

But he had no beard, and he didn't chuckle in the least.

However, he kept his word, and their friendship was untroubled by the comments he let slip occasionally and which their vigilant wives promptly drowned with shouts of surprise or bursts of laughter for which they subsequently made up a reason.

41

Uncle Jules very quickly became my great friend. He often congratulated me on having been as good as my word in keeping their secret when he and my aunt had their many rendezvous in Borély Park; he would say to whoever wished to hear it that 'this child would make a great diplomat' or 'a first-class officer' (notwithstanding its offer of an alternative, this prophecy has so far remained unfulfilled). He was always anxious to see my school reports, and would reward me—or comfort me—with toys or bags of caramels.

However, when I suggested to him one day that he should build a little house in his beautiful Borély Park, with a balcony to watch the cyclists, he confessed to me airily that he had never been its owner.

The sudden loss of such a beautiful patrimony filled me with consternation, and I was sorry that I had admired an impostor for so long.

Moreover, I discovered that day that grown-ups could lie just as well as I, and it seemed to me that I could no longer feel quite safe with them.

On the other hand, this disclosure, which justified my own lies past, present and future, brought me peace of mind, and whenever I found it imperative to lie to my father and my little conscience would feebly protest, I silenced it with a 'Look at Uncle Jules!' and then, with candid eye and clear brow, I would lie admirably.

CHAPTER NINE

TWO years passed. I mastered the rule of three, I learnt, with irrepressible delight, of the existence of Lake Titicaca, then about *Louis le Hutin*,* about '*hibou–chou–genou*'† and the appalling rules that govern past participles.

As for my brother Paul, he had thrown away his ABC and familiarized himself, at night, in bed, with the congenial philosophy of *Les Pieds Nickelés*.‡

A little sister was born to us, and this happened just when we were staying with Aunt Rose, who had kept us with her for two days to toss Candlemas pancakes.

This untoward invitation prevented me from checking fully a bold hypothesis, put forward by my class-mate Mangiapan, that children came out of their mother's navel.

This idea had at first struck me as absurd: but one evening, after a rather long scrutiny of my navel, I had to admit that it really did rather look like a buttonhole, with a kind of little button in the middle. I concluded from this that an unbuttoning was possible and that Mangiapan had spoken the truth.

However, it immediately occurred to me that men don't have children: they just have sons and daughters who call them 'papa', but the children most certainly came from the mother, just as they did with dogs and cats. And so my navel didn't prove

---

* Louis X, nicknamed the Headstrong.

† Three of the few French words ending in 'ou' which take an 'x' in the plural.

‡ Popular magazine stories for boys, the title roughly means 'Those who won't budge'.

a thing. On the contrary, its existence in the male considerably weakened Mangiapan's authority in my eyes.

Whom was I to believe? What was I to think?

In any case, since a little sister had just been born, this was the time to keep my eyes and ears open and penetrate the great secret.

On our way back from Aunt Rose's, as we were passing through La Plaine, I suddenly made in retrospect, as it were, an important discovery: for the last three months, my mother's shape had been changing, and she would walk with her bust thrown back, like the postman at Christmas. One night, Paul had asked me with a look of alarm: 'What's she got under her apron, our Augustine?'

I didn't know what the answer was. . . .

We found her smiling, but pale and weak, in the big bed. Next to her, in a cot, a grimacing little creature emitted feeble, piping cries. Mangiapan's theory seemed to me proven, and I tenderly kissed my mother, while thinking of the pain she must have felt when she had to unbutton her navel.

The little creature at first seemed a stranger to us. Moreover, our mother gave her the breast, which shocked me deeply and frightened Paul. He said: 'She's eating our Mummy four times a day!' But as soon as she began to toddle and prattle, she made us conscious of our strength and wisdom, and we definitely adopted her.

★

On Sundays, Uncle Jules and Aunt Rose would come to see us, and I would go, with Paul, to lunch with them almost every Thursday.

They lived in a beautiful flat in the Rue des Minimes. It was lit by GAS, my aunt cooked by GAS, and she had a charwoman.

I noticed one day with surprise that dear Aunt Rose was swelling in her turn, and I immediately deduced from this an impending unbuttoning.

This diagnosis was confirmed when, soon after, I overheard a few snatches of a conversation between my mother and Mlle Guimard.

While the butcher was cutting a fine four-*sous* steak in the loin end, Mlle Guimard was saying in a worried voice:

'The children of elderly parents are always delicate. . . .'

'Rose is only thirty!' my mother protested.

'For a first child, that's quite old enough. And don't forget that her husband is forty!'

'Thirty-eight,' said my mother.

'Thirty and thirty-eight, that makes sixty-eight!' said Mlle Guimard.

And she shook her head, thoughtfully and ominously. . . .

One evening, our father told us that Mama would not be coming home because she was staying with her sister 'who wasn't well'. All four of us dined in silence, then I helped my father to put my little sister to bed.

This was a difficult operation, because of the pot, the nappies, and our fear of breaking her.

While pulling off my socks, I said to Paul: 'D'you know, they're unbuttoning Aunt Rose.'

He was reading his beloved *Pieds Nickelés* in bed, and he did not answer. But I had decided to initiate him in the great mysteries, and I persisted:

'Do you know why?'

He still did not move, and I saw that he was asleep.

So I softly pulled the book out of his hands, straightened his knees and blew out the lamp at the first try.

*

Next day, which was a Thursday, my father said to us:

'Come on, hurry! Get up! We're going to see Aunt Rose and I promise you a lovely surprise!'

'This surprise of yours,' I said, 'I know what it is already. . . .'

'Oho!' he said. 'And what is it?'

'I don't want to tell you, but I promise you I know.'

He looked at me with a smile, but did not pursue the matter.

The four of us walked down the street. Our little sister was rather quaintly turned out: we had buttoned her dress at the front and had been unable to do anything about her hair, because of her howling protests.

A great anxiety was preying on my mind. We were about to see a child born of old parents: Mlle Guimard had said so. But she hadn't specified anything except that it would be sixty-eight years old. I imagined that it would be quite shrivelled up, and that it would probably have grey hair and a grey beard like my grand-father—a smaller one, of course, and the hair would be finer: a baby beard. It would not be a pretty sight. But perhaps it would talk at once and tell us where it came from! Now that would be interesting.

I was to be utterly disappointed.

We were taken in to Aunt Rose's bedroom to kiss her. She looked perfectly buttoned up, though a little pale. My mother was sitting on the edge of the bed, and between them there was a baby, a baby without beard or moustache, and his big, chubby face was peacefully asleep under a crest of fair hair.

'That's your cousin,' my mother said softly.

They both looked at it, moved, marvelling, delighted and with such excessive worship, and Uncle Jules who'd just come in was so flushed with pride that Paul, disgusted, dragged me off to the dining-room, where we gobbled up the four bananas in the cut-glass bowl which had caught his eye on the way in.

CHAPTER TEN

ONE evening in April, I was coming home from school with my father and Paul. It was a Wednesday, the most beautiful day of the week,* for what makes our days most beautiful is looking forward to the morrow.

As we were walking along the pavement in the Rue Tivoli, my father said to me:

'Little toad, I shall be needing you tomorrow morning.'

'What for?'

'You'll see. It's a surprise.'

'What about me? D'you need me too?' enquired Paul anxiously.

'Certainly,' said my father. 'But Marcel will come with me, and you'll stay at home to supervise the charwoman who's going to sweep the cellar. That's very important.'

'Generally, I'm afraid of going down into the cellar,' said Paul. 'But if the charwoman is there, I'll be all right.'

Next morning, my father woke me about eight with a ringing imitation of a bugle-call, then he dragged the blankets off me.

'You must be ready in half an hour. I'm going to shave.'

I rubbed my eyes with clenched fists, stretched myself, and got up. Paul had disappeared under the bed-clothes, all that could be seen of him was a shock of golden curls.

*

Thursday was the day for great ablutions, and my mother used

* There is no school on Thursdays in France.

to take this sort of thing very seriously. I first got myself dressed from top to toe, then went through the motions of having a thorough wash: that is to say that, twenty years before the first radio sound-effects, I composed a whole symphony of 'noises off' to indicate a boy having a bath.

I first turned on the tap of the wash-basin, and skilfully adjusted it so that the pipes groaned, thus advising my parents of the start of the operation.

While the jet of water was loudly splashing into the basin, I would look on from a safe distance.

After four or five minutes of this, I abruptly turned off the tap. This produced a hammering that made the walls shudder, thus broadcasting to the house that I had finished drawing my bath.

I waited for a moment, and made use of this pause to brush my hair. Then I rattled the small tin tub on the tiled floor and turned on the tap, but slowly, and twisting it a little at a time. It whistled, mewed and then resumed its gasping groans. I let it run for a full minute, the time it took to read one page of the *Pieds Nickelés*. At the very moment when Croquignol, after tripping up the policeman, was taking to his heels above the words 'To be continued', I turned it off with a jerk.

I was completely successful, for I brought off a double bang which made the pipes buckle.

With a final kick at the tub's tinny side, I had in the prescribed span of time completed a plausible ablution without a drop of water having touched me.

I found my father sitting at the dining-room table. He was counting money. My mother, opposite him, was drinking her coffee. Her black hair, which had a blue glint to it, was hanging down over the back of the chair. I was given my coffee and milk.

'Did you wash your feet?' my mother asked me.

As I knew she attached a particular importance to this futile operation, the need for which seemed to me inexplicable (since feet aren't seen), I answered without hesitation:

'Both of them.'

'Did you cut your nails?'

It seemed to me that, by confessing an omission, I would lend colour to the truthfulness of the rest of my story.

'No,' I said, 'I forgot to. But I cut them on Sunday.'

'All right,' she said.

She seemed satisfied. So was I.

While I was munching my bread and butter, my father said:

'Do you know where we're going? Well, I'll tell you. Your mother needs some country air. So I've rented a villa up in the hills, half shares with Uncle Jules, and that's where we're going to spend the summer holidays.'

I was awe-struck.

'Where is this villa?'

'A long way from the city, high up, among pine-trees.'

'A very long way?'

'Oh yes,' said my mother. 'We'll have to take the tram, and then walk for hours.'

'It must be quite wild, then?'

'Fairly,' my father said. 'It's on the edge of a lonely moorland which stretches from Aubagne to Aix. A real desert!'

Paul arrived, barefoot, wondering what was going on, and he asked:

'Any camels there?'

'No,' said my father. 'No camels.'

'What about rhinoceroses?'

'Haven't seen any.'

I wanted to ask a thousand questions, but my mother said:

'Eat up.'

And as the excitement had made me forget my slice of bread, she pushed my hand towards my mouth.

Then she turned towards Paul:

'As for you, go and put your slippers on first, otherwise you'll be down with another sore throat. Go on, be off with you.'

And off he went.

'So you're taking me to the hills this morning?' I asked.

'No,' said my father, 'not yet! The villa's quite empty, and we'll have to furnish it. But new furniture is very expensive. So this morning, we're going to see the secondhand dealer in the Quatre-Chemins.'

★

Buying old junk from secondhand dealers was my father's one great passion.

Every month, on his way back from the town hall where he had been to draw 'his fees', he would bring back strange and wonderful things: a broken dog-muzzle (o.50 frs.), a pair of pointless dividers (1.50 frs.), a bass bow (1 fr.), a surgeon's hand-saw (2 frs.), a naval spyglass, in which you saw everything upside down (3 frs.), a scalping knife (2 frs.), an almost oval hunting-horn with the mouthpiece of a trombone (3 frs.), to say nothing of other mysterious objects whose possible use no one had ever been able to discover and which cluttered up the house.

These monthly arrivals were a real beano for Paul and me. My mother did not share our enthusiasm. She would stare in blank amazement at the long-bow from the Fiji Islands or the precision altimeter whose needle had once soared to 13,000 feet (as a result of a climb on Mont-Blanc, perhaps, or else a drop on the stairs) and had refused to come down ever since.

Then she would say peremptorily: 'Whatever happens, the children are not to touch these things!' and she would dash into the kitchen, whence she would return with methylated spirit, disinfectant, washing-soda, and begin energetically to scour this flotsam.

I must explain that in those days microbes were quite a novel thing, since the great Pasteur had only just invented them, and she visualized them as so many tiny tigers, ready to pounce on us and devour us, innards first.

While she was shaking the hunting-horn, which she had filled with Jeyes' fluid, she would say with a look of great distress:

'My poor Joseph! What *are* you going to do with all this muck?'

But poor Joseph would merely reply, triumphantly:

50

'Three francs!'

I realized, much later, that for him the point of a bargain was not the thing he purchased, but the price he paid.

'Well, that's three francs wasted!'

'But, my dearest, if you wanted to *make* this hunting-horn, think of the cost of copper, of the special tools you'd need, of the hundreds of hours' work required to mould the copper. . . .'

My mother gently shrugged her shoulders. It was plain that she had never dreamt of manufacturing this or any other hunting-horn.

Then my father said with condescension:

'You don't seem to realize that this instrument, though of no use as such, perhaps, is an absolute *mine* of things that may be highly useful! Just think for a moment: if I saw off the mouthpiece I shall have an ear-trumpet, a megaphone, a funnel, a gramophone loudspeaker. The rest of the tube, when twisted into a spiral, can form a coil for a still; or again, I can straighten it out and turn it into a blow-pipe or a water-main—a copper one, mind you! If I cut it up into fine slices, there'll be twenty dozen curtain-rings for you! If I drill a hundred small holes in it and adapt it to the rubber enema tubing, we'll have a shower-bath! It would make an air-gun. . . .'

In this way, before his marvelling sons and disconsolate spouse, he would transform the useless contrivance into an untold variety of objects—all equally useless but infinitely more numerous.

That's why my mother, at the mere mention of the 'second-hand dealer', began to move her head from side to side, with a slight air of alarm.

But she did not express her thoughts and merely asked me:

'Have you got a handkerchief?'

Of course I had a handkerchief. It lay, clean as a whistle, in my pocket where it had been for a week. For I had the knack of extracting from my nostrils, with the nail of my forefinger, the snuffling substances that impeded my breathing, and the use of a handkerchief seemed to me a piece of parental superstition.

Just occasionally I could find a job for it, such as making my shoes shine or wiping the bench at school. But the idea of blowing mucus into this dainty fabric and storing it away in my pocket seemed to me both absurd and disgusting. However, as children arrive too late to educate their parents, one must respect the latter's incurable manias and simply try not to upset them. That is why I pulled out my handkerchief, keeping my hand over a rather fine ink-stain—which might have started another kind of conversation—and waved it at my dear, reassured Mama, as if I were on a station platform. I then followed my father out into the street.

CHAPTER ELEVEN

THERE, drawn up at the kerb, I saw a small two-wheeled cart which he had borrowed from a neighbour. On its side, in fat black letters, one could read:

BERGOUGNAS
Coal and Firewood

My father stepped backwards into the shafts.

'I shall need you,' he said to me, 'to put on the brakes when we're going down the Rue Tivoli.'

I looked at the distant street which rose towards the sky in a perfect toboganning slope.

'But, papa,' I said, 'the Rue Tivoli goes uphill!'

'Yes,' he agreed. 'It does now, But I have a very strong feeling that it'll be going downhill on the way back. And on the return trip we'll be laden. Meanwhile, you can climb onto the cart.'

I clambered up and sat down right in the centre, to ensure an even balance.

My mother watched us leave from behind the bulging iron-work of the window.

'Do mind the trams!' she cried.

Whereupon my father uttered a joyous whinny, as a mark of self-confidence, tittupped once or twice, and then cantered off towards adventure.

*

We stopped at the bottom of the Boulevard de la Madeleine, in front of a dark, grubby shop. The shop spilled over on the pavement, which was cluttered up with assorted furniture. Its centre-piece was a very ancient stirrup-pump, on which hung a fiddle.

The man who presided over this bric-à-brac was very tall, very lean and very dirty. He wore a grey beard, and a troubadour's flowing mane emerged from his wide-brimmed artist's hat. He had a melancholy air and smoked a clay pipe.

My father had paid him previous visits and earmarked certain pieces of 'furniture': a commode, two tables, and several bundles of polished wood which, according to the dealer, could be made to reconstitute six chairs. There was also a small sofa which was losing its entrails like a picador's horse, three split box-mattresses, some half-empty straw pallets, a cabinet with the shelves lacking, a goblet in the shape of a stylized cock, and various household utensils uniformly decorated with rust.

The junk-dealer helped us to load the lot onto the hand-cart which, with its prop lowered to the ground, looked like a donkey in spring. The load was secured with ropes rendered hairy by long wear and tear. Then the two men got down to settling their accounts. After what seemed profound meditation, the dealer fixedly gazed at my father and said:

'That'll be fifty francs.'

'Oho!' said my father. 'That's too dear!'

'It's dear, but it's lovely stuff,' the junk-man said. 'The com-mode is a period piece!' And he pointed at the worm-eaten ruin.

'I gladly believe it,' my father said. 'It certainly belongs to some period, but not ours!'

The dealer made a *moue* of disgust and said:

'Are you so fond of modern stuff?'

'The point is,' my father said, 'I'm not buying this for a museum but to make use of it.'

The old man seemed saddened by this confession.

'Does it mean nothing to you,' he asked, 'that this commode may have seen Queen Marie-Antoinette in her night-shift?'

'By the state it's in,' my father said, 'I shouldn't be surprised if it had seen King Herod in his drawers!'

'Now there you're wrong,' the junk-dealer replied, 'and I'll tell you why: King Herod may have worn drawers or he may not, but he didn't have a commode! Nothing but gold-studded coffers and all sorts of wooden stools. I'm telling you because I'm honest.'

'I'm much obliged,' my father retorted. 'And since you're honest, you'll charge me thirty-five francs for the lot.'

The dealer looked first at my father, then at me, shook his head with a regretful smile, and declared:

'I'm afraid I can't, because I owe fifty francs to my landlord, who's coming to collect the money at noon.'

'Why!' said my father indignantly, 'so if you owed him a hundred francs, you'd dare to charge me a hundred?'

'I'd have to! Where do you expect me to get them from? Mind you, if I only owed forty, I'd charge you forty. If I owed thirty, then thirty. . . .'

'In that case,' my father said, 'I'd better come back tomorrow when you've paid him and won't owe him anything. . . .'

'Ah! It's too late!' the dealer cried. 'It's past eleven. You've fallen into the trap—you can't get out of it now. You were out of luck in coming today, I admit. But there it is! Each must bear his burden. Still, you're young and strapping, your back's straight as a ramrod, and you have two perfectly good eyes. As long as there are hump-backed and one-eyed fellows in the world, you've no right to complain. So fifty francs it is.'

'All right,' said my father, 'in that case we'll unload this scrap, and go and help ourselves elsewhere. Undo the straps, my boy!'

The dealer held me back by the arm and cried: 'Wait!'

Then he looked at my father with pained indignation, shook his head and remarked to me: 'Isn't he a violent man!'

He walked up to him and said solemnly:

'No good arguing about the amount: it's fifty francs. I just can't reduce it. But we might perhaps increase the merchandise.'

He walked into the shop; my father winked at me triumphantly, and we followed him in.

There were ramparts of cupboards, peeling mirrors, helmets, clocks, stuffed animals. He plunged his arm into this jungle and extracted various objects from it.

'First,' he said, 'since you like modern stuff, I'll give you this bedside table in *enamelled iron* as well, and this swan-necked tap, *nickel-plated by galvanoplasty*! You can't say this isn't *modern*! Secondly, I'm giving you this damascened Arab rifle, which isn't fired with a flint, but a cap. Just look at the length of the barrel: it might be a fishing-rod! And have a look at these initials,' he added in a lowered voice. 'In Arab letters, engraved on the butt!'

He showed us some signs which looked like a lot of commas, and whispered:

'A and K. You catch the meaning?'

'You're not claiming this is Abd-el-Kader's own rifle?' my father said.

'I'm not claiming anything,' the dealer declared, with deep conviction. 'But greater wonders *have* been seen! A word to the wise, that's all. What's more, I'm going to give you this fretted brass fire-guard, this shepherd's umbrella—it'll be like new once you've changed the cover—this tom-tom from the Ivory Coast—which is a *collector's piece*—and this tailor's flat iron. Will that do?'

'It's fair,' my father said. 'But I also want this old chicken-coop thrown in.'

'Now! Now!' the dealer said. 'I grant you it's old, but it will still serve as well as a new one. Never mind, since it's you, I'll let you have it.'

My father handed him a mauve fifty-franc note. He took it gravely, with an inclination of his head.

At last, when we had almost finished squeezing our booty under the already bursting ropes, he suddenly said as he was re-lighting his pipe:

'I feel like making you a present: a bed for the boy!'

And back he went into the shop, disappeared behind the forest of cupboards, then re-emerged triumphantly. He was holding at arm's length a bed-frame made of four old planks so badly joined that, at the slightest pressure, the square became a lozenge. A rectangular piece of fraying sack-cloth had been fixed with studs to one of the planks and drooped like the grimy flag of poverty.

'To tell you the truth,' he said, 'there should be a second frame, exactly like this, to make a trestle. But with four bits of wood you can make another, and this young man will sleep like a pasha!'

He crossed his arms over his chest, gently inclined his head to one side, and pretended to be dozing off with a blissful smile.

We thanked him profusely; he seemed touched and, raising his right hand which showed a blackened palm, he cried:

'Wait! I've another surprise for you!'

And once more he ran back into his shop. But my father, who had slipped the harness over his head, moved off suddenly and cantered down the Boulevard de la Madeleine at a lively pace, while the generous old man, back on the kerb, was brandishing an enormous Red Cross flag, for which we decided it was unnecessary to go back.

CHAPTER TWELVE

WHEN my mother, who was watching out for us at the window, saw this cargo arrive, she promptly disappeared from sight and re-emerged on the doorstep. As was her wont, she said: 'Joseph, you're not going to bring all this trash into the house?'

'This trash,' my father told her, 'will be the foundation of a suite of rustic furniture which you'll never tire of looking at. Just give us time to smarten it up! I've made my plans, I know what I'm doing.'

My mother shook her head and sighed, while little Paul came running out to help us unload.

We carted all the stuff into the cellar, where my father had decided to set up our work-shop.

The first job—which I was charged with—was to steal a battered iron spoon from the kitchen-table drawer.

My mother searched for it for a long while and came across it more than once. But she always failed to recognize it, for we had flattened it out with a hammer and turned it into a trowel.

With this tool, worthy of Robinson Crusoe, we fixed four pieces of iron to the cellar-wall and fastened them, in turn, with four screws, to a rickety table; its stability thus assured, it was promoted forthwith to the rank of a work-bench.

On it we fixed a groaning vice which we pacified with a drop of oil. Then we sorted out the tools: a saw, a hammer, a pair of pliers, nails of various sizes but all equally twisted from earlier extractions, some screws, a screw-driver, a plane and a chisel.

I admired those treasures, those *Machines*, which little Paul did not dare to touch, for he believed in the active malice of all sharp or pointed things, and made little difference between a saw and a crocodile. However, he quite understood that great things were in the making, for he suddenly dashed off and brought us back, with a radiant smile, two bits of string, a pair of small celluloid scissors, and a nut he had found in the street.

We welcomed these additions to our set of tools with shouts of grateful delight, and Paul blushed pink with pride.

My father installed him on a wooden stool and advised him not to budge from there.

'You'll be of great help to us,' he told him, 'because tools are always up to tricks: as soon as you start looking for one, it somehow seems to know and promptly hides. . . .'

'Because it's frightened of getting struck by the hammer!' Paul said.

'Exactly!' my father agreed. 'So you up there on your stool can keep a sharp eye on them: that'll save us a lot of time.'

Every night at six, my father and I would leave the school-house together. We would talk over our lessons as we walked home and, on the way, we'd buy little odds and ends that were missing in the work-shop: carpenter's glue, more screws, a pot of paint, a rasp. We often stopped at the junk-dealer's shop, for he had become our friend. There I stepped into a real fairyland, for by now I was allowed to forage everywhere. In his shop could be found everything under the sun—yet one never found what one was looking for. . . . We would come to buy a broom and would leave with a cornet or an assegai—the very one, according to our friend, which had killed Prince Bonaparte. As soon as we got home, my mother, following a well-established rite, would strip us of our booty, hasten to wash my hands, then scour our trophies with disinfectant. After this drastic treatment I'd skip downstairs into the cellar where I would find my father, with Paul in attendance, busy in the 'work-shop'.

The cellar was lit by a paraffin lamp. This rather dented brass lamp had what was called a 'Matador' burner, that is to say, its

59

circular wick emerged from a brass tube and sat under a small brass mushroom which forced the flame to open out in a corolla. It was a fairly large corolla and, to contain it, the glass-chimney bulged most beautifully at its base. My father considered this lamp the last word in modern technique, and it is a fact that it diffused a bright radiance as well as a most pungent modern smell.

The first task we undertook was to put the chairs together. This proved a jig-saw puzzle, all the more difficult to solve as the rungs did not fit into the holes in the legs, nor were they all of the same length.

We complained about it to the antique dealer who at first feigned surprise, then gave us another bundle of bars. He insisted on adding a little present in the shape of a pair of Mexican stirrups.

With lashings of glue, slabs of which I melted down in warm water, the six chairs were re-assembled, and then varnished. My mother wove thick string seats for them, and a touch of unforeseen stylishness was added by a treble row of red cord round the edges.

My father, after setting them out around the dining-room table, gazed at them for a long while; he then declared that these chairs in their present state were worth at least five times the price we had paid for them, and once again he called on us to admire the fabulous 'bargains' he managed to dig up at the junk-shop.

Then it was the commode's turn. Its drawers were so tightly stuck that we had to dismantle the entire chest and make free use of the planes.

Though these occupations were spread over no more than three months, they fill an important place in my memory, because it was in the light of the Matador burner that I first discovered the intelligence of my hands and the wonderful efficiency of the simplest tools.

*

One fine Thursday morning we were at last able to range our 'holiday furniture' in the passage downstairs. Uncle Jules had been summoned as a prospective admirer, and our friend the junk-dealer was called in as an expert.

My uncle duly admired, the junk-man appraised expertly. He extolled the tenons, approved the mortices, and declared the assemblage perfect. Then, as the finished suite looked like nothing on earth, he decreed that its style was 'Rustic Provençal', and this was sententiously approved by Uncle Jules.

My mother marvelled at the beauty of this furniture and, just as my father had prophesied, she never tired of looking at it. She admired above all a small pedestal table which I had given three coats of 'mahogany varnish'. It was really a joy to the eye, but it was wiser to look at it than to touch it, for if you put your hands flat on the table-top, you could lift the table up and carry it about, as mediums do. I believe everyone noticed this inconvenience but nobody said a word that might have spoilt the triumph of our exhibition.

It so happened that I later had the pleasure of discovering that a minor error can have major advantages, for this pedestal table, placed like a precious period piece in a well-lit corner, caught so many flies that it ensured the silence and hygiene of the dining-room, at least throughout our first summer holidays.

When the time of departure approached at last, the generous expert opened an old trunk which he had brought with him. From it he pulled an enormous pipe, whose bowl, carved from a root, was as big as my head, and he offered it to my father 'as a curio'. Then he presented my mother with a shell necklace which Queen Ranavalo had worn and, after apologizing for not having foreseen the presence of Uncle Jules—'who would lose nothing by waiting'—he took his leave with the flourish of a *grand seigneur*.

CHAPTER THIRTEEN

THE first fortnight of July never seemed to end.

The furniture was marking time in the passage downstairs, and we were marking time at school, where we weren't doing much.

Our teachers read out to us tales by Andersen or Alphonse Daudet, then we would go and play in the school-yard for most of the day. But the fun had gone out of our schoolboy games which suddenly seemed silly and unexciting as, slowly but surely, we approached the never-ending games of the summer holidays.

I kept repeating certain magic words to myself: 'villa', 'pine-woods', 'hills', 'cicadas'. There were some cicadas, true enough, at the top of the plane-trees in the school-yard. But I had never seen them at close quarters, whereas my father had promised me thousands and almost all of them within reach of my hand. . . . That is why, as I listened to the stray invisible singers flouting us from their high leafy hide-outs, I would think, unstirred by any lyrical feeling: 'Just you wait, old thing! When we're up in the hills, I'll stick a straw up your arse!' Such is the angelic sweetness of eight-year-old boys.

One evening, Uncle Jules and Aunt Rose came to dine with us. It was a dinner-cum-conference, on the eve of the great departure which was to take place the next day.

Uncle Jules, who flattered himself on being an organizer, started the proceedings by declaring that, due to the state of the roads, there was no question of hiring a sizeable conveyance, which would have cost a fortune, anyway—as much as twenty francs perhaps!

He had, therefore, hired two carts: a small removal-van which would transport his own furniture, as well as his wife, his son and himself, at the price of 7.50 francs.

That sum included the services of a removal man who would be at our disposal all day long.

As for us, he had found a farmer called François, who had a piece of land a few hundred yards away from the villa. This man François came to town twice a week to sell his fruit in the Marseilles market. On his way back he would carry our furniture for the reasonable charge of four francs. This arrangement greatly pleased my father, but Paul asked:

'What about us? Do we climb on the cart?'

'You'll take the tram,' the Organizer said, 'as far as La Barasse where you'll meet your farmer and continue by *pedibus cum jambis*. There'll be just enough room for Augustine on the cart, and the three men will follow on foot, with the farmer.'

The three men joyfully agreed to this idea, and the conversation then became absolutely entrancing and went on till eleven o'clock, for Uncle Jules talked of shooting, and my father talked of insects, and I drank it all in so fervently that I kept shooting at centipedes, grasshoppers and scorpions until I woke up next morning.

At 8 a.m. we were ready and decked out in our holiday clothes: canvas breeches and short-sleeved white shirts embellished with blue ties.

These clothes were my mother's handiwork, whereas our peaked caps and *espadrilles* had been bought at a big store.

My father wore a half-belted sports jacket with two large patch-pockets, and a navy-blue cap, while my mother looked young and pretty in a white print dress with a small red flower pattern, which she had run up most successfully.

As for our little sister who, under her blue bonnet, opened wide her big black eyes, she seemed apprehensive because she realized that we were leaving home.

The farmer had warned us: the hour of departure would not depend on his eagerness to start, but on his customers' eagerness to clear his stock of apricots.

The rate of clearance was not very fast that day, for by noon he still had not arrived.

So we lunched off sausages and cold meat in the flat which already had a deserted look, and every now and then we dashed to the window, hoping to glimpse the herald of the holidays.

At last he arrived.

*

The cart was painted blue, but the colour had faded and the grain of the wood showed through.

There was a lot of play in its very high wheels, and whenever they came full circle, there was a resounding shock. The iron hoops jumped on the cobble-stones, the shafts groaned, the mule's hoofs struck sparks. . . . It was the chariot of Hope and Adventure.

The farmer who led it wore neither jacket nor smock, but a knitted waistcoat of thick wool so caked with dirt, that it was like felt. On his head sat a shapeless cap with a wilting peak. Fine white teeth, however, gleamed in a Roman emperor's face.

He spoke Provençal, laughed, and cracked a long whip-lash at the end of a plaited reed.

Helped by my father and much hampered by young Paul (who hung on to the biggest pieces on the pretext of removing them), the farmer loaded the cart, that is to say, he stacked up the furniture in a pyramid. He then ensured their balance by trussing them with ropes, cords and string and flung a canvas cover, full of holes, over the lot.

Then he shouted in Provençal:

'Here we go now!' and he grasped the mule's reins and made the beast move off by goading it with insulting oaths, which he accompanied by a few violent jerks at the rather insensitive creature's bit.

We followed the cart that carried our chattels as if it were a funeral hearse, until we reached the Boulevard Mérentié. There we left the farmer and went to take the tram.

With a shattering clang of iron, a clicking shudder of windowpanes, and long shrill shrieks at the curves, that fabulous vehicle hurtled off into the future.

As we had not been able to find a seat inside, we were standing —to my delight—on the forward platform. I could see the driver's back while he, with his hands placed on the two handles, alternately released and braked the monster's speed, with sovereign calm. I was spellbound by this omnipotent figure whose mystery was further enhanced by an enamelled plate which forbade anyone to speak to him—because of all the secrets he knew.

Slowly, patiently, turning to account each jolt and sudden braking, I wormed my way between my neighbours and finally wriggled through to him, leaving Paul to his sad fate: wedged between the long legs of two gendarmes, he was propelled, nose forward, by every jolt of the tram, against the thighs of an enormous lady, who was wobbling dangerously.

Up at the front, the shining rails dizzily sped towards me, the rush of air produced by our great speed lifted the peak of my cap and hummed in my ears: in two seconds we had overtaken a horse at a gallop. I have never recaptured, on the most high-powered modern engines, this triumphant pride in being an offspring of Man, the conqueror of space and time.

However, this meteor of steel and iron, which brought us closer to the hills, did not actually lead us on to them: we had to leave it on the farthest outskirts of Marseilles, at a place called La Barasse; from there it continued its mad race towards Aubagne.

Father, who had unfolded a map, conducted us to a point at which a narrow dusty road fled the city between two *bistros*. We stepped out firmly behind our Joseph, who was carrrying our little sister on his shoulders.

This Provençal track was a pretty lane. It ambled between two long, sun-baked stone walls, above which broad fig-leaves, bushy clematis and ancient olive-trees bowed over us. At the foot of the walls, a border of rough grass and brambles showed that the roadmender's efforts did not extend to the whole width of the track.

I could hear the cicadas singing, and on the honey-coloured

wall, motionless '*larmeuses*' were drinking in the sunshine, open-mouthed. They were small grey lizards, with a slatey sheen. Paul promptly set out to hunt them, but he only brought back some quivering tails. Father explained to us that these charming little creatures gladly abandoned them, as a thief might leave his jacket in the hands of the police, when dashing off. They would grow another tail in a matter of days, anyhow, to ensure a future escape.

After just under an hour's walk, our road met another at a perfectly round and empty crossroads. In the middle of one of its quadrants, however, there stood a stone bench, and on it my mother sat down.

My father now consulted the map and said:

'That's where we left the tram. Here's where we are now, and this is the Four Seasons crossroads where our removal-man will be waiting for us, unless we're the ones who have to do the waiting.'

I looked with astonishment at the double line on the map which represented our lane: it made an enormous détour.

'The roadmakers must be mad,' I said, 'to have built such a round-about road!'

'There's nothing wrong with the roadmakers,' my father said, 'but with the society we live in.'

'Why?' my mother asked.

'Because this enormous détour is forced on us by four or five large estates which the road couldn't cut across and which are behind those walls. . . .' He pointed to a spot on the map: 'Here's our villa. As the crow flies, it's four kilometres from La Barasse. . . . But because of the big landowners we'll have to walk nine.'

'That's a lot for the children,' my mother said.

But I was thinking that it was a lot for her. That's why, when my father got up to go on again, I asked for a few minutes' grace, pretending that my ankle was aching.

We walked for another hour, always flanked by walls on both sides, as if we were the tiny balls in a game of Pigs-in-Clover. . . .

Paul was about to go hunting lizard-tails again, but my mother dissuaded him with a few touching words which brought tears to his eyes. So he forsook this cruel game in favour of catching grass-hoppers which he squashed between two stones.

Meanwhile, my father was explaining to my mother that in the society of the future, all the châteaux would be hospitals, all the walls would be torn down, and all the roads would run straight as a bow-string.

'So you want to start a revolution all over again?' she asked.

'A revolution isn't what's wanted. It's an ill-chosen word, for a revolution means a full turn of the wheel. Consequently, those who are on top go to the bottom but then rise again to their former place—and everything starts all over again. These iniquit-ous walls weren't built under the *ancien régime*: our Republic not only tolerates them, it actually erected them!'

I loved these socio-political lectures of my father's. I used to interpret them after my own fashion and wondered why the President of the Republic never thought of calling him in, at least during the holidays, for he would have brought about mankind's happiness in three weeks.

Our road suddenly joined a highway which, though much wider, was no better cared for.

'We've almost got to our meeting-place,' my father said. 'The plane-trees you can see over there are at the Four Seasons cross-roads. And look!' he said suddenly, pointing to the bushy grass at the foot of the wall. 'This promises well!'

Deep in the grass lay immensely long iron rods, completely covered with rust.

'What are they?' I asked.

'Rails!' said my father. 'Rails for the tram-lines. It's only a question now of laying them.'

They ran all along the side of the road. But the vegetation which covered them showed that those responsible for laying the lines were unaware of the urgency of the matter.

We arrived at the Four Seasons. This was a small rustic bar at the crossroads, hidden by two tall plane-trees and obscured by a high fountain made of moss-grown boulders. Gleaming water spouted from four angled pipes, and murmured a refreshing song in the leafy shade.

How pleasant it must be to sit at the small green tables under the vault of the plane-trees. But we did not walk into this 'dram-shop', whose very charm spelled danger.

*

Instead, we went and sat on the parapet which lined the road; my mother opened the picnic parcel, and we began to devour the crisp, golden bread of those days, the tender, white-mottled sausage (in which I would look for the peppercorn first, as for the bean in the Twelfth Night cake), and the orange cradled to ripeness on Spanish cargo boats.

Meanwhile, my mother was saying, with a worried look on her face:

'It's a long walk, Joseph.'

'And we aren't there yet!' my father retorted gaily. 'There's at least another hour's walk!'

'Today we haven't any parcels to carry, but when we have to take supplies up there. . . .'

'We'll carry them up,' my father said.

'We're three men, mama,' Paul chimed in. 'You won't have to carry anything.'

'Quite so!' said my father. 'The walk may be on the long side, but it's very healthy! Besides, we'll only be coming here at Christmas, at Easter, and in the summer holidays: three times a year, that's all. And we'll start early in the morning and have a picnic luncheon halfway along the road. Then we'll stop once more, at tea-time. And later, well, you've seen those rails. I'll drop a word to Michel's brother. He's a journalist. It's outrageous that they should be left to rust all this time. I bet you that before six months are out the tram will drop us at La Croix, that's six hundred yards from here. And that'll leave less than an hour's walk!'

At those words, I saw the rails spring from the grass and wriggle into place between the paving-stones, while the deep growl of a tram could be heard in the distance. . . .

*

However, as I raised my head, what I saw coming wasn't the powerful engine but the wobbling pyramid of our removal-cart.

Paul gave a shriek of joy and ran to meet the mule. The farmer lifted him up by the haunches and dumped him astride the animal's neck. Sitting there he was level with us. Clutching the halter, drunk with pride and fear, he wore an uncertain smile halfway between joy and terror, while I was devoured by a disgraceful jealousy.

The cart stopped and the farmer said: 'Now we'll make the lady comfortable.'

He folded a sack in four, and spread it over the floor of the cart, near the shafts. My father installed my mother on it, with her legs dangling, then he placed my little sister, whose mouth was wreathed with smudges of chocolate, in her arms, and began to walk at their side, while I, having clambered onto the parapet, was dancing along it in the wake of the caravan.

Paul, by now not only reassured but triumphant, was swaying gracefully backwards and forwards, to the rhythm of the mule's step, and I was hard put to it to contain a burning desire to jump onto the crupper behind him.

Ahead of us the horizon was hidden by the high, leaf-crowned trees which bordered the twisting track.

But after walking for twenty minutes, we suddenly came upon a small village, perched on a hilltop between two valleys: to the right and left the outlook was blocked by two rocky cliffs which the people of Provence call 'barres'.

'That's the village of La Treille!' my father announced.

We were at the foot of a steep ascent.

'Madame will have to get down here,' the farmer said, 'and we'll have to push the cart for a bit.'

The mule had stopped of its own accord, and my mother jumped down on the dusty ground.

The farmer dethroned Paul, then opened a sort of drawer beneath the cart's under-belly and pulled two big wooden wedges out of it. One of them he held out to my mother, who looked surprised.

'They're chocks,' he said. 'When I tell you to, you put this one on the ground, behind the wheel at this end.'

She seemed happy to collaborate in a man's job and gripped the big chock in her little hands.

'And I,' said Paul, 'will put the other one down!'

His proposal was accepted, and I was deeply vexed at this fresh violation of the law of primogeniture. But I was to have a re-sounding revenge for the farmer handed me his whip, a very thick waggoner's whip, and said:

'As for you, you can whip the mule.'

'On its behind?'

'Everywhere, and use the handle!'

Then he spat into his hands, ducked his head between his shoulders, and with both arms outstretched, he buttressed himself against the back of the cart, till his body was almost horizontal. My father, of his own accord, adopted the same position. Then the farmer hurled some scathing insults at the mule, shouted at me: 'Pico! Pico!' ('lash him!'), and pushed with all his might. I struck the mule, not brutally, but just to let him know it was time to make an effort: the whole equipage started off, moved some thirty yards; then the farmer, without raising his head, shouted between two gasps:

'The chocks! The chocks!'

My mother, who was walking behind the wheel, swiftly placed the wooden wedge under the iron felloe; Paul imitated her with remarkable ease, and the vehicle came to a stop for five minutes' rest. The farmer made use of this to tell me that I must strike much harder and, preferably, under the belly. Paul yelled:

'No! No! Don't do that!'

And just as my father began to look touched by the little

70

fellow's kind heart, Paul pointed at the amazed farmer and cried:

'We ought to pluck his eyes out!'

'Oho!' said François indignantly. 'Pluck my eyes out, would you? What sort of a savage is this? I think I'd better lock him up in the drawer!'

He made as if to open it. Paul ran to cling to the paternal trousers.

'You see,' my father said gravely, 'what comes of wanting to pluck people's eyes out: you end by getting locked up in drawers!'

'It isn't true!' Paul screamed. 'I won't!'

'Monsieur,' my mother said, 'perhaps we might wait a bit: I think he only said it in fun!'

'It's not a thing to say even in fun,' said François. 'Pluck my eyes out, indeed! And on the very day that I've bought myself a pair of sun-glasses!'

And he actually pulled out of his pocket a pair of pince-nez with dark lenses, which a hawker sold for four *sous* in the market.

'You could wear them all the same,' Paul remarked, from a safe distance.

'Why, you wretched boy,' the farmer said, 'when your eyes are plucked out and on top of that you wear dark glasses, you can no longer see anything at all! However, for this once, I won't say any more. . . . Let's go.'

Everyone resumed his place. I struck the mule under his belly, not too hard, but yelling orders into his ears at the same time, while the farmer called him 'carcass', 'carrion', and accused him of feeding on excrement.

With an extreme effort we reached the village, or rather the hamlet, whose ruddy roof-tiles were abnormally long, as in ancient times. Very small windows were let into the thick walls.

On the left, there was a long terrace lined with plane-trees and supported by a backward-leaning wall which was quite thirty feet high. On the right was the street—I would say the main street, if there had been others. But the only other one was a narrow side-lane, no more than ten yards long but still managing to swerve into two right-angled turns before it reached the village square. This tiny square, smaller than a school-yard, was shaded by a very old mulberry tree with a deeply creviced trunk, and by two acacias; these seemed determined to meet the sun and were doing their best to outstrip the steeple.

In the middle of the square, a fountain was talking to itself. This was a basin of undressed stone surrounding a square column like a sconce, with a copper pipe emerging from the top.

After he had unhitched the mule—for there was no room for the cart to follow it—François led it to the fountain, and the animal took a long draught, flicking its flanks with its tail.

A peasant passed. He was a huge man, although rather on the lean side. Under his dirt-caked felt hat a pair of red eyebrows jutted out, as big as barley-ears. His small black eyes glinted as if looking out of a deep tunnel. A thick red moustache hid his mouth, and his cheeks were covered with a week's stubble. As he passed by the mule, he spat but made no other comment. Then he dropped his eyes and shambled away.

'Now there's an unlikeable sort of fellow,' my father remarked.

'They aren't all like that,' the farmer said. 'That one hates me, because he's my brother.'

This motive seemed to him self-explanatory, and he began to drag the mule away. The mule dropped some buns, then turned his rectum inside out till it looked just like a tomato.

I thought he would die of it, but my father reassured me.

'He does that for hygiene,' he told me, 'it's his way of keeping clean.'

CHAPTER FOURTEEN

W E left the village, and then enchantment began: I felt welling up in me a love that was to last all my life.

A vast landscape rose before us in a semi-circle reaching to the sky. Black pine-woods, divided by valleys, died away like waves up to the foot of three rocky peaks.

Around us, the brows of lesser hills surrounded our path, which meandered along a crest between two valleys. A great, black, motionless bird marked the middle of the sky, and from all sides there rose, like a sea of music, the coppery hum of cicadas. They were in a hurry to live and knew that death would come with darkness.

The farmer pointed out the peaks which seemed to hold up the sky in the background.

On the left, a big white crag glistened in the sunset at the top of a huge reddish cone.

'That one,' he said, 'is *Tête Rouge*—the Redhead.'

On its right, there gleamed a bluish peak, a little higher than the other. It consisted of three concentric terraces which widened towards the bottom, like the three flounces of Mlle Guimard's fur tippet.

'That one,' the farmer said, 'is the Taoumé.'

Then, while we were admiring this mass of rock, he added:

'They also call it the Tubé.'

'What does that mean?' my father asked.

'It means that you call it the Tubé, or else the Taoumé.'

'But what's the origin of those words?'

'The origin is that it has two names, but nobody knows why. You too have two names, and so have I.'

To cut short this learned explanation (which did not strike me as conclusive), he cracked his whip near the mule's ears, and it responded by breaking wind.

In the background, to the right, but much farther away, a slope rose into the sky, carrying on its shoulders the third rocky peak, tilting backwards and dominating the whole landscape.

'And that's Garlaban. Aubagne is on the far side, right at its foot.'

'I was born at Aubagne,' I said.

'Then you are from hereabouts,' the farmer said.

I looked proudly at my family, then at the imposing scenery with a new feeling of tenderness.

'And I was born at Saint-Loup,' said Paul anxiously. 'Am I from hereabouts?'

'A little,' the farmer said. 'A little, not much. . . .'

Paul fell behind me, vexed. And as he was beginning to show a gift for conversation, he said to me under his breath:

'He's a bloody fool!'

There was not a hamlet, not so much as a farmstead, not the smallest shack to be seen. The path was now no more than two dusty furrows separated by a ridge of wild grass which caressed the mule's belly.

On the plunging slope to our right, beautiful pine-trees towered over a thick undergrowth of kermes-oak, which stand no higher than a table but carry real full-size acorns, like dwarfs with the heads of full-grown men.

On the far side of the valley rose an elongated hill. It was the shape of a three-decker man-o'-war, each deck recessed on the other. Three long pine-woods sprang from them, separated by cliffs of white rock.

'The cliffs over there,' the farmer said, 'are the *barres* of the Holy Ghost.'

At this plainly 'obscurantist' name, my father frowned an agnostic brow and asked:

'Are people very priest-ridden around here?'

'A bit,' the farmer said.

'You go to mass on Sundays?'

'Depends. . . . When there's a drought, I meself don't go till it rains again. You've got to make the good Lord understand. . . . '

I was tempted to disclose to him that God did not exist, which I knew from very reliable sources. But as my father said nothing, I modestly kept silent.

I suddenly noticed that my mother was walking with some difficulty, due to the high heels of her button boots. Without saying a word, I went up to the cart and managed to pull off the small suit-case which had been wedged under the ropes at the rear of the vehicle.

'What are you doing?' she said, surprised.

I put the suit-case down on the ground and extracted her sandals from it. They were no bigger than mine. She gave me a wonderfully tender smile and said:

'You big silly, we can't stop here!'

'Why not? We'll catch them up.'

Sitting on a boulder by the roadside, she changed her shoes, watched by Paul who had come to view the operation, which he seemed to think rather bold from the standpoint of modesty, for he looked in all directions to make sure that nobody could have caught a glimpse of his mother's stockings.

She took us by the hand and, at a fast trot, we caught up with the wagon and I put the precious suit-case back on it. How small she was now! She looked fifteen years old, her cheeks were pink, and I saw with pleasure that her calves seemed thicker.

The path was still climbing, and we came closer to the pine-woods.

On the left, the hill sloped down in narrow terraces to the very bottom of a green valley.

The farmer said to my father:

'That one there has two names, too. You call it the "Vala" or else the "Brook".'

75

'Oho!' my father said, charmed, 'is there a brook?'

'Of course,' the farmer said. 'And a fine brook, too!'

My father turned round to us:

'Children, there's a brook at the bottom of the valley!'

Whereupon the farmer turned round, too, and added:

'After it rains, of course. . . .'

The terraces of the Vala were covered with olive-trees; each of them had four or five trunks planted in a circle. As they all slanted back from the centre, there was room for their foliage to open and form a single bouquet. There were also tender green almond-trees and shimmering apricot-trees.

I did not know the names of these trees but I loved them right away.

All around them lay untilled land, covered with a yellowish-brown grass which, the farmer told us, was '*baouco*'. It looked like dried hay, but this was its natural colour. In spring, to share in the general gaiety, it made a feeble effort to turn green. But despite its poor appearance, it was hardy and vigorous, like all useless plants.

Here I first saw, amid the *baouco*, some dark green tufts that looked like miniature olive-trees. I left the path and ran to touch their tiny leaves. A powerful perfume rose like a cloud and enveloped me entirely.

It was an unknown scent, sombre and intense, which filled my head and penetrated right to my heart.

It was thyme, which springs from the gravel of the *garrigues*: those few plants had clambered down to meet me, to herald for the small schoolboy the future fragrance of Virgil.

I tore off a few sprigs and ran back to the cart, holding them to my nostrils.

'What's that?' my mother said.

She took them, inhaled deeply, and declared:

'It's fresh thyme. It'll make lovely jugged hare.'

'Thyme!' said François, with some disdain. 'It isn't a patch on *pèbre d'aï*. . . .'

'What's that?'

'It's a sort of thyme and at the same time a sort of mint, too. But you can't put it into words. I'll show you some.'

He then talked of marjoram, rosemary, sage, fennel. You had to 'stuff the hare's belly' with it or else 'mince it fine-fine-fine' with 'a thick piece of fat bacon'.

My mother listened, much interested; I was sniffing the sacred sprigs and I felt ashamed.

The road was still going uphill, hoisting itself now and then over some small plateau. Looking back, one could see the long valley of the Huveaune, under a swathe of mist which stretched down to the glistening sea.

Paul was trotting all over the place, striking the trunks of the almond-trees with a stone, and swarms of cicadas would fly out, buzzing with indignation.

There was a last climb, as steep as the first one. Thanks to a volley of cudgel-blows, the mule, his back strained in an arc which would suddenly slacken, and his head nodding with every push on his collar, jerked the rocking cart uphill. The load, swaying like the rod of a metronome, tore off olive-branches in passing. But there was one branch that proved stronger than a table-leg which fell resoundingly on the head of my astonished father.

While my mother was trying to prevent a bump by pressing a two-*sous* piece on the bruise, little Paul was dancing around with peals of laughter. As for me, I picked up the guilty leg and was glad to see that the long, bevelled split looked easy to repair. I hastened to bring this comforting news to my father, who was pulling a face under the forceful pressure of Napoleon III's effigy.

When we joined the wagon again, it had drawn up in a spinney at the top of the rise to let the martyred mule recover his breath. He was breathing with great snorts, blowing out his meagre ribs which looked like hoops in a sack, and threads of transparent spittle hung from his long, rubbery jowls.

My father pointed with his left hand—for he was still rubbing his aching skull—to a small house on the hill opposite, half-hidden by a huge fig-tree.

'There!' he said. 'That's the *Bastide Neuve*, our holiday hide-out! The garden on the left is ours too!'

The garden, surrounded by a rusty fence, was at least a hundred yards wide.

All I could distinguish was a grove of olive and almond-trees, whose straying branches interwove above a tangled wilderness. But this miniature virgin forest was just the one I had imagined in my dreams and, with Paul following, I raced forward, shouting with delight.

CHAPTER FIFTEEN

A SMALL van was drawn up between the big fig-tree on the terrace and the house, and its two horses were crunching oats in bags hanging from their cheeks.

Uncle Jules, in shirt sleeves and with bare arms, was about to finish unloading his furniture, i.e. he was toppling it from the edge of the van onto the broad back of the removal man.

Aunt Rose, settled in a wicker arm-chair on the terrace, was giving cousin Pierre his bottle, and he manifested his joy by wriggling his toes.

Uncle Jules was rather flushed, and much gayer than I had ever seen him before: he talked in a loud voice and rolled his r's like a wooden rattle. On a round iron table there were two empty bottles and a third still half-full of red wine.

'Ah! There you are, Joseph!' he cried with exaggerated joy. 'There you are at last! I was beginning to wonder whether you hadn't foundered on the r-r-road!'

My father looked at him rather coldly:

'At all events, you've had something to help you wait for us!' he said, pointing at the three bottles.

'My dear fellow,' my uncle said, 'you will learn that wine is an indispensable item in the diet of heavy labourers, and above all of removal men. I mean *natural* wine, and this one is home-grown. Besides, you yourself will be jolly glad to swig a tumblerful when you've finished unloading your stuff.'

'My dear Jules,' said my father, 'I may drink two drops, perhaps, to pay tribute to the product of your vineyards. But I certainly shan't "swig a tumblerful", as you so well put it. A tumbler of this wine probably contains twelve centilitres of pure spirit. I'm not sufficiently immune to this poison to stand a dose which, if injected subcutaneously, would be enough to kill three large-size dogs. Anyway, you need only look at the state to which Alcohol has brought this man!'

He motioned towards the furniture-remover who was sucking his drooping moustache and reeling towards the cart, with bloodshot eyes and breathing stertorously. He took a bedside table under one arm, two chairs under the other, and tried to charge through the doorway with them. But he remained wedged between the groaning furniture, and the pressure of the bedside table produced a resounding belch from his vast paunch.

My mother turned away to laugh, and Aunt Rose giggled. Paul was overcome with glee, but I didn't feel like laughing: I expected to see him collapse any moment in spasms of agony, among the débris of our furniture.

Instead of rushing to help the wretched man (whose liver I could imagine!), Uncle Jules flew into a towering rage.

'The idea of it!... Why, *saperlipopette,* the idea of it! You can see yourself that the door is too narrow for the ...'

'You're certainly right there,' the removal man hiccoughed, 'but I ain't the one who made it.'

'The gentleman is right,' my father said, 'he didn't make the door, and he didn't make himself either. ... Since one won't go with the other, there's no point in persevering. Anyhow, your furniture is unloaded, and I don't need him for mine. Moreover, he's sure to be tired, and as his working-day is finished, he'd better get back to town.'

'Now there's a man who talks sense,' the removal man declared. 'It's already past five, and I'm the father of a family, with a hernia to boot. That may surprise you, but if you like, I'll show it to you.'

'You're a drunkard and an idiot,' said Uncle Jules.

The man with the hernia assumed a threatening scowl.

'I don't know what's preventing me from bashing your face in!'

My aunt and my mother had risen in fright. My father stepped between the two men, but the old soak pushed him away, repeating:

'I dunno wha's preventing me!'

Paul hid, white as a sheet, behind the trunk of the fig-tree. My eyes were searching for a sharp stone when a voice spoke up:

'Just look in this direction, and you'll see what's preventing you!'

It was François who stepped forward very calmly, holding in his fist the *taravelle*, i.e. the hard wooden billet which was the single spoke of his cart-winch.

The removal man turned towards him in high dudgeon, shouting:

'Wha'sh'at? Wha-sh'at?'

'The stick! The stick!' François shouted back.

'That's a bit thick!' said the man.

'Very thick!' François agreed, weighing the spoke appraisingly. Then he turned to Uncle Jules:

'Have you paid him?'

'Not yet,' Uncle Jules replied. 'I owe him seven francs fifty.'

'Pay him,' said François.

Uncle Jules handed the drunken fellow three pieces of silver.

'What about my tip?' the removal man wanted to know.

'You've tippled enough as it is,' my father said. 'And believe me it does you no good.'

'You're a lot of skunks!' the removal man growled.

'Be off with you!' said François, 'get up on your box. I'll help you turn round.'

He was looking at him in such a way that the drunkard suddenly became maudlin.

'You're a pal, you are,' he said. 'You understand life. But those bourgeois, oh la la! . . . I may have burst my bowels with that mucky bedside table of theirs, and they have the cheek to refuse me a tip! But they haven't heard the last of it, it'll cost them more than their income tax, you'll see!'

He had some trouble collecting the reins, whilst François turned the two horses, holding them firmly by their bridles. When they were once more facing the right way, he went back to his cart and picked up his whip, and while the removal man was shaking his fist at us and muttering obscure threats, François, shouting wildly, whipped the nags as hard as he could: in a cloud of dust, creaks and curses, the van hurtled off into the past.

CHAPTER SIXTEEN

THERE now began the most beautiful days of my life. The house was called the New Bastide, but it had been new for a very long time. It was a tumbledown old farm-house, which had been patched up thirty years earlier by a city gentleman, who sold tent-canvas, floor-mops and brooms. My father and my uncle paid him an annual rent of eighty francs (that is to say, four *luois d'or*), which their wives considered rather a lot. But the house looked like a villa, and there was 'water available at the sink': that is to say, the enterprising broom-merchant had had a big tank built on to the back of the house, as large and almost as tall as the building itself. All you had to do was to turn on the copper tap that was set above the sink to see the cool, clear water flow. . . .

This was an extraordinary luxury, and it was only later that I grasped the miracle of this tap. The whole region, from the village fountain to the peaks of *L'Etoile*, was as dry as dust; within a radius of twenty kilometres there were only a dozen wells (most of them dry from May onwards) and three or four 'springs'—a 'spring' being a crack in the rock, at the bottom of some small cave, which would weep in silence into a beard of moss.

That's why, whenever a peasant woman walked into our kitchen to bring us eggs or chick-peas, she would shake her head with awe as she stared at the gleaming Tap of Progress.

There was also, on the ground-floor, a vast dining-hall (quite five yards by four) which boasted a small fireplace made of genuine marble.

A curving staircase led to the four rooms on the first floor. By an artful modern contrivance, the bedroom windows were fitted with movable window-frames between the glass-panes and the shutters, and these frames were covered with a fine wire-mesh to keep the insects out at night.

Lighting was provided by paraffin lamps and some emergency candles. But as we had most of our meals out on the terrace, under the fig-tree, there was above all the Hurricane Lamp.

Miraculous Hurricane Lamp! My father extracted it one night from a big cardboard box, filled it with paraffin, and lit the wick. A flat, almond-shaped flame spurted out and he covered it with an ordinary chimney. This he enclosed in an egg-shaped globe which was protected by a nickel-plated grille topped by a metal lid. This lid was a windtrap: it had holes in it which inhaled the night-breeze, made it coil around itself and pushed it dead on the impassive flame which devoured it. . . . Whenever I looked at it, hanging from a branch of the fig-tree, burning brightly and as serene as an altar-lamp, I'd forget all about my grated cheese soup and decide to dedicate my life to science. . . . That almond of fire still illuminates my childhood, and I found the sight of the Planier lighthouse, when I visited it ten years later, much less astonishing.

Anyhow, just as the Planier beacon lures quail and lapwings, it attracted all the insects of the night. As soon as one hung it up on its branch, it was surrounded by a swarm of fleshy moths, whose shadows danced on the table-cloth: consumed by a hopeless love, they would fall, cooked to a nicety, onto our plates.

There were also enormous wasps, called *cabridans*, which we brained with our napkins, knocking the jug over sometimes, and the glasses invariably. There were also capricorn-beetles and stag-beetles, which shot out of the night as if catapulted, making the lantern tinkle before diving into the tureen. The shiny, black stag-beetles bore on their heads huge flat pincers with two antlered branches. This fabulous tool was of no use to them because it could not be articulated, but it was most convenient for attaching string harnesses, thus enabling the tamed stag-beetles to drag the enormous weight of the flat-iron very easily over the oil-cloth.

84

The 'garden' was nothing more than a very old, overgrown orchard, fenced in by wire-netting, most of which had been gnawed away by the rust of time. But by christening it a 'garden', we confirmed the status of the 'villa'.

Moreover, my uncle had bestowed the title of 'housemaid' on a bemused-looking peasant-wench who came to wash the dishes in the afternoon and sometimes to do the laundry, which gave her an opportunity of washing her hands. We were thus linked, three times over, to the upper class, the class of distinguished bourgeois.

In front of the garden spread poorly cultivated wheat and barley fields, divided by age-old olive-trees.

Behind the house, the pinewoods formed sombre islands in the vast *garrigue* which stretched over mountains, valleys and table-lands right up to the mountain-range of Sainte-Victoire. The *Bastide Neuve* was the last building on the doorstep of the desert, and one could walk for forty kilometres without coming across anything but the squat ruins of three or four mediaeval farm-houses and a few deserted sheep-pens.

We went to bed early, exhausted by the day's play, and little Paul had to be carried upstairs, limp as a rag-doll: I would catch him just in time as he fell from his chair, gripping in his clenched hand a gnawed apple or half a banana.

Every night as I went to bed, half-asleep, I'd resolve to wake up at dawn, so as not to lose a minute of the miraculous morrow. But I didn't open my eyes before seven o'clock, as vexed and querulous as if I had missed a train.

Then I'd call Paul, who'd start to grunt plaintively and turn to face the wall; but he could not resist the window which suddenly shone resplendently as the wooden shutters banged open, while the song of the cicadas and the scents of the *garrigue* rushed into the expanding room.

We went downstairs stark naked, carrying our clothes in our hands.

My father had fixed a long rubber hose to the kitchen-tap. It stuck out of the window and ended in a copper nozzle on the terrace.

I would spray Paul, then he would drench me. This method was a brainwave of my father's, for the abhorred 'washing' had become a sport; it lasted till my mother shouted out of the window: 'Stop it! When the tank's empty, we'll be obliged to leave!'

After this appalling threat, she would conclusively turn off the tap.

We quickly washed down our bread and butter with milky coffee and then the great adventure began.

We were forbidden to leave the garden, but no watch was kept on us. My mother believed the fence to be impassable—and my aunt was cousin Pierre's slave. My father often went into the village 'shopping' or up into the hills to collect herbs. As for Uncle Jules, he spent three days a week in town, for he had only twenty days' holidays and had spread them over two months.

Thus left to ourselves most of the time, we would climb up to the nearest pinewoods. But these explorations, knife in hand and ears cocked, usually ended in a headlong flight towards the house, following some unforeseen encounter with a boa constrictor, a lion, or a troglodyte bear.

Our earliest sport was hunting the cicadas which sucked the sap of the almond-trees as they sang. To begin with, they escaped us, but we had soon acquired such skill and efficiency that we came home surrounded by a halo of music, for we brought back dozens of them which went on chirping in our jolting trouser-pockets. Then came the capture of butterflies, the two-tailed sphynx with its large, blue-bordered white wings that left a silvery dust on your fingers.

For several days we threw Christians to the lions: that is to say, we flung handfuls of small grasshoppers into the diamond-studded cobwebs woven by big, black, velvety spiders with yellow stripes. Their captors swaddled them in silk in a matter of seconds, daintily drilled a hole in their victims' heads and sucked at them for a long while with a gourmet's delight. We would break off these innocent games to feast on the gum of almond trees, a reddish gum like honey. This was a sweet and marvellously sticky delicacy, but strongly disapproved of by Uncle Jules who claimed that this gum would 'eventually stick our guts together'.

My father, anxious to see us pursue our studies, advised us to give up our futile games. He recommended the minute observation of the habits of insects and, to begin with, those of the ants, in whom he saw the models of good citizens.

That's why, next morning, we spent a long time tearing up the dry grass and the *baouco* around the main entrance to a fine ant-heap. When the place was nice and tidy within a radius of at least two yards, I managed to slip into the kitchen while my mother and my aunt were picking almongs behind the house, and stole a big glass of paraffin and a few matches.

The ants, with no evil forebodings, marched to and fro in double file, like stevedores on a ship's gangway.

I first made sure that nobody could see us, then I poured a big dose of paraffin into the principal opening. The head of the column broke up in great confusion, and scores of ants came up from below; they ran hither and thither, completely bewildered, and those who had big heads opened and closed their strong mandibles, looking for the invisible enemy. I then shoved a paper spill into the hole. Paul coveted the honour of setting light to it, which he did very efficiently. A red, smoky flame rose, and our studies began.

Unfortunately, the ants turned out to be too easily combustible. Instantly blasted by the heat, they disappeared in a blaze of sparks. These little fireworks were rather amusing but too short-lived. Moreover, after the sublimation of the extra-mural workers, we vainly awaited the exit of the mighty subterranean legions and the noisy explosion of the queen, on which I had firmly counted; but no more appeared, and all that remained before our eyes was a small, smoke-blackened funnel, sad and solitary like the crater of an extinct volcano.

However, we soon consoled ourselves for this failure with the capture of three big *pregadious,* or praying mantises which, clothed entirely in green, were wandering on the green twigs of a verbena bush: fine subjects for scientific observation.

Papa had told us (with a certain agnostic glee) that the so-called 'praying' mantis was in fact a fierce and pitiless creature; that it could be considered 'the tiger among insects,' and that a study of its habits was deeply engrossing.

I therefore decided to study them, that is to say, in order to provoke a fight between the two biggest ones, I presented them to each other at very close quarters, with claws at the ready.

This enabled us to advance our studies by observing that these creatures could live without claws, then without legs, and even without half their heads. . . . After a quarter of an hour of these innocent joys of childhood, all that remained of one of the champions was its upper half which, after devouring its opponent's head and torso, unhurriedly got to work on the lower limbs which were still twitching nervously. Paul, who was kind-hearted, went to steal a small tube of seccotine ('makes even iron stick') and attempted to glue the two halves together to make them one again, to which whole we could then solemnly give back its freedom. He could not bring this generous operation to a happy end, for the top half managed to escape.

But there still remained the third tiger in the glass jar. I decided to confront it with ants, and this happy initiative allowed us to enjoy a delightful spectacle.

I briskly up-ended the jar, and placed it over the main entrance of a busy ant-heap. The tiger, being taller than the jar was wide, stood up on its hind-legs and swivelled its head about with a tourist's curiosity. Meanwhile, a horde of ants foamed out of the tunnel and attacked its legs so effectively that it lost its calm and began to dance, at the same time thrusting its two pincers right and left: with each thrust it picked up a cluster of ants which it lifted to its jaw, from which they dropped, snapped in two.

As the thickness of the glass distorted the beauty of the spectacle, and as the tiger's uncomfortable posture irked its movements, I thought it my duty to remove the jar. The *pregadiou* fell into its natural position, its pincers folded and its six feet on the ground. But at the end of each foot four ants implacably clung on, their jaws locked, their claws clutching the gravel: thus overpowered by these Lilliputians, the tiger was as helpless as Gulliver.

Meanwhile the *pregadiou's* pincers attacked each of the mooring-parties in turn and wrought havoc among the personnel. But even before the truncated insects fell from the snapping jaws, others had taken their place, and the *pregadiou* had to start all over again.

I wondered how this situation could evolve, since it seemed stabilized—I mean, fixed in an immutable cycle—when I noticed that the reflexes of the grabbing pincers were no longer as swift nor as frequent as before. I concluded that the *pregadiou* was beginning to lose courage because of the inefficiency of its tactics and that no doubt it would change them. And, indeed, after a few minutes, the lateral attacks stopped altogether.

The ants promptly abandoned its neck, chest and back, and it remained upright and motionless, its pincers in prayer and its thorax held almost straight up on its six long, faintly twitching legs.

Paul said to me: 'He's thinking.'

His thoughts seemed to me rather prolonged, and the ants' disappearance intrigued me; so I lay down flat on my belly and discovered the tragic truth.

Under the three-pronged tail of the pensive tiger, the ants had enlarged the natural orifice: one stream filed in, another filed out, as if it were the door of a big store on Christmas Eve. Each one carried away its booty: the diligent housewives were removing the inside of the *pregadiou*.

The unfortunate tiger, still motionless and, with a kind of introspection, apparently attentive to what was going on inside him, had no means of indicating his torture or despair, being by nature unequipped with facial or vocal expression. His agony therefore was unspectacular. We realized that he was dead only when the mooring-parties let go of his legs and began to carve up the thin envelope which had contained him. They sawed off the neck, cut up the chest into neat slices, peeled the legs and elegantly dismantled the terrible pincers, as a cook does with a lobster. The lot was then dragged underground and stored away in the depths of a warehouse, in a different arrangement.

All that remained on the ground were the lovely green wing-sheaths, which had fluttered so gloriously above the green jungle and had terrorized quarries and enemies alike. Scorned by the housewives, they sadly confessed that they were inedible.

That is how our studies of the 'habits' of the praying mantis and of the 'diligence' of the toiling ants came to an untimely end.

'Poor beast!' Paul said to me. 'He must have had an awful bellyache!'

'Serves him right,' I said. 'He eats grasshoppers alive, and cicadas too, and even butterflies. Papa told you: he's a tiger! I don't care a hang about a tiger's belly-ache.'

CHAPTER SEVENTEEN

JUST as we were beginning to tire of our entomological studies, we discovered our true vocation.

After lunch, when an African sun rained fire on the dying grass, we were compelled to 'rest' for an hour in the shade of the fig-tree, in those folding-chairs called 'deck-chairs' which are difficult to open correctly, which cruelly pinch your fingers and even collapse at times under the startled sleeper.

This 'rest' was torture for us, and my father, pedagogue that he was—i.e. a great sweetener of pills—made us accept it by bringing us books by Fenimore Cooper and Gustave Aymard.

Little Paul, with wide-open eyes and gaping mouth, listened to me reading aloud *The Last of the Mohicans*. This was a revelation to us, which *The Pathfinders* was to confirm: we were Red Indians, sons of the Forest, buffalo-hunters, grizzly-bear killers, stranglers of boa constrictors, and scalpers of Palefaces.

My mother consented to sew together—without knowing what for—an old table-cloth and a blanket full of holes, and we set up our wigwam in the wildest corner of the garden.

I had a real bow, which had come straight from the New World via the junk-shop. I fashioned arrows from reeds and, hidden in the undergrowth, I fiercely shot at the door of the lavatory, which stood like a sort of sentry-box at the end of the garden-path. Then I stole the Pointed Knife from the kitchen-drawer. I held it by its blade—Comanche fashion—between thumb and forefinger, and hurled it with all my strength against the trunk of a pine-tree, whilst Paul would utter a piercing whistle to make it sound more dangerous.

However, we soon came to realize that, the only really interesting game being war, we could not go on belonging to the same tribe.

So I remained a Comanche, while Paul became a Pawnee, and this enabled me to scalp him several times a day. In exchange, towards evening, he killed me with a cardboard tomahawk.

Feather head-dresses, contrived by my mother and my aunt, and war-paint made with glue, jam and the dust of coloured chalks gave the final touch to the compulsive reality of this Red Indian life.

Sometimes, the two enemy tribes would bury the hatchet and unite to fight the Palefaces, the ferocious Yankees come down from the North. We followed imaginary tracks, bent double in the tall grass, watchful of broken boughs or invisible footprints and, fiercely frowning, I would scrutinize a thread of wool clinging to a golden plume of fennel. When the track divided, we parted in silence. . . . Now and then, to maintain communications, I would utter the cry of the mocking-bird—'so perfectly imitated that it would have deceived the female'—and Paul would answer with 'the hoarse bark of the coyote'. A perfect imitation, too— except that, for lack of a coyote, it reproduced the bark of the baker's dog, a mangy pug which sometimes attacked the seats of our trousers.

At other times, we were pursued by a coalition of trappers, commanded by 'Long Rifle'. To mislead the enemy, we would then walk backwards for a long while, so as to invert our footprints.

Then, in the middle of a clearing, I'd motion Paul to stop and, in the great silence, I'd put my ear to the ground. . . . I listened with sincere alarm to the approaching sound of our pursuers, for I heard, deep in the distant savannas, my galloping heart-beat.

When we returned home, the game continued.

The table was laid under the fig-tree. Lying in a chaise-longue, my father was reading one half of a newspaper, for Uncle Jules was reading the other.

We introduced ourselves with the grave dignity that is fitting
for chiefs, and I said:

'Ugh!'

My father answered:

'Ugh!'

'Do the great white chiefs wish to receive their red brothers
under their stone wigwam?'

'Our red brothers are welcome,' my father said. 'Their road
must have been long, for their feet are dusty.'

'We've come from the Lost River and we've marched for three
moons!'

'All the children of the Great Manitou are brothers: let the chiefs
share our pemmican with us. We only ask them to respect the
sacred customs of the White Man: let them go and wash their
hands first!'

CHAPTER EIGHTEEN

AT night during dinner, under the hurricane-lamp, with its halo of gnats, I sat opposite my pretty mother, gently swinging my sleep-heavy legs and listening to the conversation of those aged males.

Quite frequently they would talk politics. My uncle made unfavourable comparisons between President Fallières and King Louis XIV. My father countered by describing a cardinal whose body was shaped like a question mark, because the king had locked him up in a small iron cage; then he talked of a certain 'Saltacks' who was ruining the people.

At other times, Uncle Jules attacked some people who were called 'Radicles'. There was a Monsieur Comble, who was a radicle and about whom it was difficult to form an opinion: my father said that this radicle was a great and honest man, whereas my uncle called him 'the finest flower of the rabble' and offered to put this down in writing and to sign, seal and deliver it. He added that this Comble was the leader of a gang of rogues who were called 'Frimmasons'.

My father then mentioned another gang, called 'Jezwits'. These were dreadful 'Hippocrits' who were undermining the ground beneath one's very feet. At this Uncle Jules would flare up and summon him to return 'the Congregation's billion francs' on the spot. But my father—though I knew he didn't care for money—vehemently retorted: 'Never! You'll never get back all the wealth that was wrested from terrorized people in their death-agony!'

Thereupon my mother and my aunt quickly asked urgent

questions about the phylloxera in the region of Roussillon, or about the undeserved promotion of a teacher to high school, and the tone of the conversation underwent a sudden change.

I wasn't much interested, anyway, in what they were talking about. What I was listening to, and waiting for, were the *words*: for I had a passion for words and secretly collected them in a little note-book, as others collect stamps.

I loved *grenade, fumée* (smoke), *bourru* (churlish), *vermoulu* (worm-eaten) and, above all, *manivelle* (crank). I'd often repeat them to myself when I was alone, for the pleasure of hearing them.

Now, in my uncle's talk, there were some brand-new ones and they were delightful: damascened, florilegium, filigree; or grandiose like: archiepiscopal, plenipotentiary.

When I saw one of these mighty three-deckers pass on the stream of his disquisition, I would raise my hand and ask for an explanation, which he never refused. It was then that I understood for the first time that grand-sounding words almost always contain beautiful pictures.

My father and my uncle encouraged this hobby which seemed to them to promise well; so much so that one day they presented me with '*anticonstitutionnellement*' (unconstitutionally), although the word did not crop up in their conversation (which indeed would have been surprising), and they revealed to me that it was the longest word in the French language. I had to write it down on the grocer's bill which I had kept in my pocket.

I copied it, with considerable effort, onto a page of my note-book and read it aloud in bed every night. It took me several days to master this monster and I promised myself I would put it to use if, by any chance, some day at the end of centuries, I'd be compelled to go back to school.

CHAPTER NINETEEN

TOWARDS August 10th, the holidays were interrupted for a whole afternoon by a thunderstorm which, as I feared, developed into a dictation lesson.

Uncle Jules, in an arm-chair by the glass door, was reading a newspaper. Paul was squatting in a dark corner, playing dominoes by himself, i.e. he was placing the pieces end to end at random, after much thought and muttered arguments. My mother was sewing by the window. My father, seated at the table, was sharpening a pen-knife on a black stone and reading aloud an incomprehensible story, of which he repeated each sentence two or three times.

It was a homily by Lamennais, which described the adventures of a bunch of grapes.

The Father of the Family picked it in his vineyard, but did not eat it: he brought it Home, to offer it to the Mother of the Family. Much moved, the latter secretly gave it to her Son who, without mentioning it to anybody, presented it to his Sister. But she did not touch it either. She waited for the Father's return. And when the Father found the Bunch of Grapes on his plate, he clasped all his Family in his arms, raising his eyes to Heaven.

The peregrinations of the bunch of grapes stopped there, and I was secretly wondering who had finally eaten it, when Uncle Jules folded his newspaper and said to me gravely:

'Now that's a page you ought to learn by heart!'

'Why?' I asked, indignant at this aggressive proposal of additional work.

'Well, surely,' my uncle said, 'you must be touched by the feelings which imbue these humble peasants?'

Through the window-pane I was watching the rain fall, polishing the boughs of the fig-tree to a shiny black, and I kept nibbling at my pen-holder.

He persisted.

'Why did this bunch of grapes pass right round the family?'

He looked at me, his eyes brimming with kindness. I wanted to please him and concentrated my whole attention on the problem. In a flash I perceived the truth, and cried:

'Because it had been sprayed with sulphate!'

Uncle Jules stared at me fixedly, gritted his teeth, and turned completely scarlet. He tried to speak, but indignation took his breath away. He attempted, one after another, three or four guttural syllables, but he was in no state to provide sequels that could shed light on their meaning. He lifted his arms to the sky, then his behind from the chair, and finally spluttered:

'*Voilà! Voilà! Voilà!*'

These three exclamations seemed to have cleared his throat, for he was at last able to cry:

'Here's the result of a Godless School for you! The inspiring effects of Love he ascribes to the fear of copper sulphate! This child, who is not a monster, has quite spontaneously given a monstrous reply. Do you realize, my dear Joseph, the gravity of your frightening responsibility?'

'Come, Jules,' my mother said, 'I'm sure he said it for fun!'

'For *fun?*' shouted my uncle. 'That makes it even worse! . . . I prefer to think that he did not properly understand my question.'

He turned towards me.

'Listen to me carefully. If you found a beautiful bunch of grapes, a marvellous, unique bunch, wouldn't you bring it home to your mother?'

'Oh yes, I would!' I said, sincerely.

'Good for you!' Uncle Jules said. 'Spoken straight from the heart!'

And he turned to my father, observing:

'I'm happy to see that, despite the abominable materialism you're teaching him, he has found the law of God in his heart and would keep the bunch of grapes for his mother!'

Seeing that he was about to triumph, I hastened to my father's rescue and added:

'But I'd eat half of it on the way.'

This displeased my uncle, and he was about to start afresh when my father declared peremptorily:

'And he's right, too! For after all, if those people had such noble sentiments, they would also deny themselves the heart of a lettuce, the white meat of a chicken, and the liver of a rabbit! And as perfect virtue is of necessity unalterable, this passing round of choice morsels must have gone on all their lives, while the poor creatures, who must after all have needed to eat, were wrangling over the duck's head, the bone in the cutlet, and the cabbage-stalk! Thanks to the boy, I've just come to realize that this story is utterly idiotic. The truth is that this Lamennais of yours was a canting parson and when he wanted to edify the faithful, he fell into sanctimonious drivel, like the rest of them.'

Uncle Jules, his moustache suddenly bristling, was about to parry this frontal attack with vigour when Aunt Rose, sensing the imminent fight, appeared at the door from the far end of the kitchen, where she had been keeping an eye on a rabbit *en civet*. She was waving the salad-basket and, holding a black oilskin cape by the hood in her left hand, she called out gaily:

'Jules! The rain's almost stopped! Quick, get some snails!'

Without giving him a moment, she shoved the wire-basket into his hands and thrust the hood of the cape down over his nostrils, as if putting a snuffer on the argument. It was hard for him, in this outfit, to embark on a diatribe. He tried, though, to roll a few r's, and we could hear:

'. . . Too sad r-r-really, too dr-readful. . . . This poor-r-r child. . . .'

But my aunt, who had laughingly swivelled him round, pushed him out into the pelting rain, closed the door after him and, through the window-pane, blew him a kiss of unfeigned tenderness. Then only did she turn on us in sudden anger:

'Joseph, you shouldn't have started it!'

Uncle Jules, who liked rain, stayed out a whole hour, and came back soaked but happy.

A fine slimy beard hung from the salad-basket, my uncle wore snail epaulets, and the chief of the tribe—who was enormous—pointed his horns in all directions.

My father was playing the flute and my mother was listening to him, as she hemmed napkins; my little sister was asleep with her head in her arms, and I was playing a game of dominoes with Paul. Uncle Jules was showered with congratulations, and no further mention was made of Lamennais.

At dinner that night, however, he took a cruel revenge.

My mother had just placed on the table the rabbit *en civet*, redolent with the scent of aromatic herbs. Normally, as a reward for my great scholastic efforts, the liver was earmarked for me, and my eyes were already searching for it in the velvety sauce. . . .

Uncle Jules caught sight of it before me, and impaled it on the end of his fork, He raised it to the lamplight, examined it, sniffed it, and said:

'This liver is admirably cooked. It's healthy and looks juicy and tender. It certainly is a titbit. I would consider it my duty, therefore, to offer it to someone, if there weren't a certain person at this table who would think it poisoned!'

Whereupon he burst into sarcastic laughter and devoured it before my eyes.

CHAPTER TWENTY

AS August 15th drew near, it became clear that great events were afoot.

One afternoon, while I was setting up a torturing-stake on a small grassy knoll, Paul arrived at a gallop, bearing strange tidings:

'Uncle Jules is busy cooking!'

I was so surprised that I promptly abandoned the matter in hand to go and solve the mystery of Uncle Jules the Cook.

He was standing at the kitchen-range, watching over a sizzling frying-pan. It contained thick, yellowish lozenges which hissed as they fried in the boiling fat. A sickening smell pervaded the kitchen, and I promptly decided that I wasn't going to eat that stuff.

'Uncle Jules, what *is* this?'

'You'll find out tonight,' he said.

And gripping the pan-handle, he gave it a short, sharp jerk, as if he were frying chestnuts.

'Are we going to eat them tonight?' Paul enquired.

'No,' said Uncle Jules, laughing. 'We shan't eat them. Not tonight, nor any other night.'

'Then why are you cooking them?'

'To give little boys something to chatter about. Now go and play outside, because if you get splashed with boiling fat, you'll have a face like a colander for the rest of your life. Go on, off you go!'

★

Once outside, Paul said to me:

100

'He's no good at cooking.'

'I don't believe he *is* cooking. I think it's a secret. We'll ask papa.'

But Papa wasn't about. He had taken his wife for an outing, leaving us behind, which seemed sheer treachery.

We had to wait till the evening.

So I devoted the afternoon to composing an admirable *Song for the Death of a Comanche Chief* (words and music):

> Farewell, prairie, oh!
> The arrow of a foe
> Has disarmed my avenging hand,
> But my heart remains pure
> Even under tor-ture,
> Thus amazing the traveller in our land.
>
> Cowardly Pawnee,
> See how I scorn thee!
> Heed my sarcastic roar!
> I'll never be licked
> By the pains you inflict:
> They're mosquito-bites, no more!

There were seven or eight verses. . . .

I went up to my room and 'rehearsed' them at length, in silence and solitude.

Then I busied myself with applying Paul's war-paint, followed by my own. At last, crowned with feathers, hands tied behind my back, I gravely advanced towards the torture-stake, to which Paul tied me firmly, raucously shouting supposed Pawnee insults. Then he danced cruelly around me, while I began to chant the Death Song.

I put so much sincerity into it and succeeded so well with my 'sarcastic roar' that my executioner prudently stepped back, a little alarmed.

But my triumph broke out in the last verse:

Farewell, my dear brothers!
Farewell, primroses and others!
My horse and my stirrups, adieu!
Go and tell my mother anon
To stop weeping—for her son
Died like a warrior true!

I ended on so poignant a tremolo that I was myself shaken by it, and my face was wet with tears. Then I let my chin sink on my chest, closed my eyes, and died.

I heard a heart-rending sob and saw Paul running away, screaming:

'He's dead! He's dead!'

It was my father who came to deliver me, and I could see that he was much tempted to add to my fictitious tortures a real clout on the ear. But I was proud of my success as an actor, and was planning to give a performance after dinner when, on my way through the dining-room to wash my hands in the kitchen, I had a marvellous surprise.

Papa and Uncle Jules had put all the extra leaves in the dining-room table, laid sacking over it, and on this vast expanse all sorts of splendours were displayed. First, there was an army of empty cartridges, and each row had its own colour: red, yellow, blue, green.

Then came small canvas bags, no bigger than a hand, and as heavy as stones. Each one bore a big black number: 2, 4, 5, 7, 9, 10.

Then there were some small scales, but with only one tray, and, clamped to the edge of the table was a strange copper contrivance, fitted with a crank and a wooden knob. And finally, right in the middle, stood the dish which Uncle Jules had cooked.

'This,' he said, 'is what I was cooking this morning. These are wads.'

'What do you do with them?' Paul asked.

'They're for cartridges!' my father said.

'Are you going shooting?' I asked.

'Certainly!'

'With Uncle Jules?'

'Certainly.'

'Have you got a gun?'

'Certainly!'

'Where is it?'

'You'll see it presently. For the time being, go and wash your hands; the soup's ready.'

CHAPTER TWENTY-ONE

THE conversation at dinner under the fig-tree was fascinating.

My father, city-bred and cooped up in schools all his life, had never killed beast or bird. But Uncle Jules had gone shooting ever since childhood, and made no mystery of it.

No sooner was the soup served than they started talking game.

'What do you think we're going to find in these hills?' my father asked.

'I made some enquiries in the village,' my uncle said.

'They're sure to have misinformed you,' my father said. 'These peasants are jealous of their game.'

My uncle smiled slyly.

'Of course they are!' he said. 'But I didn't let them know we were going shooting! I merely asked what sort of game they could sell us!'

'Now that's crafty!' my father said.

I admired this artfulness, though I wasn't sure that it did not go against our principles.

'And what did they offer to sell you?'

'To begin with, small birds.'

'Very small ones?' my mother asked, shocked.

'Well, yes,' Uncle Jules said. 'These savages will kill anything that flies.'

'Not butterflies?' asked Paul.

'No, butterflies are reserved for little boys. But they even kill warblers!'

'The soil around here is so barren,' my father said. 'And what can you grow without water? Most of these people are awfully poor, and shooting helps them to eke out a living. They sell the big birds and eat the small ones themselves.'

'Not forgetting,' said Uncle Jules, 'that a nice skewer of black-caps. . . .'

But Aunt Rose interrupted him, crying: 'Whatever happens, I forbid you to kill canaries!'

'No canaries, and no parrots! That's a promise. . . . But white-tails and ortolans. . . .'

'Ortolans are delicious,' my aunt agreed. . . .

'And what about thrushes?' my uncle said, winking. 'Will you allow us to have a go at thrushes?'

'Oh yes!' cried my mother. 'Joseph knows how to roast them on a skewer. We had some last year at Christmas.'

'When I see a thrush, I eat all of it!' Paul declared with enthusiasm. 'But not the beak.'

'Furthermore,' Uncle Jules said, 'I think we may count on rabbits.'

'I'm sure of it!' I said. 'There are even some around the house. They've made their lavatory near the big almond-tree: there are droppings all around it!'

'That will do!' my mother said sternly.

'Moreover,' Uncle Jules continued, 'we're sure to run across partridge and—what's more—*red* partridge!'

'Red all over?' Paul wanted to know.

'No, they're brown, with a black throat, red legs and beauti-ful red feathers on the wings and tail.'

'That would be lovely for playing at Indians!'

'There's also been talk of hare,' my uncle went on.

'Yet François assured me there weren't any,' said my father.

'Just offer him six francs per hare and he'll bring you some all right! He sells them five francs apiece at the Pichauris Inn! I hope our guns will save us this painful expense.'

'That would be grand,' my father agreed.

'I grant you hares are worth shooting, my dear Joseph. But

there is something better to come: in the ravines around the Taoumé there is the King of the Chase!'

'And what's that?'

'Guess!' said Uncle Jules.

'Elephants!' cried Paul.

'No!' said my uncle, but when he saw my little brother's disappointment, he added: 'I don't *believe* there are elephants, but you never can tell. Come on, Joseph, make an effort: the rarest, finest, wariest game! The game all sportsmen dream about?'

I broke in:

'What colour is it?'

'Brown, red and gold.'

'Pheasant!' my father cried.

Uncle Jules shook his head and said:

'Pah! . . . The pheasant is a pretty sight, I admit, but he's stupid and, when you flush him, as easy to shoot as a paper-kite. From the gourmet's point of view, the meat's tough and tasteless: to make it more or less fit for eating, you have to hang it and let it get high; in other words, let it rot! No, the pheasant is not the King of the Chase!'

'Then who *is* the King of the Chase?' my father asked.

My uncle rose, his arms folded, and said:

'The *bartavelle*!'

He had pronounced the word with studied emphasis and eyes rolling with wonder. However, he did not produce the hoped-for effect, for my father asked:

'What's that?'

My uncle was not in the least put out of countenance.

'You see!' he cried with satisfaction. 'The bird is so rare that Joseph himself has never heard of it! Well, the *bartavelle*—or rock partridge—is the royal partridge, and more royal than partridge, for it's huge and gleaming red. Actually, it's almost a woodcock. It lives on the heights above rocky valleys, but it's as suspicious as a fox: they always put up two sentries, and the covey's very difficult to approach.'

Paul said: 'I know what I'd do! I'd lie flat on my belly, and I'd crawl towards them like a snake, holding my breath!'

'Now that's a good idea,' Uncle Jules said. 'As soon as we see some *bartavelles*, we'll come and fetch you.'

'Have you often killed them?' my mother asked.

'No,' my uncle admitted modestly. 'I've seen them several times in the *Basses-Pyrénées*, but I've had no opportunity to shoot them.'

'But who told you there were *bartavelles* around here?'

'The old poacher who goes by the name of Mond des Parpaillouns.'

'Is he a nobleman?' I asked.

'I don't think so,' my father replied. 'It stands for Edmond des Papillons—Butterfly Ted.'

The name delighted me, and I promised myself that I'd go and pay a call on this mysterious lord.

'Has he seen any?' my father asked.

'He killed one last year. He took it to town and was paid TEN FRANCS for it!'

'Good Heavens!' my mother said, clasping her hands. 'If you could bring one home every day . . . that would suit me fine!'

'So it's not only the sportsman's dream,' my father said, 'but also the housewife's pipe-dream! Stop talking about *bartavelles*, my dear Jules: I'll probably dream of them tonight, and my dear wife will lose her head over them!'

'What bothers me,' said Aunt Rose, 'is that, if the peasants are to be believed, there are wild boar too.'

'Wild boar!' my mother repeated, alarmed.

'Yes, wild boar,' Uncle Jules said smilingly. 'But don't worry, they won't come up to the house! At the height of summer, when the springs have run dry in the Sainte-Victoire mountains, they go down to the little creek called Mulberry Well, the only spring in these parts which never dries up. Baptistin last year killed two of them!'

'But that's frightening!' my mother exclaimed.

'Not at all,' Joseph reassured her. 'The boar does not attack man.

On the contrary, he runs away as fast as he can, and you must stalk it very cautiously if you want to get near it.'

'Like the *bartavelles*!' cried Paul.

'Unless,' my uncle added gravely, 'unless a boar's been wounded!'

'And you think it can kill a man?'

'Goodness, yes!' Uncle Jules said. 'I had a friend—a chap called Malbousquet, who I used to go shooting with. He had been a wood-cutter, but he had lost an arm as the result of an accident at work. So, since he could no longer handle his axe, he took to poaching.'

'With only one arm?' Paul marvelled.

'Well, yes . . . with only one arm! And I assure you he was a marksman! Every day he'd bring back partridge, rabbits, hares, and he'd sell them on the sly to the chef at the Château. Well, one day, Malbousquet found himself face to face with a wild boar . . . not a very big one—seventy kilogrammes, to be precise, we weighed it afterwards. . . . Well, Malbousquet couldn't resist the temptation. He fired and he didn't miss. But the beast still had the strength to charge, knocked him over and tore him to pieces. Literally to pieces,' Uncle Jules repeated. 'When we found him, the first thing we saw lying in the middle of the path was a long greenish-yellow rope, quite ten yards long: that was Malbousquet's guts.'

My mother and Aunt Rose uttered a sickened 'Oh!', while Paul burst out laughing and clapped his hands.

'Jules,' my aunt said, 'you oughn't to talk about such horrors in front of the children.'

'On the contrary!' said my father (who could always discern some educational value in any catastrophe). 'It's excellent for their enlightenment. They can learn from this that the wild boar is a dangerous animal. So if by any extraordinary chance you should happen to see one, climb the nearest tree at once.'

'You must promise me, Joseph,' my mother said, 'that you too will climb a tree without firing a single shot.'

'That would be a fine thing!' cried my uncle. 'Malbousquet, as I told you, had no buck-shot. Whereas we have plenty.'

He went to fetch from a drawer a handful of cartridges which he put down on the table.

'They're longer than the others, because I filled them with a double dose of gunpowder,' he explained. 'That's enough to lay the feller out! . . . Provided,' he added, turning to my father, 'you aim just below the left shoulder. Mark my words, Joseph . . . I said the *left* one!'

'But if he's running away,' Paul objected, 'all you can see is his backside. So what is one to do?'

'Easy as anything. I'm surprised you haven't guessed.'

'You aim at his left buttock?'

'Not at all,' my uncle said. 'You only have to know that the wild boar is very fond of truffles. . . .'

'Well?' my mother asked, much interested.

'Why, Augustine,' Uncle Jules said, 'you lean over to your *left* and you shout—as loud as you can—towards the *left*: "Oh! The beautiful truffles!" So the wild boar spins round, beguiled, pivoting on his *left* foot, and presents you with his *left* shoulder!'

My mother burst out laughing, and so did I. My father smiled, and Paul said:

'You're only saying that for fun!'

But he himself didn't laugh, for he wasn't so sure.

CHAPTER TWENTY-TWO

THIS sportsmen's dinner had taken up much more time than usual, and it was nine o'clock when we left the table to begin making the cartridges. I was allowed to be present, having remarked that this was really an 'object-lesson'.

'Half an hour, no more,' my mother decreed; and she carried off Paul, who feebly groaned in protest though he was already asleep.

'First of all, let's have a rifle inspection!' my uncle said.

From behind the plates in the sideboard he took out a beautiful fawn-coloured leather-case (I was quite ashamed at having failed to discover it sooner), and extracted from it a very pretty gun which looked brand-new. The double barrel was a fine dull black, the trigger was nickel-plated, and on the polished wood of the butt a dog recumbent was carved.

My father took the gun from my uncle's hands, examined it, and gave a short, admiring whistle.

'It was a wedding-present from my elder brother,' Uncle Jules said. 'A Verney-Carron. Sixteen-bore. Central percussion.'

He took it back, slipped the breech-bolts. The gun opened with a jolly 'click', and he peered through the barrels at the hanging-lamp.

'Perfectly oiled,' he declared. 'But we'll give it a closer look tomorrow.'

Then he turned to my father.

'Where's yours?'

'Up in my room.' And he strode out to fetch it.

I had no idea that he possessed a shot-gun, and was indignant at his having kept such a beautiful secret to himself. I awaited his return with sharp impatience, trying to guess from his footfalls and the noise of the key where exactly he had hidden it. But my aural spying was unsuccessful, and we heard him hurrying down the stairs.

He was carrying a big brown case which he must have bought from the junk-dealer without my knowing it, for long scratches on it betrayed its age and revealed, in their whitish depths, that the case was the work of a papier-mâché manufacturer.

He opened this ludicrous cardboard box and said, with a somewhat embarrassed smile:

'It'll make a poor showing next to a modern weapon like yours. But it was given to me by my father.'

Having thus transformed the antiquated fire-arm into a respectable family heirloom, he extracted from the case the three parts of an enormous rifle.

Uncle Jules picked them up, adjusted and bolted them together with magical speed, then stared at the size of the weapon and exclaimed:

'Heavens alive! Is this a harquebus?'

'Almost,' said my father. 'But it's supposed to be very accurate.'

'That's not impossible,' Uncle Jules said.

The butt was uncarved and had lost its varnish; the trigger wasn't nickel-plated, and the hammers were so clumsy they looked as if they'd been forged by a blacksmith. I felt a little humiliated.

Uncle Jules opened the breech and scrutinized it pensively.

'Unless this is some unknown calibre of bygone days, it must be a twelve-bore.'

'It is a twelve-bore,' my father confirmed. 'I bought twelve-bore cartridge-cases!'

'Pin-fire, I take it?'

'Yes, pin-fire.'

He took two or three empty cartridges from a cardboard box and handed them to my uncle. From their copper base emerged a small, headless pin. Uncle Jules slipped one of them into the barrel.

'It's slightly dilated,' he said, 'but it *is* a twelve-bore pin-fire. . . .

The system was abandoned quite a long while ago, because it involves a certain risk.'

'What risk?' my mother demanded.

'A small risk,' my uncle said, 'but a risk all the same. You see, Augustine, the hammer striking this little copper pin sets the powder alight. But the pin is on the *outside*, nothing protects it: so it may go off under an accidental shock.'

'Such as?'

'Such as . . . suppose a cartridge dropped from one's hand and landed on the pin, it could explode at one's feet.'

'That wouldn't be fatal,' Joseph said in a reassuring voice. 'And anyway, I'd never drop a cartridge.'

'I once saw a singular accident,' my uncle said musingly. 'I was very young at the time, since it was still in the days of pin-fire guns. The man who ran our shoot, Monsieur Bénazet' (he pronounced it: Bénazette) 'was so fat that at night, from a distance, you might have mistaken him for a hogshead. He had to have two cartridge-belts sewn together to make up one for him. . . . One day, after a big hunting breakfast, he slipped and rolled down the stairs from top to bottom, with this enormous cartridge-belt round his waist. It was fitted with pin-fire cartridges. . . . Well, you'd have thought it was a firing-squad, by the sound of it. . . . And I regret to have to tell you that it was the death of him. . . .'

'Joseph,' said my mother, who had gone white, 'you'll have to go and buy another gun or you're not going shooting!'

'Come, come!' my father said, laughing. 'In the first place, I'm not the least like a hogshead, and moreover, I won't be presiding over a "big hunting breakfast" in a country of great wine-bibbers— for I'm quite sure that Monsieur Bénazette's explosion was accompanied by a gushing geyser of red wine!'

'That's likely enough,' said Uncle Jules, laughing. 'And besides, Augustine, I assure you that this has been the only accident of its kind so far.'

He suddenly got up from his chair and shouldered the twelve-bore gun.

My mother shouted to me: 'Stay where you are! Don't move!'

Uncle Jules repeated the manoeuvre five or six times, aiming in turn at the clock, the overhead light and the spit. At last he gave his verdict.

'This is a very old gun and it ought to weight three pounds less. But it's handy and shoulders well. To my mind, this is an excellent gun!'

My father beamed, and while he was looking around at the audience with a certain pride, Uncle Jules added:

'Always assuming, of course, that it doesn't explode.'

'What?' cried my mother, appalled.

'Don't be afraid, Augustine, we'll test it out thoroughly first and we'll fire the first shots at a distance with a string. If the thing explodes, Joseph will have lost his gun, but he'll have kept his right hand and his eyes.'

He examined the breech once more, and said:

'It may also happen that under the impact of a rather heavy charge, its bore will change and turn into a punt-gun. We'll know tomorrow, anyhow. Tonight let's get our ammunition ready!'

He adopted a tone of command.

'First of all, put out all the fires in the house! This paraffin lamp is quite dangerous enough!'

He turned to me and said emphatically:

'*You can't trifle with gunpowder!*'

My mother, terrified, ran into the kitchen and emptied a stew-pan full of water over the last crumbling embers that smouldered in the grate. Meanwhile my father made sure that the brass lamp was air-tight and that the hanging-lamp held fast.

When these precautions had been taken, Uncle Jules sat down at the table and made my father sit opposite him.

Aunt Rose, who seemed to be familiar with this dangerous ceremony, unconcernedly went up to her room to give little Pierre his bottle, and she did not come down again.

My mother had sat down on a chair, two yards away from the table. I stood in front of her, between her knees. I hoped that in this position my body would shield her effectively, should there be an explosion.

Then my uncle picked up one of the metal phials and carefully scraped off the gummed band which kept it air-tight. I saw there was a small black thread protruding from the stopper; my uncle seized it delicately between thumb and forefinger, pulled, and the stopper came out.

Then he tipped the phial over a sheet of white paper, and a pinch of black powder fell out. I drew closer, hypnotized. . . . So this was *it*, GUNPOWDER, the dreadful substance that had killed so many animals and so many men, that had blown up so many houses, and had blasted Napoleon all the way into Russia. . . . It looked just like ground charcoal, no more. . . .

Uncle Jules picked up a big copper thimble which was attached to the top of a small, dark, wooden stick.

'That's the gauge for measuring the charge,' he told me. 'It's marked in grammes and decigrammes, so we're sure to be quite accurate.'

He filled it to the brim and emptied it onto the tray of the small precision balance. The tray fell, then slowly rose again and remained poised.

'It isn't damp,' he said, 'it weighs its proper weight, and it glistens: it's perfect.'

He then proceeded to fill the cartridge cases, and my father played his part in this operation: he stuffed into them, on top of the powder, the fat wads that Uncle Jules had cooked. Then the small-shot was put in, followed by another wad, and this was topped by a round cardboard disc bearing a big black number to show the size of the shot.

After that, the cartridges were sealed: the small crank contrivance pressed down the upper rim, turning it into a crimped roll which sealed off the murderous mixture once and for all.

'A number sixteen,' I asked, 'is that bigger than a twelve?'

'No,' my uncle said, 'it's a little smaller.'

'Why?'

'Yes, why?' my father said. 'Why is it that the smaller the number the bigger the bore?'

'Nothing mysterious about that,' Uncle Jules said masterfully, 'but it's a good question. A sixteen-bore is a shot-gun for which sixteen bullets can be made from one pound of lead. For a twelve-bore, the same pound of lead will only provide twelve bullets. And if there were such a thing as a one-bore, it would fire bullets that weighed a pound.'

'Now that's a very clear explanation,' my father said. 'Did you grasp it?'

'Yes,' I said. 'The more bullets you can make from a pound, the smaller they are. And that's why the bore-hole of a gun is smaller when it's a big number.'

'You do mean five hundred gramme pounds, don't you?'

'I don't think so,' my uncle replied. 'I believe it's the old pound, which weighs four hundred and eighty grammes.'

'Splendid!' my father said, and he suddenly looked very interested.

'Why?'

'Because I can see a gold-mine of problems for the intermediate class here: "A sportsman who owned seven hundred and sixty grammes of lead could cast twenty-four bullets for his rifle. Knowing that the old pound equalled four hundred and eighty grammes, and that the figure representing the calibre stands for the number of bullets that can be cast from one pound of lead, what would be the bore of his rifle?" '

This schoolmasterly inventiveness alarmed me a little, for I was afraid my father might put it to the test at the expense of my games. But I was reassured by the thought that he seemed far too much taken up with his new passion to sacrifice his own holidays to the spoiling of mine, and the future was to prove the accuracy of my reasoning.

The evening had been a deeply interesting one for me, and at the end of it we found ourselves with a battalion of multicoloured cartridges, drawn up like tin soldiers.

I felt, however, a sort of malaise, a vague dissatisfaction, the cause of which I could not quite make out.

As I was pulling off my socks, I suddenly hit upon it.

Uncle Jules had talked all evening like a specialist, a teacher, whereas my father, who was a School Certificate examiner, had listened attentively, as if he were an ignorant schoolboy.

It made me feel ashamed and humiliated.

Next morning, while my mother was pouring coffee into my milk, I told her how I felt.

'Do *you* like the idea of Papa going shooting?'

'Not very much,' she admitted. 'It's a dangerous pastime.'

'You're afraid he might fall downstairs with his cartridges?'

'Oh no,' she said, 'he wouldn't be so clumsy. . . . But all the same, gunpowder is treacherous stuff.'

'Well, *I* don't like the idea for a different reason.'

'Don't you? What reason?'

I hesitated for a moment and made use of this pause to take a big gulp of my milk-and-coffee.

'Didn't you notice the way Uncle Jules spoke to him? He's the boss all the time and does all the talking!'

'It's only because he wants to teach your father, he does it out of friendship.'

'Yes, but I can see he's jolly glad to be one up on Papa. And I don't like that at all. Papa always beats him at bowls, and at draughts too. But this time I'm sure he's going to be licked. I think it's silly to play games one isn't good at. I never play football because I haven't the legs for it and the others would make fun of me. But I always play marbles or hop-scotch or prisoners' base, because I win almost all the time.'

'But, you big silly, shooting isn't that kind of game! It's going for a walk with a gun, and since it amuses him, it'll do him a lot of good. Even if he doesn't shoot anything.'

'Well, I for one shall be fed up if he doesn't. Yes, thoroughly fed up. And I shan't love him any more.'

I felt rather like crying and quickly gulped down my tears with my bread and butter. My mother saw it, and she came over and gave me a kiss.

'You're not altogether wrong,' she said. 'It's quite true that at first Papa won't be as good as Uncle Jules. But at the end of a week he'll be as good a shot as your uncle, and in a fortnight just see if he isn't handing out advice!'

She was not telling fibs to reassure me: she had confidence. She was sure of her Joseph. But I was as consumed by worry as the children of our revered President would be, if he confided to them his intention of taking part in the Bicycle Tour of France.

CHAPTER TWENTY-THREE

THE whole of the next day was even more galling.

While he was cleaning the rifles, whose parts were spread out on the table, Uncle Jules began to talk of his triumphs as a shot.

He said that in his native Roussillon, among the vineyards and pinewoods, he had bagged dozens of hares, hundreds of partridges, thousands of rabbits, not to mention 'rarities'.

'One evening, I'm returning home empty-handed, and I'm in a dr-readful temper for I've missed two hares, one after the other!'

'Why?' asked Paul, his mouth agape and his eyes goggling.

'For the life of me I don't know!... The fact is I'm ashamed and discour-raged... But on coming out of Taps' Spinney, I walk through Brouqueyrol's vineyar-rd—and what do I see?'

'Yes, what *do* I see?' Paul asked anxiously.

'A *bartavelle*!' I cried.

'No,' said my uncle. 'Something that doesn't fly and is much bigger. So, as I was saying, what do I see? A badger-r! A huge badger-r, which had r-ravaged a whole r-row of dessert-gr-rapes! I take aim, I fire....'

It was always the same story, and yet always new.

Uncle Jules would fire, then, as a precaution, make a 'covering' shot, and the animal fell as if thunderstruck and would be added to the interminable list of his victims.

My father listened to these tales of triumph, but made no comment. Obediently, like an apprentice, he cleaned the barrel of his gun with a round brush on a long stick, while I sadly polished the trigger and the safety-catch.

At noon, the greased and polished guns were reassembled, and Uncle Jules announced:

'We'll try them out this afternoon!'

★

The serial story of his exploits continued right through the meal and swept up to the Pyrenees for the story of a chamois hunt.

'I take my binoculars, and what do I see?'

Listening to him, Paul would forget all about his food and I was so engrossed that my mother and my aunt, after the demise of the second chamois, begged the narrator to break off his epic tale, which seemed to flatter him considerably.

This break allowed me skilfully to broach a personal question.

Since the start of the preparations, I had never for a moment doubted that I would be allowed to follow the sportsmen. But neither my father nor my uncle had specifically said so, and I had not dared to ask the question point-blank for fear of a categorical refusal: so I adopted a roundabout way.

'What about a dog?' I said. 'Won't you need a dog?'

'It would be as well to have one,' my uncle agreed. 'But how can we get hold of a trained dog?'

'Don't the shops sell them?'

'They do,' my father said. 'But they cost at least fifty francs!'

'That would be madness!' my mother exclaimed.

'That it would not,' my uncle replied. 'And if you could get a good retriever for as little as fifty francs, believe me, I wouldn't hesitate! But at that price all you'd get is a useless mongrel who'd lose the scent of a hare and lead you to a rat-hole! A trained dog fetches something like eighty francs, and you *can* go up to as much as five hundred!'

'Besides,' my aunt said, 'what would we do with it at the end of the season?'

'We'd have to sell it at half-price! And anyway,' my uncle added, 'it's dangerous to have a dog in the house with a baby.'

'That's true,' Paul said. 'He might eat our little cousin!'

119

'I don't think he would. But he might unwittingly pass some illness on to him.'

'Tonsillitis!' cried Paul. 'I know what that's like. But with me, it wasn't a dog, it was a draught!'

I didn't pursue the subject: there would be no dog. So they were counting on me to retrieve the game they'd shot. It hadn't been said in so many words, but it was obviously implied: there was no need to obtain a solemn promise, especially in front of Paul, who had expressed his intention of following the shoot 'at a distance', with cottonwool in his ears—an untenable claim which could have done mine a lot of harm.

So I kept a prudent silence.

After lunch, the grown-ups took a nap. We made use of this interval to equip the cicadas with rudders; that is to say we stuck into the backside of the poor songsters, who suddenly became mute, the stalk of an almond-leaf, and I then flung them into the air. They fluttered at random, and their fanciful circuits would make us laugh wholeheartedly.

Just before three, my father called us.

'Come here!' he shouted. 'And keep behind us. We're going to try out the shot-guns!'

Uncle Jules had firmly fastened the 'harquebus' to two big, parallel branches, and he was unwinding a long string, the end of which was attached to the trigger. He stopped ten paces away from the rifle.

My mother and my aunt hurried out of the house and made us retreat even farther.

'Look out!' Uncle Jules said. 'I've put in a treble charge, and I'm going to fire two shots at once! If the rifle explodes, the pieces may come whistling past our ears!'

The whole family withdrew to shelter behind the olive-trees, and each of us took the risk of having a quick look.

The men alone remained heroically out in the open.

Uncle Jules pulled the string: a violent explosion shook the air, and my father ran towards the captive weapon.

'It's stood up to it!' he cried, and he happily cut its bonds.

My uncle opened the breech and scrutinized it minutely.

'It's perfect!' he declared at last. 'No crack, no expansion. Augustine, now I can answer for Joseph's safety: this rifle is as strong as a howitzer!'

And as the women began to go back into the house, their minds at rest, he added to my father in a lowered voice:

'Still, you mustn't overdo it. You can be sure, of course, that prior to this test the weapon *was* perfect! But it sometimes happens that the test itself impairs the soundness of the barrel. . . . It's a risk to be run. We must now check the spread of the bullets.'

He pulled a newspaper from his pocket, unfolded it, and strode off to the lavatories at the end of the iris-bordered path.

'Has he got a stomach-ache?' Paul asked.

But Uncle Jules did not go into the sentry-box: he spread out the newspaper, fastened it to the door with four tacks and strode back to my father.

He loaded his rifle with a single cartridge. 'Look out!' he said.

He levelled the gun, took aim, and fired.

Paul, who had covered his ears, ran back to the house.

The two sportsmen walked up to the newspaper: it was riddled with holes.

Uncle Jules examined it carefully and seemed satisfied.

'They're well spread. I pulled the choke. At thirty yards it's perfect.'

He took another newspaper from his pocket and said as he opened it:

'Your turn, Joseph!'

While Uncle Jules was putting up the new target, my father was loading his gun. My mother and my aunt, drawn to the terrace by the first shot, had come back. Paul was half-hidden behind the fig-tree, one eye peering out, his fingers in his ears.

My uncle, retreating at a trot, called out:

'Go ahead!'

My father took aim.

I was trembling for fear that he should miss the door: that

would have been the final humiliation and, to my mind, would oblige him to drop shooting altogether.

He fired. The report was terrifying, and his shoulder jerked violently. He seemed neither upset nor surprised, and walked calmly up to the target; I had preceded him.

The shot had hit the centre of the door, for the entire newspaper was covered with holes. I felt a glow of pride and expected Uncle Jules to express his admiration.

He advanced, inspected the target, turned round and simply said: 'This isn't a rifle, it's a watering-can!'

'He hit it bang in the middle!' I expostulated.

'Not a bad shot!' he admitted condescendingly. 'But a flying partridge hasn't much in common with a lavatory-door. . . . We shall now try out shots number four, five and seven.'

They fired another three rounds each, and each shot was followed by my uncle's inspection and comments.

Finally he cried:

'We'll use buck-shot for the last two. Hold the butt tightly, Joseph, for I've put in a charge and a half. And you, ladies, cover your ears, for you'll hear a deafening thunder-clap!'

They fired simultaneously. The din was ear-splitting, and the door shook violently.

They both walked towards it, smiling and pleased with themselves.

'Uncle,' I asked, 'would that have killed a wild boar?'

'It certainly would,' he cried, 'provided he was hit . . .'

'Below the left shoulder!'

'Exactly.'

He tore off the layers of newspapers and I saw, deeply embedded in the wood, a score of small lead pellets.

'Pretty hard wood, this,' he remarked. 'They didn't go through! If we'd used bullets . . .'

It was a good thing they hadn't, for through the battered door we heard a small and shaky voice asking:

'May I come out now?'

It was the 'housemaid'.

CHAPTER TWENTY-FOUR

THE first day of the season was approaching, and at home we no longer talked of anything but shooting.

After his long series of epic tales, Uncle Jules had reached the stage of technical details and demonstrations. At four o'clock, after the midday siesta, he said:

'Joseph, I'll analyse for you the "King's shot", which is also the king of shots. First, listen carefully. . . . You're hiding behind a hedge, and your-r dog is descr-ribing a cir-rcle r-round the vine-yard. If he knows his job, the par-rtr-ridges will come str-raight towards you. Now you take a step backwards, but you don't level your gun yet, because the game would see it and would have time to get away. As soon as the bir-rds appear in your field of vision, you level the gun and take aim. But just as you'r-re about to fire, you jerk the barrel up four-r inches, while you press the trigger, duck your head and hunch your shoulders.'

'Why do I do all that?' my father asked.

'Because if your aim was well adjusted, a two pound bird whizzing down at thirty-five m.p.h. would fall slap in your face. Now let's get down to some practice. Marcel, get me my gun.'

I ran into the dining-room and returned slowly, reverently carrying the precious weapon.

Uncle Jules always opened the breech, to make sure that the gun wasn't loaded.

Then he took up his position behind the garden hedge. My father, Paul and I formed a semi-circle round him. With puckered brow, cocked ears and stooping, Uncle Jules peered through the foliage, trying to get a glimpse not of the dry, stony path, but of the golden vineyards of Roussillon. Suddenly he uttered two short shrill barks. Then, blowing hard through his nose, he imitated the droning flight of a covey of partridges. Then he took a step backwards and gazed intently at the sky just above the hedge. He quickly levelled his gun, giving it a small sharp jerk, and shouted: 'Bang! Bang!' Whereupon we all ducked our heads, hunched our shoulders and remained motionless, with our eyes closed, ready to withstand the shock of a 'two pound bird whizzing down at thirty-five m.p.h.'.

Uncle Jules released us by saying: 'Plomp! Plomp!', for two partridges had dropped behind us. He looked around searchingly for a moment, then went to pick them up, one by one—for in these demonstrations he invariably fired a 'double'. At last, whistling to his dog, he withdrew to the shade, dragging his feet like a tired sportsman. My father said thoughtfully:

'That doesn't look very easy.'

'Oh, it takes some practice! I've never heard of a beginner pulling it off first shot, I admit. . . . But if you're gifted—which I can't judge yet—next year you might quite possibly. . . . Why don't you try it right away?'

And my father obediently took his turn with the rifle and faithfully repeated Uncle Jules' pantomime.

Sometimes in the mornings he would take me with him on the road to the Rapon valley, which was lined with bushy hedgerows. And there we'd secretly rehearse the 'King's shot': I'd play the part of the partridge, then at the moment of taking flight, I'd hurl a stone over the hedge as hard as I could, and my father would try and follow it with his abruptly levelled gun. . . .

Later, rehearsing for the rabbit shoot, I'd fling into the grass without warning a mouldy old wooden ball, the relic of a long-forgotten game of skittles, which I had found in the garden.

At other times, he would send me off to hide in a bush and order me to shut my eyes. There I'd wait, with my ears pricked for the slightest sound of cracking twigs. Suddenly he would put his hand on my shoulder and say: 'Did you hear me coming?'

In this way my father prepared for the 'Opening Day', and applied himself to it so humbly and conscientiously that, for the first time in my life, I doubted his omnipotence, and my anguish grew from day to day.

CHAPTER TWENTY-FIVE

AT last dawn broke on the morning before the Great Day. My father and uncle first tried on their sporting outfits. Papa had bought a blue cap, which seemed to me most impressive, brown leather leggings and rope-soled boots. Uncle Jules wore a beret, laced boots, and a very special jacket about which I must say a word, because it was really quite a remarkable garment.

When she first saw it, my mother declared:

'That isn't a jacket: it's just thirty pockets sewn together!'

Even in the back there were slits and flaps. I later realized that this multiplicity of pockets had its drawbacks.

When my uncle was looking for something in his pockets, he first fingered the cloth, then the lining, then both together at the same time, in an effort to locate the missing object. The most difficult part followed, and that was to find a way of getting at it.

Thus, a small blackbird, which had got lost in the labyrinth, advertised its presence a fortnight later by an appalling smell. Aunt Rose easily traced it with her nose, and was also helped by the sight of a sad yellow beak, which had poked its way through the lining. My uncle thereupon started going through all his pockets and, in so doing, discovered a rabbit ear, some half-stewed snails, and an old tooth-pick which promptly got stuck under his finger-nail. . . . But to extricate the corpse he had to resort to scissors.

However, on the day of the dress rehearsal, the jacket produced a great effect and seemed to hold forth promise of game in plenty.

The ceremony in front of the looking-glass took quite a long time, and the sportsmen seemed to derive great pleasure from it. But their wives proceeded to strip them while they were still admiring themselves, and took charge of the clothes to secure a button here and there.

The rifles were polished and greased all over again, and I had the honour of inserting the cartridges in the leather loops of the belts.

They then studied the ordnance maps with a magnifying glass.

'We'll climb behind the house,' Uncle Jules said, 'up to Redouneou, which is here' (and he stuck a black-headed pin into the map); 'we shan't be seeing much till we get there, except perhaps an occasional thrush or blackbird. . . .'

'That'll be quite interesting,' said my father.

'Small fry!' my uncle said. 'Our game certainly won't be the *bartavelle*—there's no point in deceiving ourselves—but at least ordinary partridge, rabbit and hare. I believe we'll find some at the Escaouprès, at least that's what Butterfly Ted told me. So from Redouneou we'll make for there. We'll climb right up to the foot of the Taoumé, which we'll skirt on the right to get to the Mulberry Well. That's where we'll have lunch, getting on for half past twelve. Then . . .'

But I did not hear the rest, for I was hatching a plot of my own.

The time had come to ask my question outright and to obtain confirmation of my certainty, a certainty which had actually been a trifle shaken by the passive attitude of those about me.

There had been no mention of an outfit for me. . . . No doubt, the idea was that my own suit was quite good enough for a sportsman's dog?

One morning, I had told the housemaid that I was impatiently waiting for the Opening Day of the Season. The dim-witted creature had laughed and said:

'Don't let yourself imagine that they'll take *you* with them!'

These were the silly words of a fool, of course, and I was sorry I had opened my mind to her. What troubled me more was that I thought I detected a certain uneasiness in my father and the fact that he had said several times at table—for no apparent reason—

that sleep was indispensable for children, all children without exception, and that it was very dangerous to wake them up at four in the morning. My uncle had entirely agreed with him, and even quoted examples of little boys who got rickets or T.B. because their parents habitually made them get up too early in the morning.

I had thought that these observations were intended for Paul to prepare him for his exclusion from the field. But they had left me with a very unpleasant impression, and I felt some small gnawings of doubt. I took my courage in both hands.

First of all I must get Paul out of the way.

He happened to be outside the door, engrossed in tickling the underbelly of a cicada, which was chirping with pleasure, or perhaps croaking with pain.

I offered him a butterfly-net and confided to him that at the bottom of our garden I had just seen a wounded humming-bird which could be easily captured. This news excited him greatly; he released the cicada and said: 'Quick! Let's get it!'

I told him I couldn't possibly go with him, because I had been ordered to take a bath, with soap.

I thought that this would, with one stroke, excite his pity and provoke the fear that similar treatment might be inflicted on him. My ploy was completely successful, for lured on by the humming-bird and fleeing the bath, he wrested the butterfly-net from me and disappeared in the tangle of gorse.

I went back into the house to find Uncle Jules folding the map and saying:

'Twelve kilometres across hill country, that isn't too bad, but it's quite a long stroll all the same.'

'And I'll carry the lunch,' I said bravely.

'What lunch?' asked Uncle Jules.

'Ours, of course. I'll take two haversacks and carry the food for all of us.'

'Wherever to?' my father asked.

The question unnerved me, for I could see he was pretending not to understand.

Desperately, I took the plunge.

'To go shooting,' I said. 'I've no rifle, so I'm the obvious one to carry the lunch. It would be a perfect nuisance for *you* to have to carry it. And even if you were to put it in your game-bag, there'd be no room left for the game. And I don't make a sound when I walk either. I've read all about Red Indians and I can move as quietly as a Comanche. You can tell that by the way I catch cicadas whenever I want to. And besides, I can see for miles. The other day I was the one who pointed out the sparrow-hawk, and even then you didn't see it right away! And you haven't got a dog, and so you wouldn't be able to find the partridges you've shot down. But I'm small and I can worm my way through the under-growth. . . . And while I'm looking for them, you'll have time to kill some more. And then . . .'

'Come here,' said my father.

He put his big hand on my shoulder and looked me in the eye. 'You heard what Uncle Jules said: twelve kilometres across hill country! Your legs are a bit short for that kind of a walk.'

'They're short but they're tough,' I said, 'Feel them, they're like iron.'

My father felt them.

'Your muscles are strong all right. . . .'

'And I'm wiry, I am. I haven't got fat thighs like Uncle Jules, and so I never get tired!'

'Ho! Ho!' exclaimed Uncle Jules, who was only too glad to change the subject, 'I don't know that I like people taking the liberty of criticizing my thighs.'

But I refused to be drawn into an argument, and went on:

'Grasshoppers aren't fat either but they can jump much further than you can and when Uncle Jules was seven his father always took him when he went shooting and I'm more than eight and a half and *his* father was awfully strict Uncle Jules said so himself and so it really wouldn't be fair . . . and anyway if you don't take me I shall be ill, in fact I'm feeling rather sick already!'

Whereupon I dashed away from them, turned my face to the

wall and, with my head against the crook of my arm, I set up a loud wail.

My father, not knowing what to say, began to stroke my hair.

My mother came in and, without a word, took me on her knee. I was in the depths of despair. For one thing because the opening day of the shoot had always seemed to me the glorious starting-point of Adventure, the opening up of the unknown uplands at which I had for so long been gazing from afar. But, more than anything, I wanted to help my father in his ordeal: I could slip into the cover and drive the game towards him. Should he miss a partridge, I could say: 'I saw him fall!' and then I'd triumphantly bring back some feathers I had previously picked up in the chicken-run, to restore his self-confidence. But I couldn't tell anybody this, and to see my love thus foiled was breaking my heart.

'There's no denying you never stopped talking about it in front of him,' my mother said reproachfully.

'It would be dangerous to take him,' my father said, 'especially on the first day. There'll be other guns in the hills. . . . He's small and, under cover, they might mistake him for game.'

'But I'd see the guns!' I shouted between two sobs. 'And if I talked to them they'd know I wasn't a rabbit!'

'Look, I promise that you can come with us in two or three days' time, when I've had more practice and we shan't be going so far.'

'No! No! I want to be there on the First Day!'

Then Uncle Jules showed himself to be a great and generous soul.

'Perhaps I'm meddling in what isn't really my business,' he said, 'but, to my mind, Marcel deserves to be in on the Opening Day. Now stop crying. He can carry our luncheon, as he suggested, and he'll follow us like a good boy, ten paces behind the guns.'

He turned to my father.

'All right with you, Joseph?'

'If it's all right with you, it is with me.'

Gratitude brought a new flood of tears which choked me. My

mother gently caressed my head and kissed my wet cheeks. Then I ran to my uncle, clambered over him and pressed his big head against my throbbing heart.

'Quiet now, quiet!' my father murmured.

I planted two fat, well-aimed kisses on my uncle's cheek and bounced down again. I kissed my father's hand and, flinging my arms up, I performed a war dance which ended in a flying leap that carried me right onto the table, from which vantage point I blew kisses at the entire audience.

'Only we mustn't say a word about it to Paul,' I said afterwards, 'because he's too little. He couldn't walk so far.'

'Dear, dear!' my father said. 'Do you mean to say you're going to lie to your brother?'

'I'm not going to lie, I just won't tell him.'

'But supposing he mentions it to you?' my mother asked.

'Then I'll have to lie, because it's for his own good.'

'He's right!' my uncle declared. Then, looking me straight in the eye, he added:

'You've just discovered an important truth. Try not to forget it: *You are justified in telling children a lie, if it is for their own good.*'

And he repeated: 'Now don't forget that.'

At this point Paul arrived, rather sheepish at not having found the wounded humming-bird, and the conversation came to an abrupt end.

★

During dinner, I was so dizzy with happiness that I could hardly swallow a bite, despite my mother's exhortations. But as my uncle had said that a good appetite was the typical mark of the sportsman, I devoured my cutlet and asked for a second helping of potatoes.

'What's come over you?' my father asked.

'I'm stoking up for tomorrow.'

'What are you planning to do tomorrow?' my uncle asked, in a tone of affectionate curiosity.

'Why,' I said, 'it's the Opening Day!'

131

'The Opening day? But that's not tomorrow!' he exclaimed. . . .'Tomorrow is Sunday! Do you think the Good Lord would allow us to kill His beasts on His Own Day? And what about going to mass? But of course, you're a family of unbelievers!' he went on. 'And that's why this child can cherish the mad idea that the Shooting season might start on a Sunday!'

I was bewildered.

'But when does it start, then?'

'On Monday . . . the day after tomorrow.'

This was distressing news, for to spend a whole day waiting was tantamount to a long martyrdom. But what could I do? I resigned myself to the fact, very reluctantly but without a word. Then, as Uncle Jules declared he was dead-tired, everybody went up to bed.

When my mother had tucked up little Paul, she came to kiss me good-night and said:

'Tomorrow while you cut the arrows, I'll finish the new Red Indian suits for you. And for lunch we'll have apricot tart with whipped cream.'

I realized that she was promising me a treat to lessen my disappointment, and I tenderly kissed her hand.

CHAPTER TWENTY-SIX

ARDLY had she gone, however, than little Paul spoke up. I could not see him, because my mother had blown out the flame of the candle. His small voice sounded calm and collected.

'*I* knew they wouldn't take you shooting with them on the first day of the season. I was sure of it!'

I replied hypocritically:

'I never asked them to. Opening Day isn't for children.'

'You're a big liar. I could see right away that your humming-bird tale wasn't true. So I ran back and stood under the window, and I heard all you said, *and* how much you cried! And I even heard you promising you'd tell me lies. But I don't care a fig about going shooting. I'm too scared of real guns. But all the same, you are a liar, and Uncle Jules is an even bigger liar than you are.'

'Why?'

'Because it *is* tomorrow. I know it. Mama cooked a tomato omelette this afternoon, and then she stuffed it into the game-bags with a long sausage and some raw cutlets, and also some bread and a bottle of wine. I saw everything. And the game-bags are hidden in the kitchen cupboard, so that you won't see them. They're starting very early, and you'll just have to whistle for it!'

This was a shattering revelation. But I refused to believe it.

'Do you have the cheek to tell me that Uncle Jules would tell lies? Why, I've seen him in a sergeant's uniform. *And* he's got a medal, Uncle has!'

'And *I'm* telling you they're going shooting tomorrow. And now stop talking, I'm sleepy.'

The small voice fell silent, and I remained, with eyes wide open, in doubt and darkness.

Have you the right to lie, when you're a sergeant? Surely not. The proof of it: Sergeant Bobillot*.

But I suddenly remembered that Uncle Jules had never been a sergeant: I'd simply invented it in my dismay. Moreover, in his past record, there was the dreadful story of Borély Park. . . .

What had he done when I'd discovered his deception? He had merely laughed, that was all, without being in the least put out of countenance.

However, I was desperately trying to make excuses for that half-forgotten fib, so as to reduce its value as evidence, when a terrible memory flashed through my mind.

That very afternoon, when I had been foolish enough to say that I would lie to Paul because it was for his own good, Uncle Jules had jumped on it at once. He had warmly approved me, to justify his own criminal play-acting beforehand.

I was stricken to the heart by this treachery. And my father had not said a word! My father had been a silent accomplice in a plot directed against his own little boy . . . . And Mama, darling Mama had thought to comfort me with whipped cream. . . . I suddenly felt so overcome by my sad fate that I began to weep in silence; the silver fluting of an owl in the distance added to my despair.

Then doubt raised its head again: Paul could be devilish at times. Supposing he had made up the story to get his own back for the humming-bird?

The whole house seemed asleep. I got up noiselessly and it took me over a minute to turn the door-knob. . . . I could see no crack of light under the doors of the other bedrooms. Barefoot, I went downstairs: not a step creaked. In the kitchen, the moonlight helped me to find matches and a candle. Then, faced with the door of the fateful cupboard, I hesitated for a moment. Concealed behind this dead wood, I should discover Uncle Jules' villainy or

* Hero of the French Expeditionary Force in the Tonkin War, 1885.

Paul's perfidy—whatever the outcome, my affections would be dealt a disastrous blow.

I turned the key, slowly . . . I pulled . . . the door opened towards me . . . I entered the deep wall-cupboard, raised the candle: there they were, the two big, light-brown leather bags, with their string pockets. . . . They were bulging to bursting-point, and from the side of each protruded the corked neck of a bottle. . . . On a shelf next to the game-bags were the two cartridge-belts which I had equipped myself. What a treat in store! Sudden indignation seized me, and I made a wild decision: I would go with them, in spite of them!

I sped back to my room as nimbly as a cat, and worked out my plan.

The most important thing was to keep my eyes open. Once I fell asleep I was lost. I had never in my life managed to wake up at four o'clock in the morning. So, I must not go to sleep.

Secondly, I must get my clothes ready. I had flung them all over the place, as was my habit. . . . On all fours, in the dark, I recovered my socks and put them inside my rope-soled shoes.

After prolonged searching, I found my shirt under Paul's bed. I turned it right side out, and did the same to my shorts. I then laid them on the foot of my bed. After that I lay down again, rather proud of the decision I had taken—and, with all my might, I strained to keep my eyes open.

Paul was peacefully asleep. Two owls were now conversing at regular intervals. One was not far from my window, probably in the big almond-tree. The voice of the other—not quite so deep, but prettier, I thought—rose from the valley. That was the wife, I imagined, replying to her husband.

A slender shaft of moonlight filtered through the hole in the shutter and made the glass top of my bedside table glisten. The hole was round, but the shaft of light was flat. I decided I would ask my father for an explanation of this phenomenon.

Suddenly, up in the attic, the dormice began a saraband which ended in a skirmish of jumps and squeals. Then silence fell, and I heard, through the partition, Uncle Jules' snoring, the peaceful, even snore of an honest man—or a hardened criminal. 'To my mind,' he had said, 'Marcel deserves to be in on the Opening Day!' Lithe Stag was right: the Palefaces have two-edged tongues!

And he had had the cheek to lie to me 'for my own good'! Was he doing me good in reducing me to despair? And I had pressed him so tenderly against my heart! I solemnly vowed that I would never, never forgive him.

Then I remembered the mute treachery of my father: I determined, however, to keep silent about this distressing episode, and I walked more quickly along a path, on either side of which thornless bushes caressed my bare calves. I was carrying a rifle as long as a fishing-rod, and it glistened in the sunlight. My dog—a red-and-white spaniel—was running ahead of me, its nose to the ground, uttering a plaintive bark from time to time, exactly like the musical cry of the owl. Another dog answered in the distance. Suddenly, an enormous bird flew up: it had a long beak like a stork, but it was a *bartavelle*! . . . It flew right at me, its mighty wings swiftly beating. The 'King's shot'! I took a step backwards, took aim, gave the sharp little upward jerk, and bang! In a cloud of feathers, the *bartavelle* dropped dead at my feet. I had no time to pick it up, for yet another bird was coming straight towards me: ten times, twenty times I pulled off the 'King's shot', to the amazement of Uncle Jules, who had emerged from the thicket, with the shifty look of an awful liar. I offered him some whipped cream all the same and let him have all my *bartavelles*, saying: 'One's justified in lying to grown-ups, when it's for their own good.' Whereupon I lay down under a tree and was on the point of falling asleep, when my dog came and whispered in my ear: 'Listen! They're going off without you!'

I woke up in earnest. Paul was standing by my bedside, gently pulling my hair.

'I heard them,' he said. 'They stopped in front of our door to listen. I saw the light through the keyhole. After a moment, they tiptoed downstairs.'

A tap was running in the kitchen. I hugged Paul and got dressed in silence. The moon had gone down, it was pitch-dark. Gropingly I found my clothes.

'What are you doing?' asked Paul.

'I'm going with them.'

'They don't want you.'

'I'm going to follow them at a distance, like a Redskin, all morning. . . . They said they were going to have lunch at midday near a well. That's when I'll show myself and if they want to send me home, I'll say I'd get lost, and then they won't dare.'

'Perhaps you'll get a whacking box on the ear!'

'Never mind! I've had my ears boxed before, and sometimes for not doing anything at all. . . .'

'If you hide in the thicket Uncle Jules might take you for a wild boar and shoot you. It would serve him right, too, but you'd be the one that was dead!'

'Don't worry about me.'

And, borrowing discreetly from Fenimore Cooper, I added: 'The bullet that can kill me hasn't been cast yet!'

'What about Mama? What am I to tell her?'

'Is she downstairs with them?'

'I don't know . . . I haven't heard her.'

'I'll leave a note for her on the kitchen table.'

Taking the greatest care, I opened the window without moving the shutters. I climbed onto the sill and glued my eye to the moon-light-hole.

Day was breaking. Above the plain, which was still dark, the summit of Mount Taoumé gleamed pink and blue. At any rate, I could see the road into the hill quite clearly: they wouldn't escape me.

I waited. I could no longer hear the tap running.

'What if you meet a bear?' Paul whispered.

'Nobody's ever seen a bear in these parts.'

'Perhaps they're hiding. . . . Do be careful. Take the sharp knife from the kitchen-drawer.'

'That's a good idea! I will.'

In the silence, we heard the thump of studded boots. Then the front-door opened, and closed again.

I promptly ran over to the window and opened the shutters a crack. The footsteps came round the corner of the house: the two traitors came in sight and began to climb uphill towards the pine-woods. Papa had donned his cap and his leather leggings, Uncle Jules his beret and laced boots. They looked handsome, despite their troubled consciences, and they were walking at a fast pace, as if they were escaping from me.

I kissed Paul, who promptly went back to bed, and ran down-stairs. I quickly lit a candle and tore a sheet out of my copy-book.

'Dear little Mama, they're taking me with them after all. Don't FRET about me. Keep some whipped cream for me. Love and two thousand kisses.'

I propped this note in a conspicuous place on the kitchen-table. Then I slipped a piece of bread, two bars of chocolate and an orange into my haversack. Finally, gripping the handle of the kitchen-knife, I set out on the track of the killers.

CHAPTER TWENTY-SEVEN

I COULD no longer see them, nor did I hear anything. But for a Comanche, finding them was child's play.

I clambered up the slope as softly as I could, until I reached the edge of the pinewoods. I stopped and listened; it seemed to me that, higher up, I could just catch the sound of footsteps on stones. I began to trot on again, skirting the thickets. I reached the point where the first pinewood ended, on the edge of a plateau: vines had once been grown here, now sumac, rosemary and Spanish juniper had taken their place. But this vegetation was rather low-growing, and in the distance I could see the cap and the beret. Their wearers were still carrying their rifles at the slope and striding along fast. Near a tall pine-tree they stopped: the beret descended the hillside, to the left, while the cap continued uphill. But it bobbed up and down, like a cap tiptoeing along, one step at a time. I realized that the chase was on. . . . My heart beat faster. . . . I held my breath and waited.

There was a sudden, loud report which echoed over and over again, seeming to skip from rock to rock as it bounced its way down the valley. . . . I dashed to the nearest pine-tree and shinned up it, frightened to death. I sat astride a big branch, fully expecting the sudden appearance of a wounded boar, perhaps the very one that had unwound the one-armed poacher's ten yards of guts.

As nothing happened, I began to fear that the charging boar was about to gore my father, and I begged God—if he existed—to lead the boar to my uncle instead, for he believed in Paradise and would consequently die more hopefully.

But the beret appeared on my left, above the junipers: its owner

139

was brandishing a black bird the size of a small pigeon, and he was shouting: 'It's a fine blackbird!' The cap, emerging from a thicket of gorse, hurried towards him. The cap and the beret seemed to be having a consultation, then they parted again.

I slid down to the ground and took counsel with myself. Should I follow them down to the bottom of the valley? The high scrub would prevent me from watching the shoot and, moreover, as my father had said, I'd run the risk of being shot at by mistake.

Whereas if I continued to follow the ridge just along the cliffs of the *barres*, but under cover of the terebinths, I would see everything without being seen. Furthermore, in the event of their wounding a boar, I'd be well out of its reach and could even finish the monster off by dropping boulders on it. So I slipped between the kermes-oaks which scratched my calves, the cades and the junipers. After making a rather wide detour on the plateau, I wormed my way through the thickets and came out on the edge of the cliff.

They were at the bottom of a wide dell of blue rock. In the centre was the dry bed of what would be a river in the rainy season. There were few trees, but thickets of gorse reached up to their waists.

Over on my side, my father could be seen walking halfway up the slope. He was holding his rifle at the ready, its butt under his elbow, his right hand on the trigger, his left under the guard. He was advancing cautiously, with bent back, stepping over the brushwood.

He was beautiful to look at—beautiful and threatening—and I was rather proud of him. On the opposite slope, my uncle was following a parallel path. From time to time he would stop, pick up a pebble, fling it into the bottom of the valley, and wait for a few seconds. I had a much better view than I should have had if I had been with them.

After my uncle had thrown the third stone, a big bird flew out of the thicket and flashed towards the far end of the field. With marvellous speed my uncle levelled his gun, aimed, fired: the bird dropped like a stone, and a few feathers floated slowly down in the sunlight.

My father ran, leaping over the spiky scrub, picked up the bird and lifted it for my uncle's distant inspection. Uncle Jules shouted: 'It's a snipe! Put it into your bag and keep on the same course, twenty yards from the cliff.'

His skill, coolness and mastery fired my enthusiasm, and I felt my grievance against him melting: a Buffalo Bill was allowed to lie!

My father and my uncle continued to walk on. But as they had passed out of my line of vision, I withdrew cautiously and again made my way in an arc over the vast *garrigue*-covered plateau, so as to catch up with them. The sparkling sun hung about two yards above the horizon, and as I ran, the early morning lavender which I crushed under my feet surrounded me with its fragrance.

When I thought I had outstripped them, I veered towards the *barre*: and there, running ahead of me, I saw a kind of golden hen, with red spots on the tip of its tail. Excitement paralysed me: a partridge! It was a partridge! . . . It scurried along as fast as a rat, and disappeared in an enormous cade. Blindly I dashed after it through the thornless branches. But already I could see red feathers emerging on the far side: the hen was not alone! I saw two others, then four, then a dozen. . . . At this, I cut across to the right, to force them in the direction of the cliff, and this manoeuvre succeeded; but they didn't flush, as if my unarmed presence did not warrant such extreme measures. So I picked up some stones and flung them ahead of me. There was an enormous rumbling noise, as if a load of stones was being tipped out of an iron bucket. I flew into a panic: for a second I expected some monster to appear, then I realized that it was the covey taking flight. It soared towards the cliff and swooped down into the valley.

As I reached the edge of the cliff, two shots rang out almost simultaneously. I saw my father, who had just fired, following the soaring flight of the beautiful partridges with his eyes. . . . But they continued to glide through the morning air, without a tremor. . . .

At this moment, the beret emerged from a thick clump of

gorse and a gun appeared above it. My uncle fired unhurriedly: the first partridge toppled to the left and dropped, as if hooked out of the sky. The others swerved sharply to the right; the rifle described a quarter circle, and a second shot rang out: another partridge seemed to explode, and plunged almost vertically. I softly shouted with joy. . . . The two sportsmen, after searching about for a bit, picked up their prizes, which lay some fifty yards apart, and waved them above their heads. My father shouted: 'Good shot!' but while he was putting the partridge into his bag, I saw him stumble and feverishly remove the empty cartridge-cases from his gun. A fine hare, which had scuttled between his feet, did not wait for the end of this operation and dived into the thicket, ears cocked and tail in the air. . . . Uncle Jules flung up his arms:

'Oh Lor-rd! You should have reloaded at once! The moment you fire, you must r-reload!'

My father disconsolately spread his arms, as if crucified, and sor-r-rowfully r-reloaded.

Throughout this rumpus I had been standing at the edge of the cliff, but the marksmen, mesmerized by the partridges, had not seen me. I suddenly realized the extent of my imprudence, and, taking a few steps back, once more concealed myself.

I was profoundly dismayed by our failure which, in my view, was a major catastrophe. My father had twice missed the 'King's shot', and the hare, as if deliberately making fun of him, had forced him to cut a ludicrous caper before rudely showing him its backside. It had been appallingly funny.

I immediately tried to make excuses for him: as he was standing just below the steep cliff, he had not had time to see the partridge coming, whereas Uncle Jules had been able to take aim at leisure, as if making a practice shot.

Furthermore, he wasn't yet familiar with his gun, and Uncle Jules himself had said that that was what counted most. . . . Besides, this was his first day's shooting, his first taste of the excitement of the chase, and that's why he hadn't thought of 'r-reloading'. But in the end I was compelled to admit that this incident justified my worst fears: I resolved never to mention it to anyone, least of all to him.

What was going to happen next? Would he succeed in pulling off an honourable shot? Could it be that my father—a schoolmaster, an examiner for School Certificate, an expert bowler and such a fine draughts-player that he would often take on the famous Raphaël himself, watched by a circle of connoisseurs—could it be that *my father* would come home crestfallen, while Uncle Jules would arrive decked out with hares and partridges like a shop-window? No, never! That must not happen! I would follow him all day long, and I'd drive back to him so many birds, so many rabbits and hares, that he just couldn't fail to kill one in the end!

I had been deep in these thoughts, leaning against a pine-tree, on which the small black cicadas of the hills were sawing up desiccated reeds, while the scent of warm resin drifted round us, and I was nervously chewing a sprig of rosemary. I set off again, still thoughtful, my hands in my pockets and my head sunk on my chest. A shot, muffled by the distance, shook me out of my reverie. I ran towards the edge of the cliff. My father and my uncle were already far away: they had almost reached the end of the valley which debouched onto a wide, rocky plain. I broke into a run to catch up with them, but I saw them turn off to the right and disappear into a pinewood, behind the slope of the Taoumé which now loomed before me.

I decided to go down to the bottom of the valley and follow their tracks. . . . But there was a sheer drop of over three hundred feet from the cliff, and I couldn't see any way down. I thought of turning back to try and find the path the others had taken when I had left them; but we had been tramping for over an hour. I calculated that it would take me at least twenty minutes to return—at a run—to the point where I had set off. I would then have to cover the entire valley, where it would be hard to run because of the spiky gorse which grew higher than my head: quite half an hour in all. And after all that time, where would they have got to? I sat down on a boulder to think the matter over.

143

Was I, then, to throw in my hand and walk home? It would certainly lower me in Paul's estimation, and my mother's tender consolations would be humiliating. However, there would still be the glory of a courageous attempt and a perilous return, and the tale could be embellished in the telling. But had I the right to abandon Joseph, alone with his preposterous rifle, peering short-sightedly through his glasses, to compete single-handed with the king of sportsmen? No, that would be a worse betrayal than his had been.

The problem, therefore, was how to find them again. Mightn't I lose my way in this lonely wilderness?

But I scornfully laughed off these childish fears: I had only to keep cool and determined like a true Comanche. Since they had marched round the base of the cliff, moving from left to right, I could not help running into them if I walked straight ahead. I examined the towering mass of the Taoumé before me. Its size was considerable, and the distance to be covered undoubtedly rather long. I decided to husband my strength by adopting the light trot of the Redskin: I tucked in my elbows, crossed my hands over my chest, drew my shoulders back and lowered my head. Run on the tips of your toes. Stop every hundred yards to listen to the sounds of the forest, and take three deep, calm breaths.

With a perfectly Indian determination, I set off.

CHAPTER TWENTY-EIGHT

THE slope before me rose so gently that I could hardly feel it. The ground under my feet was one huge slab of bluish limestone, furrowed with cracks which were adorned with an embroidery of thyme, rue and lavender. . . . Here and there, emerging from the bare rock, was the Gothic shape of a cade, or a pine-tree, whose thick, gnarled trunk contrasted with the stunted height of the tree, which was no taller than I. One could see that the starveling had for years been waging a fierce struggle against the hard rock, and that it must have cost long days of patience to produce a single drop of sap. On my left, the peak of the Taoumé, after being left for so long to soak in the sky, was pale blue, a laundry-blue, and I was trotting towards its left shoulder through a vaporous haze which quivered in the heat. Every hundred yards, according to the Indian 'rite', I stopped and made my chest swell three times.

After twenty minutes, I found myself immediately below the peak, and the scenery changed. The rocky plateau was slashed by a deep and rugged ravine: tall pine-trees and high brushwood rose between crumbling boulders. I clambered down to the bottom easily enough but found it impossible to climb up the other side: from a distance its height had deceived me; accordingly I kept to the foot of the cliff, convinced that I would find a chimney.

The Indian chief's trot was now slowed down by curtains of clematis and tangles of terebinth. The small leaves of the kermes-oak, which are adorned with four symmetrical spikes, insinuated themselves into my canvas shoes, where the sides gaped a little as I walked on tiptoe. From time to time I stopped to take them off, and slapped them against the rock until they were empty.

More than once, birds rose from under my feet, or flew over my head. . . . I could not see further than ten yards in any direction. The trees, thickets and the steep sides of the gorge hid the rest of the world from me.

I began to feel vaguely disturbed, and took the redoubtable sharp knife out of my haversack; I clutched its handle tightly.

The air was calm, and the poignant scents of the hillside filled the bottom of the gully like an invisible smoke. Thyme, lavender and rosemary added a green pungency to the golden smell of resin which, in the luminous shade, glistened in long, suspended tears on the black bark of the trees. I was walking soundlessly in the silent solitude when, a few paces away, terrifying noises broke out.

There was a cacophony of frantic trumpeting, heart-rending sobs and desperate cries. These mysterious sounds had a nightmare intensity, and as they echoed round the gorge they seemed to grow louder with each repetition.

I stood rooted to the spot, trembling all over, ice-cold with fear. All of a sudden the racket stopped, and there was a motionless silence which seemed to me even more frightening. At that moment, on the cliff behind me, a running rabbit loosened a stone: it dropped on a fan-shaped heap of blue pebbles, which stood on a kind of steeply sloping balcony. The heap started to move down the incline with a ghastly, hail-like rumble and came to rest in a pool of stones round my ankles. At this, the wretched Comanche chief jumped like a startled animal, and found himself suddenly halfway up a pine-tree, clasping its trunk to his breast as if he were hugging his mother. I took a deep breath and listened to the silence. I would have liked to hear the sound of a cicada—there was not a single chirp.

Around me, the branches twined impenetrably. Far below, on the dry twigs, I could see the blade of my knife gleaming.

I was about to slide noiselessly down, when the awful cacophony broke out afresh, more violently than before. Panic-stricken I climbed almost to the top of the tree, without being able to suppress a faint whimper. . . . Then suddenly I saw, on the topmost branches of a dead oak, about ten shimmering birds: their wings were a very bright blue with two white stripes. They had sand-coloured necks and rumps, blue-and-black tails, and their beaks were canary-yellow. Without any reason and apparently just for the fun of it, they threw their heads back and screamed, howled, moaned and keened, making a devilish din. Fear gave way to wrath. I slid down to the foot of the tree. I picked up my knife, then a splendid flat stone, and ran up to the tree on which these maniacs had alighted. But at the sound of my running feet, the whole swarm rose and took themselves and their ridiculous racket to a pine-tree at the top of the cliff.

I sat down on the scorching gravel, on the pretext of emptying my shoes again but really to recover from these nerve-racking experiences, and munched a bar of chocolate.

I spent some time listening for some sound from the hill, but heard only a deathly silence. Was it possible? Not a single gun out on the first day of the season? I was to learn later that the local people never went out on that day: they would have blushed at the indignity of taking out a 'licence' to go shooting on their own native ground, and they were wary of the gendarmes of Aubagne, who were spurred to particular zeal by the Opening Day.

I looked back to gauge the distance I had covered, and saw high in the sky an unknown mountain whose rocky peak sprawled for five hundred yards at least. It was the Taoumé, but as all I'd ever seen of it was its face, I did not recognize it. Thus the first astronomer to see the other side of the moon will probably register a new astral body.

I was perplexed at first, then uneasy. I kept on looking in all directions. There was no familiar landmark. At last I decided to head for home, or rather in the direction of home: for, in an effort to save face, I was determined not to show myself. I would await the guns' return in the shadow of the pinewood, and go home with them.

So I started to retrace my steps, which seemed an easy task, on the face of it. But I had reckoned without the malice of things.

The paths you leave behind you take advantage of you by changing in appearance no sooner is your back turned. The track that forked off to the right has changed its mind: it now forks to the left on your way back. Before, it fell away in a gentle slope; now it rises in an embankment, and as for the trees, they seem to be playing puss in the corner.

However, as I was at the bottom of the gully, there was no room for doubt: all I had to do was to face about and climb up the ravine again, refusing to be bothered by all this hocus-pocus.

Knife in hand, I turned back. Like a good Comanche, I looked for my tracks: a footprint, a displaced stone, a broken bough. I saw nothing, and I thought of the remarkable shrewdness of Tom Thumb, the genius who had invented the prefabricated track. It was much too late to start imitating him.

I suddenly came upon a sort of crossroads: the valley divided into three gorges which spread like crows' feet over the side of the mysterious peak. . . . I had not noticed the other two gorges on my way down. . . . How could I have missed them, I wondered as I examined each of the three in turn. . . . Suddenly I understood: the brushwood was taller than I; on the way down, looking straight ahead, I had only seen the cleft I was following and this, as I have said, was rather crooked. But which was my path? If I had reasoned it out I would have realized that I had climbed down the first ravine on my left, since I had not crossed either of the other two when I was on the plateau. But the unhappy Comanche chief completely lost his bearings: he slumped in a heap on the ground, and began to cry.

However, it was not long before I grasped the shameful futility of such despair: I had to do something, and do it quickly, like a man. And first of all I had to recover my strength for, despite the incredible muscularity of my legs, I felt most alarmingly weary.

At the mouth of one of the ravines stood an ilex with seven or eight trunks branching out in a circle, and its dark green foliage emerged from a clump of undergrowth, in which thorny gorse mingled with kermes-oaks. This mass of prickly greenery seemed impenetrable: but in the emergency my knife became a *machete*, and I was determined to hack my way through.

After struggling for more than fifteen minutes and suffering a thousand fiery pricks, I finally broke through the defensive circle: in the centre of the tree-trunks I discovered a big tuft of *baouco*. I sat down on it, with a comforting feeling of safety: I was invisible and, moreover, I noticed that one of the trunks looked easy to climb: an appreciable advantage should a wounded wild boar appear. I lay down on my back in the soft grass, my hands crossed behind my head. Through a gap in the ilex I could see a big round patch of sky: and right in the centre of it, an almost motionless bird was taking stock of the landscape.

The thought came to me that this vulture—or condor—could see my father and uncle at this very moment grilling their cutlets over glowing rosemary twigs, for the sun was at its zenith.

After a few moments' rest, I opened my haversack, and ate my bread and chocolate hungrily. But I had brought nothing to drink with me, and my throat was quite parched.

I felt a strong desire to devour my orange, but a Comanche is careful to provide for adversity, and I put it back into my haversack, for there were other ways of dealing with the problem: I knew—from reading Gustave Aymard—that all you had to do was suck a pebble to have a feeling of being delightfully refreshed. Provident nature, in this spring-less region, had not been sparing with pebbles. I picked one which was perfectly round, quite smooth and the size of a chick-pea. And, according to approved technique, I placed it under my tongue. . . .

On my right hand, the ravine rose steeply skyward. I saw, however, that it came to an end some five hundred yards ahead, where crumbling boulders on a gentle slope would probably let me clamber up to the plateau. From there I should be able to survey the whole of the surrounding country at last, perhaps detect our village, perhaps even my home. The thought at once filled me with confidence, and I resumed my tramp with a lighter step.

CHAPTER TWENTY-NINE

THIS ravine, like the other, bristled with brushwood, but cade and rosemary predominated. These plants seemed much older than any I had seen so far. I admired one cade which was so wide and tall that it looked like a small Gothic chapel, and the rosemary shrubs were taller than I. There was little life in this wilderness: a pine-tree cicada chirped rather zestlessly, and three or four small, azure-blue flies followed me untiringly, buzzing about like grown-ups.

Suddenly a shadow passed over the thicket. I raised my head and saw the condor. He had soared down from the zenith and was gliding majestically: the span of his wings seemed to me twice the breadth of my outspread arms. He moved away to the left. I thought he had hovered over me out of sheer curiosity, casting a glance on the intruder who had dared to penetrate into his kingdom. But I saw him swoop in a wide circle behind me and come back on my right; I then realized in terror that he was describing a circle of which I was the centre, and this circle was gradually lowering over me.

This made me think of the famished vulture which one day had followed the wounded Pathfinder across the prairie, seeing that he was about to die of thirst. 'These ferocious creatures follow the exhausted traveller for days and patiently wait until at last he falls, when they pounce and tear off bleeding chunks of his still quivering flesh.'

Consequently, I gripped my knife—which I had been imprudent enough to put back in my haversack—and ostentatiously sharpened it on a stone. It seemed to me that the circle of death had stopped drawing in. Then, to prove to the ferocious creature that I was far from exhausted, I performed a wild dance which ended in an outburst of defiant laughter that reverberated so loudly in the echoing ravine that I was frightened myself. . . . But this batterer on bleeding flesh did not seem intimidated for all that and resumed his fatal descent. My eyes—those eyes he would gouge out with his hooked beak—searched desperately for a refuge. What a blessing! Twenty yards away to my right, an ogival arch opened in the rocky wall. I held my knife pointing upwards and, shouting threats in a choking voice, I seized my last chance and made for the shelter. . . . I stumbled straight ahead, through cades and rosemary, my calves torn by the small kermes-oaks, over the pebbles that rolled away under my feet. . . . The shelter was no more than ten paces away: too late, alas! The murderer hung motionless some eighty feet above my head; I saw his vast wings quiver, his neck craning towards me. . . . And suddenly he swooped down, as swift as a falling stone. Frightened out of my wits and covering my eyes with my arm, I flung myself flat on my stomach under a big juniper, screaming with despair. At that very moment there was a dreadful uproar, a shattering din like a barrow tipping out its load: a covey of partridges flew upwards in panic ten yards ahead of me, and I saw the bird of prey soaring in a broad and powerful sweep; in his talons he was carrying a trembling partridge, after which a despairing trail of feathers floated in the sky.

I was hard put to suppress the nervous sobs which Faithful Heart would have reproved, and although the danger was past, I took refuge in the cave to try and recover my composure.

It was a tent-shaped crevice, hardly taller than I, and only two paces wide. I gave a few kicks against the *baouco* that carpeted the floor, then finding a seat against the wall, I reviewed the situation.

The first thing I realized was that the vulture had never intended to attack me, but had been following the partridges; the unfortunate birds had fled before me for some time, not daring to take wing because of the soaring murderer above, who was waiting for them to take flight. . . . This theory reassured me when I thought of the course of future events: the vulture would not return for me.

Then I congratulated myself on having chosen a pebble that was both smooth and round to slake my thirst, for I discovered that in my bewilderment I had swallowed it.

The skin of my right cheek felt drawn up. I put my hand up to rub it, but the palm of my hand got stuck: when I had leaned against the pine-tree, scared by the blue birds, I had coated it with resin. I knew from experience that when no oil or butter was available, there was nothing to do but bear the tautness and the feeling that one's cheek was made of cardboard. But once one has chosen the status of a Comanche, such small miseries aren't even worth mentioning.

The state of my legs was more alarming. They were striped with long red weals, criss-crossed like wire-netting, and a great many thorns were still stuck in them. I patiently pulled them out one by one, using my finger-nails as pincers. Then, as all these small wounds were smarting, I went to collect some plants: everyone knows that hill plants help wounds to heal quickly. . . . I probably did not pick the right ones, for after rubbing my legs thoroughly with thyme and rosemary, they burned so sharply that I began to dance, hopping from one foot to the other and howling with pain. . . . To comfort myself, I promptly ate half the orange, which did me a world of good.

I then tried to climb up to the plateau, but the last mass of rocks was harder to scale than I had expected, and I discovered that a landslide has a natural tendency to slide: each time I had almost reached the top by advancing on all fours, I would slither down again as if on a conveyor-belt of pebbles. I had almost despaired of succeeding when I discovered a negotiable chimney which, though a trifle narrow for a man, was just right for me.

I was up on the plateau at last. It was vast and sparsely wooded.

There were only the ubiquitous kermes-oak, rosemary, cade, thyme, rue and lavender. There were the same short, gnarled pine-trees, leaning in the direction of the *mistral*, and the big blue stone-slabs. I scanned the horizon: I was surrounded by hills which, in their turn, were hemmed in by a distant circle of mountains that I had never seen.

CHAPTER THIRTY

I DECIDED that the first thing to do was to get my bearings. My father had told me a hundred times: 'If you face due East, then the West will be behind you. The North will be to your left, and the South to your right. It's as simple as that!'

Very simple, indeed. But where was the East? I looked at the sun. It was no longer in the middle of the sky, and as I knew that it was past noon, I was rather pleased that I had discovered the West.

I therefore turned my back to it, spread out my arms and said aloud: 'On my right, the South. On my left, the North.'

Whereupon I realized that, as I had no landmark to go by, this marvellous piece of knowledge was of no earthly use to me. In which direction did my home lie? Those damned ravines had made me go round in circles. . . . I was utterly disheartened, and so deeply and hopelessly discouraged that I decided to play some different game.

I began to hurl stones, as shepherds do, by flicking my wrist against my hip. There was, on this plateau, a marvellous selection of thin, perfectly flat pebbles of all sizes. They whizzed through the air, spinning over and over with fantastic ease. And as my technique grew better and better, they flew further and further. The tenth pebble hit a cade, and a wonderful green lizard, as long as my arm, emerged from it. Flashing like an elongated emerald, it vanished into a clump of junipers . . . I ran forward, a stone in each hand. Hoping to scare the lizard, I flung the first after it. As I did so, I saw an extraordinary creature leap from the thick green cluster: it was as big as a field-rat, and it jumped at least five yards, plumping down on a wide table of rock. It stayed there only half a second, but I had time to see that it was like a miniature kangaroo. Its disproportionately long hind-legs were as black and smooth as a chicken's foot, while its body was covered with beige fur and topped by small straight ears. I recognized it as a jerboa, for Uncle Jules had described one to me. It sprang up again, as light as a bird, and in three bounds it had reached the miniature forest of kermes-oaks. I vainly tried to pursue it but it was nowhere to be seen. While I was looking for it, I discovered a sort of cone-shaped hut, made of flat stones very ingeniously arranged. Each circular row was inset by the thickness of a finger on the one below, so that the dwindling circles eventually joined at the summit. The last circle left a hole as wide as a plate, which was topped by a beautiful flat stone. The sight of this shelter reminded me of my sad situation: the sun was sinking towards the horizon, and this shepherd's hut might perhaps save my life. . . .

I did not enter it at once: everyone knows that in the prairie an abandoned shack sometimes hides a Sioux or an Apache, whose tomahawk is raised in the shadow, ready to split the skull of a too trusting wayfarer. . . . Moreover, I might find a snake there, or poisonous spiders.

I stuck a pine-twig through the hole that served as an entrance, and waved it in all directions, while uttering mumbled threats. Only silence answered me. Through a slit in the wall, I inspected the inside. There was nothing bar a layer of dry grass on which some sportsmen had probably had a nap.

I slipped into the hut and found it cool and safe. I could at least spend the night there, secure from such nightly prowlers as the puma or the leopard, but I discovered to my dismay that there was no door to the entrance-hole! . . . It occurred to me at once to collect a safe number of flat stones and block the entrance with a small wall when the time should come for me to take refuge in my fortress. So I dropped the rôles of the trapper and the crafty Comanche and began to practise, instead, the stout-hearted patience of Robinson Crusoe.

First setback: there was not a single flat stone near the hut.

Wherever had the shepherd found the ones he had used ? I realized, with a flash of genius, that he must have found them precisely there where none was left. I merely had to look further afield; this I did with conspicuous success. . . .

While I was transporting these building materials—and grazing my hands in the process—I thought to myself: 'For the time being, nobody is worrying about me. The guns think I'm at home, and my mother thinks I'm with them. . . . But once they get back, what a calamity! Maman, perhaps, will collapse in a faint! At any rate, she'll cry.'

At this thought I began to cry myself, clutching a perfectly flat stone—but which weighed as much as I did—against my flattened stomach.

I would have liked to 'address a fervent prayer to Heaven', as Robinson did, to enlist the support of Providence. But I didn't know any prayers. And moreover, Providence—which doesn't exist but knows everything—had very little reason to take an interest in me.

However, I had heard it said that 'Heaven helps those that help themselves'. So in the belief that courage was worth a prayer at least, I continued to work in spite of my tears. 'One thing is certain,' I thought to myself, 'they'll come and search for me. . . . They'll call out the peasants and, at nightfall, I'll see a long file of "resinous wooden torches" climbing towards me and I'd then have to light a fire "on the highest point of the mountain".'

Unfortunately, I had no matches. As for the Redskin method which is known to kindle dry moss to a flame without the slightest difficulty, by simply rubbing two pieces of wood together, I had tried several times to put it into practice. Yet even with Paul's help—and he blew hard enough to burst—I had never been able to produce the slightest spark. My failure struck me as definitive, since it was presumably due to the absence of a special American wood or a particular type of moss. The night therefore would be black and fearful—perhaps it would even be the last of my life.

This was what disobedience had brought me to—that and Uncle Jules' treachery.

At this stage in my reflections, there rose to the surface of my mind a sentence which my father often repeated and which he had made me copy out several times when giving me lessons in handwriting—running hand, round hand, slanting. 'Hope is not needed to undertake a task, nor success to carry it through.'

He had explained its meaning to me at length and told me that it was the most beautiful sentence in the French language.

I repeated it out loud several times and, as if it were a magic formula, I felt manliness welling up within me. I was ashamed of having cried, ashamed of having given way to despair.

I had got lost in the hills: what of it? Ever since I had left home, I had been climbing steeply almost all the time. All I had to do was go downhill and I was sure to find a village, or at least a proper road.

I gravely ate the second half of my orange, then, with smarting legs and sore feet, I set off at a jog-trot down the gentle incline of the plateau.

As I skipped over the cades and junipers, I kept repeating the magic sentence to myself. On my right, the sun was beginning to redden behind scarves of cloud, looking just like the chocolate-boxes that aunts give one at Christmas.

I ran like this for over a quarter of an hour, at first nimbly like a jerboa, then like a goat, then like a calf, until I stopped to get my breath back. When I turned round, I found that I had covered at least a kilometre, and I could no longer see the three ravines: they had been swallowed up by the vast plateau.

To the West, however, I thought I could discern the opposite side of the valley. I advanced towards it at a walking pace to save my strength before breaking into a run again.

Yes, there was no doubt this was a valley which seemed to burrow more deeply as I drew nearer. Could it be the same valley that I had seen in the morning?

I stepped forward, thrusting aside the terebinth and gorse which were as tall as I. . . . I was still fifty paces from the cliff when a shot rang out, then, two seconds later, another! The sounds came from below me: I leapt forward, wild with joy, when a flight of very big birds, surging up from the valley, came swooping straight towards me. . . .

But the leader of the covey suddenly turned a somersault, closed his wings and, lurching over a tall juniper, heavily struck the ground. I bent forward to seize it when a violent shock half stunned me and flung me on my knees: another bird had hit my head, and for a moment I was dazed. I rubbed my throbbing skull vigorously and saw that my hand was red with blood. I thought the blood was mine and was about to burst into tears when I realized that the two birds were themselves blood-soaked, and this at once set my mind at rest.

I picked them both up by their claws, which were still twitching with a last, agonized quiver.

They were partridges, but their weight surprised me: they were as big as barnyard cocks and, however high I raised my arms, their red beaks still brushed the ground.

Then my heart gave a leap: they were *bartavelles*! The royal partridges! I carried them towards the edge of the cliff—could it have been a 'double shot' by Uncle Jules?

But even if the game were not his, the marksman who must be looking for them would surely give me a great welcome and would take me home: I was saved!

I was painfully groping through a thicket of gorse when I heared a sonorous voice, rolling reverberating R's: Uncle Jules' voice, the voice of salvation, the voice of Providence!

I could see him through the branches. The valley, which was quite wide and sparsely wooded, was not very deep. Uncle Jules, who was approaching from the opposite bank, was shouting ill-temperedly:

'Why no, Joseph, no! You shouldn't have fired! They were coming towards me! It was your—perfectly futile—shots that made them turn tail!'

I then heard my father's voice. I could not see him because he was just below the cliff.

'They were well within my reach, though, and I do believe I hit one!'

'Come, come,' Uncles Jules replied scornfully, 'You might perhaps have hit one if you'd let them pass over! But you had the presumption to fire the "King's shot", and a double at that! Not content with missing one this morning, when a whole covey was bent on suicide, there you go again, with *bartavelles* this time, and *bartavelles* coming right towards me!'

'I admit I was in a bit of a hurry,' my father said guiltily. 'And yet . . .'

'And yet,' Uncle Jules said trenchantly, 'there you are: you've missed royal partridges, as big as a child's kite, with a spread wide enough to cover a bed-sheet. And the saddest part of it is that this was a unique opportunity, we'll never get another like it! If you had given me a chance, we'd have them in the bag now!'

'I know I was in the wrong,' my father said, 'but I did see some feathers fly. . . .'

'So did I,' Uncle Jules sneered, 'I saw some fine feathers carrying away the *bartavelles* at thirty-five m.p.h. and flying right up to the top of the cliff where they must now be laughing their heads off!'

I had got quite close, and I could see poor Joseph. His cap was awry, and he was nervously chewing a rosemary stalk and sadly shaking his head. So I bounded onto a rocky promontory which jutted out above the valley, and, my body arched like a bow, I yelled with all my strength: 'But he did kill them! Both of them! He did kill them!'

And raising my small, bloody fists, from which four golden wings were dangling, I brandished my father's glory high in the sky against the setting sun.

CHAPTER THIRTY-ONE

THE bearer of good tidings, even if he be a criminal, is never cold-shouldered.

My father looked up at me from below, radiantly smiling. All he said was: 'Both of them, Jules, both of them!'

Then suddenly taking the situation in, he cried: 'What are *you* doing there?'

But his voice expressed only happy surprise.

I flung the birds, one after the other, at the victor's feet, and slithered down a chimney in the rock-face. As I touched the ground, I jumped to one side, for a hail of pebbles had followed me.

My father, meanwhile, was admiring the birds and, with a trembling hand, he groped for the place where the fatal shots had entered.

'What are you doing, so far from home at six o'clock at night?' Uncle Jules asked sternly. 'Don't you know that you might have got lost?'

'I did get lost,' I said, 'and I'll tell you all about it. But first of all give me something to drink: I've been dying of thirst since this morning. . . .'

'What's that?' my father cried. 'Didn't you have lunch at home?'

'No, I followed you at a distance. I'll explain, just give me a drink. My tongue is all swollen. . . . It makes it hard to talk. . . .'

'There's only white wine left,' my uncle said.

And he poured out a small tumblerful.

'Just a sip,' my father said. 'You can have a drink when you get home.'

I obeyed, then recounted my odyssey. I informed them proudly that I had been the one who had driven the first partridges back to them.

'I had guessed there was someone up there,' Uncle Jules said. 'But I thought it was another gun. . . . Your disobedience has been of some use, after all: I don't approve of you, but I must admit that.'

'And the *bartavelles*!' my father said. He was blowing at their feathers so that he could admire their flesh. 'Without him we'd never have found them—we wouldn't even have looked for them. And I would have returned home, chapfallen and dishonoured!'

'I would have given you credit for the blackbirds,' my uncle said magnanimously.

'That would merely have been a lie!'

'Pah! A sportsman's lie!' said Uncle Jules. 'It isn't even worth mentioning when you go to confession!'

We were sitting on big boulders, all three of us.

'What *have* you got on your face?' my father suddenly asked, as if coming out of a dream.

'It's nothing: just resin.'

Then I told them of my silent departure, the note left for my mother, my intention of joining them at the Mulberry Well, and the dreadful incident with the condor. My uncle insisted on shrinking the fierce bird to the proportions of a sparrow-hawk, and he declared that he had killed two of them with stones, at the age of ten.

Thoroughly disgusted, I did not allude to my fears, my solitude, or to my despair, and I decided to reserve that poignant story for my sensitive mother and the attentive Paul.

In any case, my father was hardly listening, because of the *bartavelles*. He kept wiping away the blood that was trickling from their beaks and smoothing their long red feathers.

Uncle Jules got up.

'My dear Joseph,' he said, 'I think it's time we were homeward bound. My feet have had quite enough for the first day!'

My feet too had had enough, and I had trouble getting on to them.

My father looked at me tenderly, and stroked my hair; then he unloaded his rifle and held it out to me:

'Take this,' he said.

Reverently I took charge of the triumphant weapon.

Then he opened his game-bag, which already contained a number of birds as well as two empty bottles.

'There's no room for them in here,' he declared. 'Besides, it would be a pity to damage them.'

Tying two bits of string round their necks, he hanged them on his cartridge-belt, one on his right, the other on his left. Then he presented his back to me, lowered himself, his hands on his knees.

'Climb up, little toad!'

The rifle slung crosswise, I settled myself on his shoulders. Uncle Jules preceded us, eyes and ears cocked for a possible last exploit.

'Perhaps a hare,' he had said.

I trembled lest he should succeed, for that hare would have tarnished the glow of the *bartavelles*: but not the smallest pair of ears came in sight, and as we emerged from a pinewood, at the moment when I least expected it, I caught a glimpse of the roof of our house a little lower down. Bordering the path, there were the olive-trees beloved of my cicadas. . . . I laughed with joy and clutched my father's curly hair in my fists. . . . As we passed by the ivy-clad olive-tree, a very small Sioux suddenly appeared from behind it. He was crowned with feathers and was carrying a quiver on his back; with a fierce grimace, he fired two pistol-shots at us and fled towards the house, yelling:

'Maman! They've killed some ducks!'

At this, my mother and my aunt, who had been sewing under the fig-tree, got up and came towards us, followed by the 'house-maid', and we made our triumphant entrance.

The three women uttered little cries of joy and admiration.

While I was descending from the height of my father's back, Paul had very skilfully detached one of the *bartavelles* and now carried it in his arms towards the three women.

The housemaid clasped her hands and, with eyes raised to heaven, exclaimed in awe-struck tones:

'Oh, Mother of God! The King's Partridge!'

Meanwhile, Uncle Jules had noisily flung down on the terrace-table two handfuls of blackbirds and thrushes, five or six partridges and two rabbits. In his turn my father emptied his game-bag, which contained three partridges and the snipe, and he said:

'Look, Rose. Jules bagged all those!'

'And what about you?' my mother asked, disappointed. 'Did you miss everything?'

'I only bagged the *bartavelles*,' he said modestly.

And I could see that their hearts were overflowing with joy.

I ran to the 'icebox'—a soap-box containing a block of ice—to get a cool drink. There I found, next to a sweating water-jug, two glass-bowls full of whipped cream, and I dashed over to kiss my mother, who insisted on scrubbing my face. After four soap-ings, the resin still needed some olive-oil (and even then I carried a brownish stain on my right cheek for over a week: it was sticky and rather repulsive but gave me a very Sioux-like complexion). Then, after seeing the sad state of my legs, she put me on a divan, sterilized a needle with the flame of a match, and began to extract the small thorns which were pricking cruelly. Paul followed this operation closely, uttering cries of pain on my behalf, while I submitted, impassive and covered with glory, like a warrior re-turned from battle.

My father, meanwhile, was relating Uncle Jules' exploits in de-tail: his uncanny flair, his noiseless gait, his unerring judgment, the extraordinary speed with which he fired, and his murderous accuracy. . . . My uncle was listening, watched by his doting wife and my admiring mother. After five or six stanzas he was com-pletely cured of his *bartavellitis* and began to sing Joseph's praises, describing his nervousness, his first clumsy attempts, his efforts to control himself, his resistance to fatigue, and finally the wonder-

163

ful inspiration which had crowned a lovely day. He ended with a sentence which made my mother's black eyes sparkle:

'A double King's shot on royal partridges, pulled off by a beginner, is something which, I may say, has never yet been seen!'

I too wanted to have my say and sing my own praises, since the sportsmen were forgetting me. But suddenly my eyelids dropped over my eyes, and I felt my mother's fingers opening my hand which gripped the arm of the lounge-chair; then she carried me into the house. I tried to protest in the name of whipped cream, but all I could articulate were faint mutterings, and then a bounding jerboa, as big as a hare and perfectly white, carried me away in four leaps towards the shadowy ravines of sleep.

CHAPTER THIRTY-TWO

NEXT morning my mother was jotting down, on a corner of the kitchen-table, the 'shopping list' for my father to take to the village.

'Little toad,' he said to me, 'get your haversack, you're coming with me. It's a long list, and I'll be loaded! It's not so much the weight as the volume. I mean to take my rifle with me; I've spotted a sparrow-hawk which often hovers over Madame Toffi's chicken-run. If we see him this morning, we'll say a word or two to him in passing!'

When the list was complete, he read it out loud. My mother had meanwhile taken the *bartavelles* out of the larder and placed them on the table.

'What are you going to do?' he asked her, with an anxious look on his face.

'I'm going to pluck and draw them, and we'll roast them to-night.'

'Wretched woman! This isn't an ordinary fowl, it's *game*! And what game! We won't eat it before tomorrow, it would be a crime to have it today. Besides,' he said, 'I have an idea. I feel very much like submitting it to the expert opinion of Mond des Parpaillouns. One must never lose an opportunity of acquiring knowledge, and that old poacher certainly knows more than many a naturalist.'

He hung up the brace of birds on his belt, then picked up his rifle and slung it crosswise.

We set off in high spirits. I was carrying the three empty haversacks, and he was walking in front of me, his eyes scanning the terraced olive-groves which lined the road. We saw some flocks of sparrows, but the *bartavelle*-killer spurned such perchers.

I was filled with happiness at being with him, and fiercely proud of his exploit—but I was trying hard not to show my conceitedness, for fear of a reprimand.

One day, Monsieur Arnaud, who was a passionate angler, had hooked an enormous hog-fish with his rod; and he had brought a snapshot, showing him and his catch, with him to school.

In those days, a photograph was a noteworthy document, which perpetuated the memory of one's tender childhood, of military service, of a wedding, or a trip abroad.

But here one could see, on a kind of picture postcard, a smiling Monsieur Arnaud, with swelling chest, a rod in his left hand, and his raised right arm holding a spiky fish by its tail.

At table, my father had described this triumphant picture and had concluded:

'I will gladly allow him his pleasure in making a fine catch, but to have yourself photographed *with a fish*! What a lack of dignity! Conceit is of all the vices definitely the most ridiculous!'

He had spoken without violence but with a pitying smile, which had ruined my admiration for Monsieur Arnaud. For this reason I considered that our visit to Mond des Parpaillouns had a purely scientific purpose.

We came to the entrance of the small squat farm-house where the famous Mond was living. In front of it lay a piece of wasteland on which two dozen olive-trees, gone wild with freedom, looked like enormous thickets, for Mond never trimmed them.

He was sitting astride a bench, in front of his porch under the mulberry tree, and was dipping thin wooden sticks in a bucket of glue. He raised his head: his thick thatch of grey hair ran into a wiry beard, white on one side, but yellowed on the other by a fag-end that drooped from the corner of his mouth.

He had black, piercing eyes, and his hairy hands were flecked with yellow freckles.

He saw the *bartavelles*, got up and came forward, open-mouthed.

'Oh, Mother of God!' he cried. 'Who's been and sold you those?'

My father gave a little smile.

'All they cost me was a couple of gun-shots.'

'A double shot!' Mond said incredulously. 'A double at *bartavelles*?'

'Why, yes,' my father said, smoothing his black moustache with the tip of his forefinger.

'And where was that?'

'In Lancelot valley, just below the cliff, over by Passe-Temps.'

Mond had picked up the two birds and was weighing them in his hand.

'The most amazing thing is that you were able to retrieve them,' he said.

'Why?'

'Because these creatures, even when they're dead in the air, still fly five or six hundred yards.'

'The youngster was up on the cliff. He was the one who saw them drop.'

'Bravo, *pitchounet*!' Mond said to me. 'I'll take you shooting with me one day!'

Then, as if it were a rule of conduct in life, he announced:

'When you haven't got a dog, you've got to have children!'

My father then put a thousand questions about the *bartavelles*—about their origins, their habits, the difficulty of approaching them, the swiftness of their flight.

From these questions and old Mond's answers, it became clear that a double hit at *bartavelles* was, if not an impossible achievement, at least a very rare one and worthy of 'a big shot'.

Once this fact has been established, we left Mond—who was beginning to tell us of his own successes, with a vaingloriousness which made me think of Monsieur Arnaud—and we walked down into the valley.

My father handed the shopping list to the grocer in the small shop where five or six women customers had already forgathered. But the grocer, with the list in his hand, had eyes only for the game and exclaimed: 'Wood-cock!'

167

My father enlightened him, and told him a thing or two about the life and lore of *bartavelles*. The grocer offered to weigh them, and this my father accepted willingly. The operation took place before the eyes of the assembled housewives.

The bigger of the two topped 1,530 grammes, the other 1,260 —for the grocer insisted on accuracy. A neat little old lady (the curé's housekeeper) advised us to stuff them with *pèbre d'aï*, before putting them on the spit, and not to bring them too close to the fire right at the start: the spit ought to be brought near the fire in —at least—three stages. As the price of her precious advice she asked for permission to take one of the tail-feathers, which was thus stolen from the head-dress of a Pawnee chieftain, and all the new arrivals gazed with respect at the sportsman capable of such beautiful slaughter. We left the list with the grocer who undertook to prepare the lot, and my father said to me: 'I must go and talk to Monsieur Vincent.'

Monsieur Vincent kept the public records at the Prefecture, and he was a friend of Uncle Jules. He was spending his holidays in the village, where he was born.

But in the street we met the postman, who himself went shooting in the Allauch grounds. It was he who stopped us, and I was astonished to see him massaging the *bartavelles'* necks between his thumb and forefinger.

'Just between ourselves,' he said in a low voice, 'didn't you catch them with a snare?'

'Not on your life!' my father replied. 'It was a double. I was lucky enough to pull it off with the "King's shot".'

But the postman was 'a jealous shot', and he kept on fingering the fowl's neck, in the hope of discovering a fracture. So my father, blowing the feathers the wrong way, showed the postman the mortal wounds, which he inspected suspiciously. He then asked what bore the rifle was, the size of the shots, the distance, the time and place. At last, getting the better of his jealousy, he consented to endorse the achievement.

'Monsieur,' he said, 'I take off my képi to you. I've been after these birds for two years now: I've fired five times, and all I've had for my pains was four feathers! Allow me to shake you by the hand!'

Meanwhile, the village children had asssembled and were loudly voicing their admiration.

When we reached the little square, we ran into Monsieur le Curé. He was reading his breviary near the fountain, while waiting, by the sound of it, for his jug to overflow.

The arrival of our little group made him raise his head, and as 'these people turn anything to account', he addressed a nice big smile to my father and said pleasantly:

'Monsieur, if these royal partridges weren't bought in a shop, allow me to compliment you on them!'

It was the first time that I saw my father face to face with the crafty enemy. To my great surprise, he answered very politely:

'They come from the Lancelot Valley, Monsieur le Curé.'

'I've rarely seen such fine specimens,' said the Curé, 'and I'm inclined to think that the great St. Hubert was with you!'

'The Great St. Hubert—and my twelve-bore!'

'And also your *skill*,' said the Curé. . . . 'You've bagged an old cock and a two-year-old hen. . . . My father was a great sportsman, that's why I know a little about it. This partridge is not a *Caccabis Rufa*, which is much smaller. It's the *Caccabis Saxatilis*, that is to say, the rock partridge which is also called the Greek partridge and, in Provence, the *bartavelle*.'

'Where does the name come from?' my father asked.

'Well,' the Curé said, 'I may seem very learned to you, but I must confess that my erudition is of very recent date. It so happens a farmer talked to me about *bartavelles* only yesterday, and I was curious enough to look up the etymology of the word. Now I am glad of it, since the question interests you. My dictionary says that it is a French word derived from an old Provençal term, *bartavélo*, which means a rough sort of lock. The bird is supposed to be so called on account of its cry which, it seems, is rather creaky. But in my modest opinion, this is not a fully satisfactory explanation. I'll speak to the Canon of La Major about it, he's lunching with me at the vicarage tomorrow, and if he tells me

169

anything interesting, it will give me great pleasure to let you know of it. Excuse me please, my jug is full, and the bell's calling me.'

Very courteously, he raised his biretta, my father raised his cap, the *curé* picked up his jug and walked away.

Still followed by the children, we went to visit Monsieur Vincent. We were told that he was away in town and would not be back until the next day. Nevertheless, my father looked for him all over the village and even went to the bowling grounds to ask whether the players had seen him pass. No, they hadn't seen him, but they saw the *bartavelles* which no one thought of hiding from them. They broke off their game, admired, weighed up, and asked a hundred questions. My father gave two hundred answers and informed them that these were not *Caccabis Rufa* at all, but *Saxatilis*.

In the end, in response to general request, he consented to give a demonstration of the 'King's shot', stressing the fact that the choke had to be kept loaded for the second shot. These technical explanations, which might have lasted till the evening, were happily cut short by the church-tower clock striking noon above our heads.

As we went to fetch our haversacks from the grocer's, we met the Curé once again. He was carrying a camera, which had the shape, size and elegance of a paving-stone. He came towards us, wreathed in smiles, and said:

'If it's no trouble to you, I would like to have a souvenir of this remarkable achievement.'

'A piece of luck,' my father said modestly, 'surely doesn't deserve so great an honour.'

'It does, it does! It will give me special pleasure to send you a print of this picture, which will be a pleasant memory of this year's summer holidays for you.'

My father obediently lent himself to the photographer's importunity: he showed me that it irked him, but that he didn't dare to be impolite. So he stood the rifle-butt upright on the ground, placed his left hand on the mouth of the barrel, and encircled my shoulders with his right arm. Monsieur le Curé gazed at us for a moment, with screwed-up eyes. Then he stepped forward, slightly rearranged the *bartavelles* to show their flecked bellies more clearly.

At last he took four steps backward, pressed the camera against his waist, lowered his head, and cried:

'We mustn't move now!'

I heard a click as loud as a key in a lock, and Monsieur le Curé counted:

'One. Two. Three. Thank you!'

'We live up at Les Bellons,' my father said, 'at the Bastide Neuve.'

'I know, I know!' the Curé said.

Then he added, on a somewhat pathetic note:

'As I have not frequently an opportunity of seeing you, I shall entrust the print for you to your brother-in-law, who is our most eminent parishioner. Good-bye, and once more my sincere compliments!'

He walked away—polite, friendly, smiling, and so nice that I felt like following him, which made me realize how dangerous these false appearances can be for society.

When we had turned the corner of the square, my father said to me:

'We are in a small village here. It would have been awkward to refuse. Perhaps that's what he was expecting, so as to accuse us of sectarianism, afterwards; but we've outfoxed him!'

CHAPTER THIRTY-THREE

WE marched at a smart pace uphill back to our home. The birds were still dancing from my father's belt, and as they were hanging by their necks, I told him that although he may have killed *bartavelles*, we'd eventually be eating swans.

They were impaled on a spit the next day—it was an historic feast, and almost a solemn one.

It was marked, however, by one untoward incident; Uncle Jules, whose peasant appetite excited the whole family's admiration, broke a—porcelain—tooth on a number seven shot, which had remained invisibly lodged in the tender flesh around one of the 'parson's noses'. But he recovered his old smile when my father declared that the village *curé* was a learned and, moreover, a most prepossessing man, whose conversation had charmed him.

The following day, as we set off for the shoot, I noticed that my father, renouncing his peaked cap, had put on an old brown felt hat—'on account of the sun', he said, 'which sometimes dazzled him through his spectacles'. But I also noticed, without saying a word, that the crown of the felt hat was surrounded by a band, which is not the case with caps—and that stuck in the band were two pretty red feathers, a symbol and a souvenir of the double 'King's shot'.

Ever since that day, people in the village would say, when talking of my father:

'You know the one I mean, the gentleman up at Les Bellons.'

172

'The one with the thick moustache?'
'No, the other! The marksman! The *bartavelle*-wizard!'

★

When Uncle Jules returned from mass next Sunday, he pulled a yellow envelope out of his pocket.

'This is from Monsieur le Curé,' he said.

The whole family crowded round: the envelope contained three prints of our photograph.

It was a success: the *bartavelles* were enormous, and Joseph glowed in all his glory: he evinced neither surprise nor conceit, but the calm confidence of a blasé sportsman who had reached his hundredth 'double' with *bartavelles*.

As for me, the sun in my eyes had made me grimace a little, which I didn't think was pretty. But my mother and my aunt saw an added charm in it, and crooned their wholehearted admiration for a long time.

As for Uncle Jules, he said good-naturedly:

'If you have no objection, my dear Joseph, I'd like to keep the third print, for Monsieur le Curé told me that he had meant it for me. . . .'

'If such a trifle gives you pleasure. . . .' my father said.

'Oh yes!' Aunt Rose said enthusiastically, 'I'll have it framed behind glass, and we'll hang it up in the dining-room!'

The thought that we would be lit up every night by luxurious Gaslight filled me with pride. As for dear Joseph, he showed no embarrassment. With my mother's chin resting on his shoulder, he gazed for a long time at the picture of his apotheosis, while justifying the length of this scrutiny by technical considerations. He informed us that this was 'P.O.P.' paper which had the property of turning black in the sunlight. Then he declared that the lighting was excellent, the focus perfect, and that Monsieur le Curé knew his business very well. At last, stroking my hair, he said:

'As we've got two prints, I'd rather like to send one to my father, to show him how much Marcel has grown. . . .'

Little Paul clapped his hands, and I burst out laughing. Yes, he

173

was as proud of his exploit as that; yes, he'd send a print to his father, and he'd show the other all round the school, just as Monsieur Arnaud had done.

I had caught my dear superman red-handed in the act of being human: I felt that I loved him even more for it.

So I sang a farandole and began to dance in the sunshine. . . .

PART TWO

My Mother's Castle

CHAPTER ONE

AFTER the epic hunting exploit of the *bartavelles*, I was automatically admitted to the ranks of the sportsmen, but in the capacity of a beater and a retriever.

Every morning, about four, my father would open the door of my bedroom and whisper: 'Coming with us?'

Neither Uncle Jules' mighty snores nor cousin Pierre's howls when he clamoured for his bottle at two a.m. were powerful enough to penetrate my slumbers, but my father's whisper would make me tumble out of bed.

I would dress silently in the darkness so as not to wake young Paul and go down to the kitchen, where Uncle Jules, with puffy eyes and the rather wild look common to half-awake grown-ups, was warming up the coffee, while my father filled the game-bags and I busied myself with equipping the cartridge-belts.

We left the house noiselessly. Uncle Jules locked the door behind us, put the key on the sill of the kitchen-window and pushed the shutter back to cover it.

The early morning air was brisk. A few white-faced planets flickered nervously. Above the cliffs of the Eagle Plateau the shrinking hem of darkness was embroidered with white strands of mist, and in the pinewood of Petit-Oeil a melancholy owl fluted a farewell to the stars.

We followed the thin strip of dawn all the way up to the red rocks of Redouneou. But we went past without making a sound, because Baptistin, François's son, was 'stationed' there, with switches and bird-lime galore, to catch ortolans: he was often steeped in lime up to his hair.

Walking in single file in the darkness, we would soon reach 'Baptiste's pen'. This was an ancient sheep-pen, where our friend François occasionally spent the night, with his goats. There, on the long plain that mounted towards the Taoumé, the red rays of the new sun would gradually conjure the pine-trees, cades and rock-roses out of the darkness, and, like a ship emerging from the mist, the high prow of the lonely peak would suddenly loom before us.

The guns would descend into the valley, sometimes to the left, towards the Escaouprès, sometimes to the right, down to La Garette and Passe-Temps.

As for me, I would follow the line of the plateau, some thirty or forty yards from the cliff's edge. I'd flush towards them everything that had wings, and if by chance I started a hare, I'd run towards the edge of the plateau and signal wildly with my arms like an old-time sailor. Then my father and uncle would hurriedly clamber up towards me and we'd mercilessly run Master Long-Ears to earth.

Never, no, never again did we see a *bartavelle*. And yet, without ever mentioning it, that's what we searched for everywhere, and especially in the hallowed ravine of sublime memory. . . . We'd approach it, crawling on our stomachs under the kermes-oaks and needle-gorse which often enabled us to surprise partridges, hares and even a badger which Uncle Jules struck down almost at point-blank range; but the royal partridges had flown away into the land of fable, where they have remained ever since: for fear of Joseph, without a shadow of doubt, and this only brightened his halo.

Secure in his glory, he had become formidable: success is often the breeding-ground of skill. Convinced that from now on he just could not miss the 'King's shot', he did indeed pull it off each time and with such complete ease that Uncle Jules at last declared:

'This isn't the King's shot any more, it's Joseph's shot!'

But he himself remained unequalled in 'peppering the back-sides' (as he put it) of all that fled before us—hares, rabbits, partridge, blackbirds—and which fled with good reason, since they fell as if struck by lightning at the very moment when I believed them to be out of range.

We brought back so much game that Uncle Jules was able to trade in it, and out of the proceeds he paid—loudly applauded by the whole family—the eighty francs for the rent of the house.

I had my share in this triumph. Sometimes at dinner at night, my uncle would say:

'That youngster is worth more than a dog. He can trot from dawn to dusk without stopping. He doesn't make the slightest noise and he ferrets out all the hiding-places! Today he flushed a covey of partridges, a wood-cock, and five or six blackbirds. The only thing he doesn't do is bark. . . .'

Whereupon Paul produced an admirable bark, after spitting his meat out on to his plate.

While Aunt Rose was scolding him, my mother gazed at me thoughtfully.

She was wondering whether it was sensible to let such spindly legs trot so many miles each day.

CHAPTER TWO

ONE morning, at about nine, I was nimbly trotting over the plateau that overlooks the Mulberry Well.

At the bottom of the valley, Uncle Jules was lying in wait in a vast clump of ivy, and my father was hiding behind a curtain of clematis beneath an ilex, half-way up the slope.

I was beating the bushes of needle-gorse with a long cade stick —a very hard timber which feels soft in your hand, because it is smooth and velvety to the touch. But there were no partridges, nor was there the famous 'flying' hare of Baume-Sourne.

However, I was conscientiously attending to my doggy task when I noticed, at the cliff's edge, a kind of short column, made up of five or six big stones, piled one on top of the other by some human hand. I walked up to it and saw a dead bird at the foot of the pile, its neck gripped in the two metal hoops of a trap.

The bird was bigger than a thrush and had a pretty plume on its head. I bent down to pick it up, when a young voice cried out behind me:

'Hi, my friend!'

I saw a boy about my age surveying me severely.

'You mustn't touch other people's snares,' he said. 'It's sacred, a snare is!'

'I wasn't going to steal it,' I said. 'I just wanted to have a look at the bird.'

He came closer. He was a young peasant-boy, swarthy and with a fine Provençal face, black eyes and long girlish eyelashes. He was wearing, under an old, grey woollen waistcoat, a brown shirt with long sleeves which he had rolled up above his elbows, short trousers, and rope-soled shoes like mine, but he had no socks.

'When you find game caught in a trap you've got the right to take it, but you must set the snare again and put it back where it was.'

He extricated the bird and said:

'That's a *bédouide*.'

He put it in his haversack, and took out of his waistcoat pocket a small reed-tube which was stoppered with a roughly-chipped cork; then he let a big, winged ant slide out of it onto his left palm. With a dexterity that roused my admiration, he corked the tube again, and seized the ant between the thumb and forefinger of his right hand, while with a slight pressure of his left hand he forced open the ends of the tiny wire pincers which were attached to the centre of the trap. Each of these ends formed a semi-circular curve and, when closed, made a tiny ring. In this ring he placed the slender waist of the ant which thus remained captive: the roots of its wings prevented it from moving backwards, and its big belly from advancing.

'Where d'you get ants like that from?' I inquired.

'They're "*aludes*"—winged ants,' he said. 'There are a few in every ant-heap, but they never come out. You've got to dig more than three feet deep for them with a pick—or else you've got to wait for the first rain in September. As soon as the sun shines again, they all fly away at once. . . . If you put a damp sack over the hole, it's easy. . . .'

He had set the trap again and put it back at the foot of the small column.

I watched the operation, deeply fascinated, and made a mental note of every detail. He finally got to his feet, and asked me:

'Who are you?'

He added, to give me confidence:

'I'm Lili, from Les Bellons.'

'I come from Les Bellons, too,' I said.

He burst out laughing.

'Oh no, you don't! You don't come from Les Bellons, you come from the city. Aren't you Marcel?'

'Yes,' I said, flattered. 'D'you know me?'

'I've never seen you,' he answered. 'But my father carried your furniture up. That's why he talked about you. Your father is the twelve-bore, isn't he, the *bartavelle* man?'

I was overcome with pride.

'Yes,' I said, 'that's him.'

'You'll tell me about them, won't you?'

'About what?'

'The *bartavelles*. Where it happened, and how he did it, and all that.'

'Yes, of course! . . .'

'Later, when I've finished my rounds,' he said. 'How old are you?'

'Nine.'

'I'm eight,' he said. 'Do you set snares?'

'No. I don't know how to.'

'I'll teach you, if you like.'

'Oh yes, please!' I exclaimed enthusiastically.

'Come along: I must get on with this round of mine.'

'I can't, just now. I'm beating for my father and my uncle. They're hiding down in the valley. I've got to flush the partridges for them.'

'Partridges? Not to-day, you won't. . . . There are three coveys up here, as a rule. But the wood-choppers passed this morning and scared them off. Two coveys flew off to La Garette, and the third swooped down towards Passe-Temps. . . . We might beat up the big hare for them. He must be hereabouts: I saw a *pétoulié*.'

He meant a layer of droppings.

So we began the round of the snares, beating the brushwood at the same time.

My new friend picked up several white-tails—or wheatears—two more *bédouides* ('a sort of lark', he explained to me), and three *darnagas*.

'The city-folk call them "cross-bills". But we call them *darna-gas*,* because they're such silly birds. . . . If there's a single one about and just one snare, you can be sure the *darnagas* will find the snare and manage to get itself throttled. . . . It's very good to eat, though,' he added. 'Look! Another *limbert*—silly bastard!'

He ran towards another upright pillar and picked up a magnificent lizard. It was a brilliant green, flecked with tiny golden dots on its sides, and pastel-blue lunulae on its back. Lili released the beautiful corpse and flung it into the bushes where I ran to retrieve it.

'Can I have it?'

He laughed.

'And what d'you think I'd do with it? . . . They say people ate them in the old days. Apparently they're quite tasty. But we don't eat coldblooded animals. I'm sure it would poison you. . . .'

I put the lovely lizard into my haversack, but ten yards further on I threw it away, for in the next snare another one was trapped, which was almost as long as my arm and even more dazzling than the first. Lili uttered some oaths in Provençal and implored the Holy Virgin to protect him against those '*limberts*'.

'But why?' I asked.

'Can't you see that they are blocking up my snares? Once a lizard's caught, a bird can't get into it any more, and that means one trap less!'

After that, it was the rats' turn. They had blocked up two traps. They were big blue rats with very soft fur. Lili became angry again and remarked:

'My grandfather used to stew those things *en civet*. They're clean creatures, live in the open air, and they eat acorns, roots and sloes. . . . Actually, they're as clean as rabbits. But even so, they're rats, and . . .'

He pursed his lips in a *moue* of disgust.

The last snares had caught four *darnagas* and a magpie.

'Oho!' cried Lili. 'An *agasse*! And what does he think he's doing

* *darnagas*, in Provençal, also means 'fathead'.

183

here? Getting himself caught in a naked snare! He must have been the fool of the family, because——'

He stopped short, put his finger to his lips, then pointed towards a thicket of needle-gorse further away.

'Something moving in there. Let's walk round it, don't make a sound!'

He moved away with a supple, stealthy step, like the true Comanche he was without knowing it. I followed him. But he motioned to me to swerve round in a wider arc, to the left. He was walking towards the gorse without haste, but I ran to complete the pincer movement.

When he was ten paces away, he flung a stone and jumped up and down several times, with outflung arms, shouting wildly. I imitated him. Suddenly, he dashed forward: I saw an enormous hare bounding, ears rigid, out of the thicket. He was so big that one could see the daylight under his belly. . . . I managed to head him off his course: he swerved towards the cliff and dived down a chimney in the rock-face. We had run to the edge of the plateau and could see him sheering straight ahead and slipping into the brushwood down in the valley. We waited with beating hearts. Two shots rang out, one after the other. Then two more followed.

'The twelve-bore was the second to shoot,' Lili said. 'We'll go and help them find the hare.'

He scrambled down the chimney as easily as a monkey.

'This looks like a hard way down,' he said, 'but really it's as easy as a flight of stairs.'

I followed him down. He seemed to appraise my nimbleness with the eye of an expert.

'For someone from the city, you manage pretty well.'

CHAPTER THREE

ONCE we had reached the foot of the rocky cliffs, we broke into a run down the slope.

Close to the well, under some very tall pine-trees, there was a small glade shaded from the sun. There stood my father and my uncle, gazing at the stretched-out hare; they turned round to us, looking rather pleased with themselves.

'Who killed him?' I asked, a little diffidently.

'We both did,' Uncle Jules said. 'I hit him twice, but he kept running, and it took your father two more shots to bring him to a standstill. . . . This sort of creature wears buckshot very easily.'

He spoke as if buckshot were something like a sports jacket or a bowler-hat.

He caught sight of my new friend.

'Aha! We've got company!'

'I know him!' my father said. 'You're François's son, aren't you?'

'Yes,' Lili answered. 'You saw me in our house, at Easter.'

'And it seems you're a rare sportsman. Your father told me so.'

'Oh!' Lili murmured, blushing, 'I just snare birds. . . . '

'Do you catch a lot?'

Lili first glanced all around him, then emptied his haversack on the grass, and I was struck dumb with admiration: there were some thirty birds.

'It isn't very hard, you know,' he said. 'The main thing is to have the winged ants. I know a willow, down by La Vala. . . . If you're free tomorrow morning, we'll go and get some, because I haven't many left.'

Uncle Jules was inspecting the 'bag' the little fellow had laid out.

'Oho!' he said, shaking a mock-minatory finger, 'you're a real poacher, aren't you?'

'Me?' Lili answered with genuine surprise. 'I was born in Les Bellons!'

My father asked him to explain what he meant.

'I mean that these hills, they belong to the people from hereabouts. Which means we aren't poachers!'

His was a very simple point of view: all the poachers hailing from the country around La Treille were sportsmen, whereas all the sportsmen from Allauch or from the city were poaching on their preserves.

We picnicked on the grass. We found Lili's conversation enthralling, for he knew every valley, every gorge, every path, and every stone of the hillsides. Moreover, he was familiar with the time-table and habits of all game; however, on this topic he seemed to me somewhat reticent. He merely answered the questions Uncle Jules put to him, sometimes replying evasively and with a sly grin.

'What this region lacks most is spring-water,' my father said. 'Aren't there any other springs here, apart from the Mulberry Well?'

'Of course!' Lili said. But he added nothing further.

'There's the Passe-Temps well,' my uncle said. 'It's marked on the ordnance map.'

'And the one at Escaouprès,' Lili remarked. 'That's where my father waters his goats.'

'That's the one we saw the other day,' Uncle Jules explained.

'There are sure to be others,' said my father. 'It's quite impossible that the rainwater doesn't break through somewhere or other in such a vast mountain mass.'

'Perhaps there isn't enough rainfall,' Uncle Jules suggested.

'Don't you believe it!' my father cried. 'The annual rainfall in Paris is 0.45 metre. Whereas here it amounts to 0.60!'

186

I proudly glanced at Lili and gave a slight wink to emphasize my father's omniscience. But he did not seem to grasp the value of this information.

'Since these table-lands are made up of impermeable bedrock,' my father continued, 'it seems to me quite certain that a substantial flow of fresh water must collect in subterranean pockets in the valleys. And it seems more than likely that some of these pockets must break the surface and ooze out in the open whereever the ground is lowest. Surely you know of other wells, don't you?'

'I know of seven,' said Lili.

'Where are they?'

The peasant-boy seemed a little embarrassed, but he gave a clear answer:

'I'm not allowed to say.'

My father was as startled as I was.

'But why?'

Lili blushed, gulped, and declared:

'Because a well is something you mustn't tell about!'

'What sort of a dogma is that?' cried my uncle.

'It's obvious,' my father said. 'In a thirsty country like this, a well is a priceless treasure.'

'Besides,' Lili said candidly, 'if people knew about the springs, they might go and drink at them!'

'What people?'

'People from Allauch or else from Peypin. And then they'd come and shoot here every day!'

Suddenly warming to his subject, he went on:

'And then there'd be all those silly fools who come on excursions. . . . Ever since someone told them of the well at Petit-Homme, at least a score of them keep going there every now and then. . . . For one thing, it disturbs the partridges—besides, they went and stole grapes from Chabert's vineyards—and sometimes, when they've drunk a lot, they piddle into the well. Once they put up a notice saying: "We've piddled into the well!" '

'Why did they do that?' my uncle asked.

'Because,' Lili answered in a completely casual voice, 'Chabert had taken a pot-shot at them.'

'A real shot?' I asked.

'Yes, but from a long way off, with smallshot. . . . He's got only one cherry-tree, and they went and pinched his cherries!' Lili explained indignantly. 'My father said he should have used buckshot!'

'These seem rather savage customs!' my uncle exclaimed.

'They're the ones that are savages!' Lili said vehemently. 'Two years ago, just to fry themselves a cutlet, they set fire to the pinewood at the Jas de Moulet! It was a small wood, luckily, and there was nothing else near. But if they did that at Passe-Temps, just imagine what it would be like!'

'It's true,' my father said, 'that townspeople are dangerous because they don't know anything. . . .'

'Those who don't know should stay at home,' Lili declared.

He was eating a tomato omelette with hearty appetite.

'But *we* aren't trippers. We don't foul wells, and you might tell *us* where they are.'

'I'd like to,' Lili said. 'But I'm not allowed to. Even in your own family, you don't tell. . . .'

'Not even in your own family?' my father cried. 'Now that beats everything!'

'He may be exaggerating a little,' Uncle Jules suggested.

'No, I'm not! It's the truth! There was a well my grandpa knew: he never would tell anyone about it. . . .'

'Then how do you know?'

'Because we have a small field, down at Passe-Temps. Sometimes we used to go and plough it up for buckwheat. And at noon, when it was time to eat, grandpa he'd say: "Don't look where I'm going!" And he'd go off with an empty bottle.'

'And didn't you look?' I asked.

'Holy Mother of God! He'd have killed the lot of us! So we all sat on the ground and ate, without so much as a glance in his direction. And after a minute or two he'd come back with a bottle full of ice-cold water.'

'And you never learnt where it was?' asked my father.

'It seems that, just as he was dying, he tried to tell the secret....
He called my father and said something like: "François, the
spring . . . the spring. . . . " When hop! he was dead . . . he had
waited too long. And however hard we looked for it, we never
found it. So now the well is lost. . . .'

'That's a stupid waste,' my uncle said.

'I suppose it is,' Lili agreed, a little sadly. 'Still, perhaps now and
then it gives a drink to a bird. . . . '

CHAPTER FOUR

A NEW life began for me with Lili's friendship. When, after the early morning coffee-and-milk, I left the house at dawn with the sportsmen, we would find him sitting on the ground, under the fig-tree, already very busy preparing his snares.

He had three dozen of them, and my father had bought me twenty-four at the general store in Aubagne, which hypocritically sold them as 'rat-traps'.

I had strongly urged that we should get some traps of a larger size, specially contrived for strangling partridges.

'No,' my father told me, 'it would be unfair to trap such lovely game.'

At this I contested the fairness of his blunderbuss which struck the unsuspecting flyers down by surprise.

'Whereas a snare's something against which a partridge can defend itself, because it's intelligent and crafty, and so it stands a chance of making a getaway. . . .'

'Perhaps it does,' he admitted. 'But nevertheless, the snare isn't a noble weapon. . . . Besides, I have another reason: the springs in those traps are too powerful. You might break a finger.'

At once I set about proving to him that I knew perfectly well how to handle them, and he was forced to admit it. As I still kept on teasing him, he eventually said in a low voice:

'And besides, they're too expensive.'

I pretended I hadn't heard and dashed off, with a shout of joy, towards a reasonably-priced catapult which was on sale for three *sous*.

The 'rat-traps', which were no bigger than a saucer, turned out to be terribly efficient: they snapped at the neck of a bird with such impact that even a big blackbird succumbed to them.

While beating the game towards our guns, we would place our snares on the ground, on the edge of the cliffs or on a forked branch which we would break to level it up, at the very heart of a terebinth which Lili called '*pételin*'.

This tree, which thrives abundantly in pastoral poems, bears clusters of red and blue seeds which all birds are fond of: a snare set in a terebinth guarantees the capture of a warbler, a thrush, a greenfinch, a blackbird. . . .

We would place them as we climbed towards the heights all through the morning, then our quartet would stop for lunch near a spring, in the luminous shadow of a pine-tree.

The game-bags were always copiously filled, but we'd gobble up the lot to the very last crumbs. While we were munching the tomato omelette—delicious when it's cold—the cutlets would sizzle over a fire of rosemary twigs. Sometimes Uncle Jules would suddenly snatch up his gun and, with his mouth full, aim skywards through the branches at something nobody else had seen: and a wood-pigeon, an oriole, a sparrow-hawk would suddenly drop from the sky. . . .

When there was nothing left but the bones of the cutlets and some cheese-rind, the guns would stretch out on a bed of *baouco*-grass and have forty winks, with a handkerchief over their faces to keep off the gnats, while we would climb back to the cliffs for a first visit to our 'sets'.

We had an infallible memory for where we had placed them—trees, bushes, rocks. From quite a distance I could see at once when a trap was not in its place. I'd race towards it with the excitement of a trapper who expects to find the body of a sable or a silver fox.

Most of the time I would discover the strangled bird with the snare round its throat, under a tree or next to the pile of stones. But when we found nothing, our excitement would reach fever-pitch, like a gambler at a lottery who hears the first three figures of his number called and is waiting for the fourth to be drawn.

The further the trap was from where it was set, the bigger the quarry that had dragged it along. We would beat the bushes in concentric circles all round the spot where the ambush had been laid.

It often turned out to be a fine blackbird, a fat thrush from the Alps, a wood-pigeon, a quail, a nut-hatch. . . .

At other times, we never found the snare, which had been carried off by some hawk together with the imprisoned prey, whose wing-beating agony had attracted the thief.

At other times again, a ridiculous disappointment was in store for us: a big rat, a huge 'limbert', a fat, honey-coloured centipede. One day, after a long and hopeful search, we even found a white owl: all its feathers a-bristle, it was dancing on its long, yellow legs, with the trap round its neck. Half strangled and whispering curses, it received us with visible displeasure, opening its feathered eyes like saucers. As I approached with some alarm, it suddenly gave an odd leap, thrusting its legs forward as high as the trap, which it seized in its claws, and fell back on its rump. It would certainly have managed to disengage itself if it had gripped only one of the brass arms. But it gripped both of them at once about its frail, wounded throat; the imminence of death made it open its beak; then, collecting its last strength, it violently pushed the trap away and at a single stroke tore off its head.

The feather-ball, propelled as it was into the air, must have thought for a moment that it was flying away, but it fell down on the gravel, its beak pointing to the sky, and its eyes still round with wonder.

When at school, years later, Monsieur Laplane taught us that the owl was Minerva's bird and that it represented wisdom, I let out such a peal of laughter that I was made to copy out four verbs, and deponent verbs at that, right up to the gerundive.

CHAPTER FIVE

AFTER making our first round, we had to wait till five or six o'clock to give the traps time to 'work'.

So, during the afternoon, we went to explore the crevices, pick *pèbre d'aï* at the Escaouprès or the Taoumé lavender. But frequently, lying under a pine-tree surrounded by brushwood—for like wild beasts we wanted to see without being seen —we would talk softly for hours.

*

Lili knew everything: what the weather would be like, where the hidden springs were, and the ravines where you could find mushrooms, wild lettuce, almond-pinetrees, sloe, arbutus; he knew where, deep in some thicket, a few vine-stocks remained which had been spared by the phylloxera and on which were ripening, in solitude, clusters of tart, but delicious, grapes. He could make a three-hole flute from a reed. He would take a very dry branch of clematis, cut off a length between two knots and, thanks to the thousand invisible channels which ran with the grain of the wood, you could smoke it like a cigar.

He introduced me to the old jujube-tree at La Pondrane, to the service-tree at Gour de Roubaud, to the four fig-trees at Précatory, to the arbutus at La Garette and then, at the top of *Tête-Rouge*—Mount Redhead—he showed me the *Chantepierre,* the singing stone.

This was a slim pillar of rock, standing at the edge of the cliff and riddled with holes and grooves. All alone in the sunny silence it sang according to which way the wind blew.

Lying on our stomachs in the *baouco* and the thyme, one on either side of the slender rock, we would hug it in our arms and, with our ears glued to the smooth stone, listen with closed eyes.

A gentle mistral would make it laugh; but when its temper rose, the stone would mew like a lost kitten. It disliked wind and rain and announced their coming, first with sighs, then with mutters of alarm. These were followed by the mournful sounds of an old hunting horn which kept moaning for a long time, as if from the heart of a rain-swept forest.

But when the Damsels' wind blew, there was real music. One could hear the chorus of ladies dressed in the swishing robes of *marquises*, dropping curtseys to one another. Then, high in the clouds, a crystal flute, high-pitched and delicate, would accompany the voice of a little girl singing on the bank of a brook.

My good old Lili never saw a thing, and when the little girl was singing, he thought it was a thrush, or sometimes an ortolan. But it wasn't his fault if he had a blind ear, and I admired him none the less.

In return for all these secrets I told him about the city: the shops where you can find just everything, the exhibitions of toys at Christmas, the torchlight parades of the 141st Regiment, and the raptures of 'Magic-City', where I'd ridden on the scenic railway; I would imitate the rumble of the iron wheels on the rails, the strident screams of the passengers, and Lili would scream in unison. . . .

Moreover, I had discovered that he in his ignorance looked upon me as a scholar. I strove to justify his opinion—which was such a far cry from my father's—by feats of mental arithmetic which, in fact, I carefully prepared beforehand. I owe it to him that I learnt the multiplication table up to thirteen times thirteen by heart.

I then made him a present of several words from my collection, beginning with the shortest ones: *javelle* (swath), *empeigne* (vamp of a shoe), *ponction* (puncture), *jachère* (fallowness), and I grasped the nettle with both hands to dazzle him with *vésicule* (vesicle). Then I found a way of placing *vestimentaire* (sartorial), *radicelle* (radicle), *désinvolture* (casualness), and the admirable 'pleni-potentiary', which title I awarded (quite mistakenly) to the cor-poral of the village constabulary.

Finally I gave him, one day, written by hand on a piece of paper: *anticonstitutionnellement*. When he had managed to read it, he complimented me warmly, while admitting that he 'would not use it very frequently'. This left me quite unruffled: my aim was not to increase his vocabulary but his admiration, which grew in proportion to the length of the words.

Our conversations, however, invariably reverted to sporting talk. I would pass on Uncle Jules' stories to him and every so often he would say to me gravely, as he leant against a pine with folded arms, nibbling a stalk of fennel: 'Tell me again about the *bartavelles. . . .*'

CHAPTER SIX

I HAD never been so happy in all my life, but sometimes remorse followed me into the hills: I had deserted little Paul. He did not complain, but I felt sorry for him when I imagined his loneliness. That's why I decided one day to take him along with us.

The night before I told the sportsmen that Lili and I would not be leaving the house early, but at a much later hour because of Paul and that we would join them at the Passe-Temps spring for lunch.

They seemed disappointed to be let down and tried—unsuccessfully—to make me change my mind.

Though I said nothing, I was savouring my triumph: they had refused to take me with them on the first day of the shoot, and now look who regretted my absence and thought me indispensable! . . . It's the kind of glee that must fill Americans when we call them to our rescue after having driven out their forebears for reasons of politics or religion.

About six in the morning we set out with Paul, who was still half-asleep but rather excited by the adventure, and he bravely marched between us.

When we arrived at Petit-Oeil, we found a chaffinch caught in the first snare.

Paul promptly released it, looked at it for a moment, then burst into tears, crying in a choking voice:

'He's dead! He's dead!'

'Of course he's dead,' Lili said. 'They kill 'em, snares do.'

'No, no! I don't like it! You must unkill it! . . .'

He tried to breathe into the bird's beak, then flung its body into the air to help it soar. . . . But the poor chaffinch dropped heavily to the ground, as if it had never had wings. . . . Then little Paul collected some stones and began to throw them at us in such a rage that I had to pick him up and carry him home in my arms.

I told my mother how sorry I was to have to leave him behind.

'Don't worry about him,' she told me. 'He dotes on his little sister and is very patient with her. He looks after her all day long, don't you, Paul?'

'Oh yes, *maman*!'

He did indeed have a way of looking after her.

He would fasten a handful of cicadas in her fine, curly hair, and the captive insects would whirr around the child's head, while she laughed, pale and terrified; or else he would set her in the forked branch of an olive-tree, six feet above the ground, and then pretend to leave her to her sad fate: one day, afraid to come down, she climbed to the highest branches, and my mother, aghast, saw the tiny face peeping above the distant silver foliage. . . . She rushed to fetch a step-ladder, and succeeded in capturing her with Aunt Rose's help, in the way firemen sometimes do with too adventurous kittens. Paul asserted that 'she had given him the slip', and our little sister was henceforward believed to be capable of breathtaking climbs, like a monkey.

At other times, he would slip down her back the fluffy contents of a hip—the fruit of the dog-rose. This berry goes in French— not undeservedly—by the name of '*gratte-cul*' or 'bottom-itcher'. And indeed, it earned her a reputation for whining without any cause. . . .

To quiet her, he stuffed her with almond-tree gum and even made her eat a liquorice drop which had not come from a chemist's but out of a rabbit. He confided this exploit to me that very night, for he was afraid that he had poisoned her.

I then confessed that I myself had treated him to black olives, which were still warm from having been picked up in the wake of a herd of goats, and that he had felt none the worse for it. He was overjoyed by this reassuring confession and continued to play his brotherly tricks without vain regrets.

But, as the great Shakespeare was to teach me later, crime will out! And so it happened that, one evening, I came back from the shoot to find him in our bedroom, sobbing on his pillow.

On that fateful day, he had invented a new game, the rules of which were extremely simple.

He would vigorously pinch our little sister's fat backside, and she promptly uttered piercing screams.

Then Paul would run towards the house, as if scared to death: '*Maman*! Come quick! A wasp has stung her!'

Twice *Maman* came running out with cottonwool and ammonia and tried to remove a non-existent barb between two finger-nails. This caused our little sister to redouble her screams, to the great joy of the sensitive Paul.

But he committed the gross error of repeating his brotherly joke once too often.

My mother, who had begun to have suspicions, caught him in the act: he received a whacking box on the ear, followed by some strokes with the strap, which he accepted without flinching. But the pathetic remonstrance which followed broke his heart, and he was still inconsolable at seven in the evening. At dinner, he condemned himself to going without any dessert, while his martyred and grateful little sister offered him, with tears of tenderness, her own share of caramel custard. . . .

As I realized from all this that he never had a dull moment, I had no trouble in rising above my qualms and light-heartedly left him to his criminal pastimes.

CHAPTER SEVEN

ONE morning we set out under an overcast sky, which had settled on the mountain-tops and scarcely reddened towards the east. A cold little breeze, blowing in from the sea, was slowly rolling dark clouds before it. My father had made me wear a cap and a windbreaker with long sleeves.

Lili arrived, crowned with a beret.

Uncle Jules gazed at the sky and decreed:

'It won't rain and this is perfect weather for shooting.'

Lili gave me a wink and said to me in an undertone:

'If he had to drink all that's going to come down, he'd be piddling till Christmas!'

This seemed to me an admirable expression, and Lili confided to me, not without pride, that he had it from his big brother Baptistin.

The morning passed as usual, but about ten we were caught by a shower near the cliffs of the Taoumé. It lasted for ten minutes, which we spent under the thick branches of a huge pine. My father turned this enforced rest to account by teaching us that in no circumstances must we seek shelter under a tree. There were no thunderclaps, and we were soon able to make for Baume-Sourne, where we had lunch.

We had set some fifty snares on the way, and the guns had brought down four rabbits and six partridges.

The weather had brightened, and my uncle affirmed:

'The sky has rained itself out. It's over.'

Lili winked at me again but did not repeat the delightful phrase.

After vainly beating the Gardener's Valley, the men left us and took the road to Passe-Temps while we climbed back to our own hunting-grounds.

While we were scaling the fallen boulders, Lili said:

'There's no hurry. The longer we leave the snares, the better.'

So we lay down, with our hands clasped behind our heads, at the foot of an old service-tree which rose in the centre of a thick clump of hawthorn.

'I wouldn't be surprised,' he said, 'if we caught some fieldfare tonight, because it's autumn today.'

I was struck dumb with surprise.

In the central and northern parts of France, when the first brief gusts of wind blow a little too sharply in the early days of September, they pick up in passing a beautiful, bright yellow leaf which turns, slides and swirls as gracefully as a bird. . . . This forecasts the forests' imminent resignation: they turn russet, then black and gaunt, for all the leaves have flown in the wake of the swallows at the sound of autumn's golden bugle call.

But in my native Provence, pinewoods and olive-groves turn yellow only when they are about to die, and the first September rains, which wash the dusty verdure clean, seem to bring April to life again. On the *garrigue*-covered plateaux, the thyme, rosemary, cade and kermes-oak remain in leaf all the year round among the ever-blue lavender, and autumn slips silently and furtively into the heart of the valleys: it takes advantage of a nocturnal shower to yellow the small vineyard and the three or four peach-trees, whose change of colour is attributed to sickness, and to cover up its coming more effectively, autumn brings a blush to the naïve arbutus berries which always mistake it for spring.

So as each day of the long holidays looked exactly like its brother, they gave no inkling of the passage of time, and there was still no wrinkle on the face of summer though it was already dead.

I looked around, unable to grasp the fact.

'Who told you it's autumn?'

'In four days it'll be Michaelmas, and the fieldfare will be coming. It won't be the big migration yet—that'll be next week, in October. . . .'

That last word chilled my heart. October! THE BEGINNING OF SCHOOL!

I refused to think of it, I repelled the painful thought with all my strength: I was then living in a state of mind which I was only to understand much later when my teacher, Aimé Sacoman, explained to us Fichte's subjective idealism. Like the German philosopher, I believed that the outside world was a personal creation of mine, and that, by an effort of will, I was able to wipe out unpleasant events, as if with an india rubber. It's this inborn belief, constantly belied by the facts, that makes children fly into such violent rages when an event which they think they have under control impudently contradicts them.

I therefore tried hard to suppress the month of October. It was somewhere in the future and thus offered less resistance than a present event. In this endeavour I was the more successful for being helped by a distant rumble which cut short our conversation.

Lili got up and stood listening: the rumbling could be heard again, further down, over Allauch, on the far side of the Taoumé.

'There you are,' said Lili. 'You'll see, in an hour! . . . It's still a long way off, but it's coming.'

When we emerged from the dog-rose bushes, I saw the sky had darkened.

'What are we going to do, now? Suppose we went back to Baume-Sourne?'

'No need to. I know of a place, almost at the top of the Taoumé, where we won't get wet and we'll see everything. Come on.'

He got going.

At that very moment, a growl of thunder—already a little closer—brought a shudder to the country all around us. He turned towards me.

'Don't be frightened. We have plenty of time.'

But he quickened his pace.

CHAPTER EIGHT

WE clambered up two chimneys, while the sky darkened. As we were reaching the shoulder of the mountain, I saw moving towards us a vast violet curtain, which was suddenly but soundlessly rent by a crimson flash of lightning.

We climbed a third chimney, which was almost perpendicular, and arrived at the last shelf but one; only a few yards above it towered the flat mountain-top.

Some fifty paces away from us, there gaped a triangular crevice in the cliff, no more than a yard wide at its base.

We entered it. It was the kind of cave which was widest at its mouth and narrowed as it shrank into the rocky darkness.

Lili collected a few stones and built with them a sort of bench facing the landscape. Then he cupped his hands like a megaphone and shouted towards the clouds:

'Now you can start!'

But start it did not.

At our feet, below the three terraced plateaux, the Gardener's Valley dropped away. Its pinewoods stretched up to the two high rock-walls of the Passe-Temps gorges which plunged between two barren plains.

To our right, and almost level with us, lay the sloping plain of the Taoumé, where our snares were set.

To the left of the Gardener's Valley, the cliff, covered with pine and holly-oak, outlined the edge of the sky.

This landscape, which I had always seen quivering in the sunlight, in the tremulous air of sweltering days, now seemed solidified, like a huge cardboard décor.

Purple clouds drifted over our heads, and the bluish light grew fainter every minute, like that of a dying lamp.

I was not frightened, but I felt a strange disquiet, a deep-seated animal anguish.

The fragrance of the hillside—and the scent of lavender, above all—now rose from the ground as a powerful, almost visible, smell.

A few rabbits scurried past, as quickly as if dogs were after them, then partridges with outspread wings, surged soundlessly up from the valley and alighted under the overhanging grey cliff, thirty paces to our left.

Now, in the solemn silence of the hills, the motionless pine-trees began to hum.

It was a distant murmur, a sound too faint to rouse an echo, but quavering, unceasing, spell-binding.

We did not stir, we did not speak. Over by Baume-Sourne, a sparrow-hawk was calling from the cliffs, a shrill, jagged cry that ended in a long-drawn-out appeal. On the grey rock in front of me the first drops fell.

Widely spaced, they burst in violet splashes as big as two-*sous* pieces. Then they fell more thickly and more quickly, and the rock-face shone like a wet pavement. At last, a sudden, brief flash of lightning, followed by a sharp, vibrant clap of thunder, rent the clouds which burst over the *garrigue* with an ear-splitting crackle.

Lili laughed out loud. I saw that he was pale and realized that I was too, but already we were breathing more freely.

A vertical sheet of rain now hid the landscape, of which all that remained was a semi-circle curtained off by white beads. Every now and then, a flash of lightning, so swift that it seemed motion-less, illuminated the black ceiling, and the dark silhouettes of trees broke through the glass curtain. It was chilly.

'I wonder where Father is,' I said.

'They must have reached the cave at Passe-Temps, or else the small ruined hut at Zive.'

He pondered for a second or two, then all of a sudden said:

'If you swear you won't tell a soul, I'll show you something. But you must swear "wooden cross, iron cross".'

This was a solemn oath, which was only demanded on great occasions. I saw that Lili had assumed a grave expression and that he was waiting. I got up, held out my right hand, and clearly pronounced the formula above the noise of the rain:

> Wooden cross, iron cross,
> If I lie, in hell I'm lost.

After ten seconds' silence—which gave the ceremony its full value—he rose.

'All right,' he said, 'Come on, now. We'll go to the other side.'

'What other side?'

'This cave goes right through. It's a passage under the Taoumé.'

'You've passed through it before?'

'Lots of times.'

'You've never told me.'

'Because it's a great secret. Only three people know about it: Baptistin, my father, and me. It'll be four, with you.'

'You think it's so important?'

'You bet! On account of the *gendarmes*! When you see them on one side of the Taoumé, you cross over to the other. *They* know nothing about the passage, and before they've run round it, you're a long way off! You've sworn: you can't tell anybody any more!'

'Not even my father?'

'He's got his licence, he doesn't need to know.'

In the depths of the cave, the crack became narrower and ran away to the left. Lili squeezed into it, one shoulder forward.

'Don't be afraid. It gets wider, further on.'

I followed him.

The corridor climbed, then descended again, turned off to the right, then to the left. We no longer heard the rain, but the rumbling thunder shook the rock all around us.

At the last turning, a glimmer of light appeared. The tunnel opened onto the other slope, and the Escaouprès must now be at our feet, but was completely covered by a shroud of fog. Moreover, grey breakers of cloud were surging towards us: they broke like rollers in a rising tide which soon drowned us. We could not see ten steps ahead.

The cave in which we found ourselves was larger than the first, stalactites hung from the ceiling, and the threshold was six feet above ground-level.

The rain was now falling furiously, thick, fast and heavy, and the flashes suddenly began to follow one another without a break. Each thunderclap merely reinforced the end of the preceding one, whose beginning was already rolling back to us in shuddering echoes.

Just outside the cave, a terebinth quivered with every falling drop, gradually shedding all its shiny leaves. To our right and left, we could hear rushing rivulets coursing over rolling stones and gravel, and seething at the bottom of invisible little waterfalls.

We were perfectly sheltered and flouting the fury of the thunderstorm, when a blood-red, howling stroke of lightning hit the cliff quite close to us, bringing down an entire slab of rock.

We heard the cracking of tree-trunks as the bouncing boulders crushed them on their way down before exploding in the distant depths of the valley, as if blasted by dynamite.

This time I was trembling with fright and shrank back deep into the tunnel.

'It's lovely!' said Lili.

But I could see he wasn't feeling too sure. He came and sat next to me, saying:

'It's lovely, but bloody silly.'

'Will it go on for long?'

'An hour perhaps, not more.'

Water was beginning to trickle from the cracks in the vaulted ceiling, the top of which was lost in darkness; before long, a jet of water forced us to move.

'What really is a pity,' Lili said, 'is that we're going to lose a dozen snares. And we'll have to dry all the others out properly by the fire, and grease them, because——'

He stopped short and stared fixedly behind me. Hardly moving his lips, he murmured:

'Bend down quietly, and pick up two big stones!'

Suddenly scared, I ducked my head and did not move. But I saw him bending slowly forward, his eyes still fixed on something that was behind and above me. . . . I bent down gently, in my turn. . . . He had picked up two stones as big as my fist. I followed his example.

'Turn round slowly,' he whispered.

I forced myself to turn my head and shoulders: high up, glistening in the darkness, I saw two phosphorescent eyes.

I said under my breath:

'Is it a vampire?'

'No. A grand duke.'

By dint of staring as hard as I could, I at last made out the bird's outline.

Perched on a shelf in the rock, the grand duke—or eagle-owl—was quite two feet tall. The water had driven it out of its nest, which must have been somewhere in the vaulting.

'Mind your eyes, if he attacks us!' Lili whispered.

Suddenly terror gripped me.

'Let's go,' I said, 'let's go! I'd rather be wet than blind!'

I jumped down into the fog; he followed me.

CHAPTER NINE

I HAD lost my cap. The rain pattered on my bare head, my hair streamed over my eyes.

'Keep close to the cliff,' Lili shouted. 'We won't get so wet, and we shan't run the risk of losing our way.'

Indeed, I could hardly see four steps ahead.

I had thought that we knew those parts so well that the sight of a single tree, a single boulder, a single bush would be enough to guide us. But the fog was not just a curtain that blotted out the shapes: it actually transformed them, because it came in patches. It would allow us to glimpse the ghost of a small, crooked pine-tree but completely efface the outline of a big oak next to it; then the small pine-tree vanished in turn, and half the oak emerged, unrecognizable. We advanced through a constantly changing landscape, and if it hadn't been for the wall of rock which we could touch with our hands, we should have been obliged to sit down under the deluge and wait for it to subside.

Happily, the sky gradually recovered its calm. The thunder-storm had passed on towards Garlaban, and the violence of the downpour subsided. The rain was now coming down, quite straight and steady, as if settling in. . . .

The cliff, however, which guided us, came to a sudden stop with the spur of the Taoumé. We abandoned it with apprehension, like toddlers letting go of the banisters.

Lili passed in front of me.

His eyes glued to the ground, he found the path, though the torrents released by the cloudburst had changed its aspect. More-over, an old cade, which reared two gnarled, dead branches in the mist, brought formal proof: we were on the right road and we set off at a trot.

Our canvas shoes, bulging with water, squelched at each step. My dripping hair felt icy on my forehead. My windbreaker and my shirt were sticking to my skin.

In the silence, now returned, we heard a kind of distant rumble, faint but continuous. Lili stopped and listened.

'That's the Escaouprès flowing down. But it's impossible to tell where it comes from.'

We listened attentively: the noise came from all sides, because of the rain-muffled echoes.

Lili remarked thoughtfully:

'It could just as well be the Garette or perhaps the Pas de Loup. . . . We'd better run, or we'll catch a cold!'

He thrust forward, his elbows close to his body, and I followed him, afraid of losing sight of the bobbing little silhouette, from which wreaths of fog were trailing.

But after running for some ten minutes, he stopped abruptly and turned towards me.

'We're going downhill all the time,' he said. 'We can't be far from Baptiste's Pen.'

'We haven't seen the three terebinths.'

'You won't see a lot to-day, you know.'

'There's one that blocks the path. Even in the fog we couldn't have missed it!'

'I haven't been looking out,' he said.

'But I have!'

'Well, perhaps they're a little lower down.'

He broke into a run again. A thousand little streams were splashing round us. A big black bird, with wings outspread, passed ten yards above our heads. I realized that we had lost the path a long way back. Lili noticed it too and stopped again.

'I wonder,' he was saying, 'I wonder. . . .'

He obviously was at a loss what to do, for he began to hurl scathing Provençal insults at the fog, the rain and the gods.

'Wait!' I suddenly said. 'I have an idea. Don't make a sound.'

I turned to my right, and with my hands cupped like a trumpet, I let out a long cry, then listened.

A faint echo repeated my cry, then another, even fainter.

'That one,' I said, 'is the echo of the Escaouprès cliff, I believe, just below Tête-Rouge.'

I then shouted straight ahead. There was no answer. I turned to my left and we both shouted at once.

A more resounding echo was followed by two further reverberations: that was the voice of Passe-Temps.

'I know where we are,' I said. 'We've strayed a little too far to our left, and if we go on this way, we'll hit the edge of the La Garette cliffs. Follow me.'

I set off, veering a little to the right. . . . Nightfall was thickening the fog: but I called to the familiar echoes, appealing to the Escaouprès one for guidance, and out of pity it drew closer.

At last my feet recognized a series of round stones which rolled under my rope-soles.

Then I stepped off the path, to my right, and I thought I could make out a long, dark mass.

I moved forward, my hands in front of me, and I suddenly clutched a handful of leaves, the fleshy leaves of a fig-tree. . . . It was the one at Baptiste's Pen, and the musty smell of the sheep-pen, revived by the downpour, told us that we were saved. The rain too realized it, for it stopped.

Our adventure now made us proud and happy; what wonderful yarns we'd be able to spin about it! But as we scrambled hastily down the steep path of the Redouneou, I heard a bird calling far behind us.

'That's a peewit,' said Lili. 'They won't stop here. . . . The peewits are leaving. . . .'

Hardly visible though they were flying low on account of the mist, they appeared in V-formation and passed over our heads in pursuit of that plaintive call. . . . They were leaving for other holidays.

CHAPTER TEN

A S usual, we reached the house from the back.
A faint glimmer flickered upstairs, lighting up the very
fine drops of a filmy mist: leaning out of the window in
the gathering night my mother had lighted, against the growing
dark, the ludicrous beacon of an oil lamp whose burning hot
chimney had been cracked by the last raindrop.

A huge fire crackled in the fireplace. My father and my uncle,
in slippers and dressing-gown, were chatting with François, while
their shooting outfit was drying in front of the fire, over the backs
of several chairs.

'There! You see they aren't lost!' my father exclaimed, overjoyed.

'Oh! They were in no danger,' said François.

My mother felt my jacket, then Lili's, and cried out, much
alarmed:

'They're drenched! As drenched as if they'd fallen into the
sea!'

'Does 'em good,' François declared, quite undisturbed. . . .
'Children thrive on water—rainwater especially.'

Aunt Rose came running down the stairs as if the house were on
fire. She was loaded with clothes and towels. In next to no time
we were standing naked in front of the fire, to Paul's great joy and
Lili's equally great embarrassment: with a peasant-boy's bash-
fulness, he hid as well as he could behind the drying sports-
jackets. But my aunt grabbed him without the least hesitation and
rubbed him down with a bath-towel, turning him round and
round as if he were an inanimate object. My mother applied the

same treatment to me, and François, watching the operation, declared:

'They're as red as rose-hips!' And once again he said: 'Does 'em good!'

Lili was then dressed in my old sailor-suit, which made him look very smart all at once; in the meantime I was wrapped, rather than clothed, in one of my father's pullovers which reached down to my knees, while my mother's woollen stockings reached up to my hips.

We were then made comfortable in front of the fire and I began to relate our odyssey. The climax was the attack by the eagle-owl who, for obvious reasons, couldn't be allowed to stay, unmoving, on his rock: he therefore swooped down on us, with fiery eyes and claws outstretched, and circled round our heads. While I beat my wings, Lili uttered the monster's shrill cries. Aunt Rose listened open-mouthed, my mother shook her head, Paul shielded his eyes with both his hands. So complete was our success that I even alarmed myself, and many a time in my dreams—even years later—the aggressive creature would come back to gouge my eyes out.

With heroic composure, Uncle Jules then described the sportsmen's day of peril.

Caught by the storm at the bottom of a gorge, they had had miraculous escapes first from the enormous boulders which crashed down ceaselessly behind and in front of them, then from a stroke of lightning which cleft the big walnut-tree at Little Spring; eventually, soaked, exhausted, and pursued by a torrent which swelled from minute to minute, they owed their safety to a desperate sprint—of which, Uncle Jules confessed, he would never have believed himself capable.

His story did not make a great impression: one doesn't tremble for sportsmen who wear moustaches.

François merely remarked as he got up:

'What can you expect? It's the time of year! . . . The fine weather is over now. . . . Anyway, it's settled for Sunday. Well, good-bye, all.'

He went out, accompanied by Lili, who was still wearing my old sailor-suit for his mother to admire.

★

At dinner, I was eating hungrily when Uncle Jules made a very simple remark to which I paid no heed at first.

'I don't think,' he said, 'that our parcels will be a very heavy load for François' cart. So it should be possible to get Rose on, the baby, Augustine, and the little girl as well. And perhaps even Paul. What do you say, young Paul?'

But young Paul was unable to say anything: I saw his lower lip lengthen, protrude, then droop towards his chin. I was well acquainted with this phenomenon, which I sometimes elegantly compared to the rim of our little sister's chamber-pot. As usual, this ominous sign was closely followed by a stifled sob, then two big tears welled up in his blue eyes.

'What's the matter?'

My mother took him on her knee at once, and rocked him in her arms, while he cried and sniffled his heart out.

'Now listen, you big baby,' my mother was saying, 'you knew all along it couldn't last for ever! And after all, we'll be coming back soon . . . Christmas isn't very far!'

I sensed disaster.

'What does she mean?'

'She means,' Uncle Jules answered, 'that the holidays are over!'

And he calmly poured himself a glass of wine.

'Over! When?' I asked in a strangled voice.

'We have to leave the day after tomorrow,' my father said. 'Today is Friday.'

'*Was* Friday,' Uncle Jules corrected him. 'And we're leaving on Sunday morning.'

'You know that Monday is the beginning of school!' Aunt Rose chimed in.

I remained uncomprehending for a moment, and stared at them in blank amazement.

'Now look,' said my mother, 'this doesn't come as a surprise! We've been talking about it for the last week!'

It was true that they had been talking about it, but I hadn't wanted to hear. I knew that this calamity was bound to happen some day, just as people know that they are bound to die some day. But they keep telling themselves: 'The moment hasn't come yet to go into this problem thoroughly. We'll think about it when the time comes.'

The time *had* come. The shock deprived me of speech and almost of breath. My father saw this and talked to me kindly.

'Come on, son, come on! You've had two long months' holiday. . . .'

'Which is excessive, anyhow,' my uncle broke in. 'If you were the President of the Republic, you wouldn't have as much!'

This ingenious argument left me cold, for I had in any case decided not to aspire to this high office until after my military service.

'Ahead of you,' my father resumed, 'lies an important year in your life: don't forget that next July you'll be sitting for your scholarship, so that you can enter high school the following October!'

'You know how important that is!' my mother said. 'You always say you want to be a millionaire. You never will be if you don't go to high school!'

She believed very firmly that riches were a kind of school prize—the unfailing reward for hard work and study.

'Besides,' my uncle said, 'you'll learn Latin at the *lycée*, and that you'll find really exciting, I can promise you! I was so keen on Latin that I used to mug it up even in the holidays, just for the fun of it!'

All these strange statements concerning a period that seemed shrouded in the dim and distant future, could not hide the tragic reality: the holidays were over; and I felt my chin trembling.

'I hope you're not going to cry!' said my father.

I hoped so, too, and I made a brave effort, the effort of a

213

Comanche at the torture stake. My despair gave way to defiance: I decided to counter-attack.

'Well, all this is up to you, of course,' I said. 'But what's worrying *me* most is that Mama could never walk all the way down to La Barasse.'

'Since that is your great worry,' my father said, 'I'm glad to set your mind at rest. On Sunday morning, as Uncle Jules has just said, the women and children will travel in François' cart, which will drop them at the foot of La Treille, at the bus terminus.'

'What bus?'

'The one that runs on Sundays; it'll take us to the tram.'

This mention of a Sunday bus which we had never seen confirmed the existence of a carefully hatched plot: they had thought of everything.

'What about the figs?' I asked abruptly.

'What figs?'

'The ones on the terrace. More than half of them are still on the tree and they won't be ripe for another week. Who's going to eat them?'

'Perhaps we shall, if we come back here for a few days on All Souls' Day, in six weeks.'

'What with the sparrows, the blackbirds and the wood-cutters, there won't be a single one left! And all those bottles of wine in the cellar, will they be wasted?'

'On the contrary,' Uncle Jules said, 'wine improves with age.'

Momentarily nonplussed by this triumphant pronouncement, I immediately tried another line of attack.

'That's true,' I admitted. 'But have you thought of the garden? Papa has planted tomatoes: we haven't eaten a single one yet! And what about the leeks? They're no bigger than my little finger!'

'I may have gone wrong in my agricultural calculations,' said my father, 'but the drought is the real culprit. We've had no rain at all, until today.'

'Well, it's going to rain now,' I said, 'and all the vegetables will grow to an enormous size! And that will really be too bad!'

'Don't worry,' my father said. 'We'll have the great pleasure of eating those vegetables at home, for François has promised to look after them. And when he comes up on market-day, he'll bring us whole crates full!'

And I went on seeking for one wild excuse after another, in the attempt to prove that such a cruelly abrupt departure was not really conceivable, and as if it were possible to postpone the beginning of term. But I was well aware of the futility of my arguments, and was on the point of giving way to despair, when I had a brainwave. . . .

'Speaking for myself,' I said, 'I know quite well I have to go to school, and I even enjoy going.'

'Splendid!' said Uncle Jules, getting up.

'You're beginning to see reason!' my father added.

'Only I'm thinking that the city air is no good for Maman. You said so yourself. Yes, you did, you did! Whereas you can see how beautiful she looks here! And it's the same with our little sister. She's climbing trees now and throwing stones! So all we have to do is what Uncle Jules does.'

'What does Uncle Jules do?'

'Well, he goes to town almost every day on his bicycle and comes back here at night! Just ask him to lend you his machine and you can put me on the handle-bars or else on your back. And Mama will stay here with our little sister, and with Paul! Because Paul, well, he doesn't do a thing at school. And besides, you saw how he cried! If we take him with us to town, he'll cry all the time! I know Paul, I do——'

My father rose and said:

'That mayn't be such a bad idea. But it's getting late now. We'll talk about it tomorrow.'

'That's right,' my uncle said. 'Now we must go to bed, so that we can get up early, because tomorrow, for our last outing, we have permission to go into the Pichauris' wood: it's the finest shoot in this part of the country!'

My father took the sleeping Paul in his arms, and we walked up the stairs behind him. I whispered to my mother:

'Don't you think it's a good idea?'

'A lovely idea. . . .' she said. 'But it would be awfully tiring for your father!'

'Well, perhaps we wouldn't come every day. Perhaps Wednesdays and Saturdays. . . .'

'I'm sure I'd be frightened to remain all alone on the other days!'

'No, you wouldn't be! First of all, I'll ask Lili to come and sleep here. . . .'

'Now that would settle everything!' Uncle Jules declared. 'If Lili accepts, we're saved.'

'He's already done some shooting!' I said. 'He really has—with his brother's gun.'

'Well,' my mother said, 'get some sleep first, you need it . . . I'll talk to your father, and we'll settle all this tomorrow.'

CHAPTER ELEVEN

A COLD draught woke me up: Paul had just opened the window, and there was a faint glimmer of daylight. I thought it was the grey light of dawn, but I heard the gutter gurgling on the roof and the melodious sound of water dripping in the echoing tank. . . .

It was at least eight o'clock, and my father had not called me: the rain had washed out the last shoot.

'When it stops,' Paul said to me, 'I'll go and look for snails.'

I jumped out of bed.

'You know we're leaving tomorrow?'

I hoped to rouse in him a spectacular despair that I could turn to account.

He did not answer, for he was busily lacing his shoes.

'We won't go out shooting any more, there'll be no more ants, no more *pregadious*, no more cicadas.'

'They're all dead!' Paul said. 'Nowadays I can't find any more.'

'In town, there are no trees, no garden, and we'll have to go to school. . . .'

'Oh yes,' he said joyfully. 'Fusier will be at school. He's lovely, Fusier. I like him. I'll tell him everything. I'll give him gum. . . .'

'So you're pleased the holidays are over?' I asked him, with sternness in my voice.

'Oh yes!' he said. 'Besides, I have my box of soldiers at home!'

'Then why were you crying last night?'

He opened wide his big blue eyes, and said:

'Dunno.'

I felt sickened by this defection, but I did not lose heart and went down to the dining-room. It was crowded with people and things.

My father was stacking shoes, utensils, books, in two wooden boxes. My mother was folding linen on the table, my aunt was cramming things into suit-cases. Uncle Jules was tying up bundles with string, my little sister in a high-chair was sucking her thumb, and the 'maid', on all fours, was picking up plums that had fallen out of a hamper she had just knocked over.

'Ah, there you are!' my father said. 'The last day's shooting has gone down the drain. Nothing to be done about it. . . .'

'It's a minor disappointment,' Uncle Jules said. 'I only hope life doesn't have any bigger ones in store for you!'

My mother found a place on the cluttered-up table for my coffee-and-milk and some big slices of bread and butter. I sat down.

'Papa,' I said, 'have you thought about my idea?'

'What idea?'

'That Mama should stay on here with Paul—and that we two . . .'

Uncle Jules interrupted me:

'My dear boy, it won't hold water.'

'But *you* did it all the time! Don't you want to lend us your bike?'

'I'd gladly lend it to you if your plan were feasible. But what you didn't think of is that I left my office at five and arrived here at half past seven! That was in summer, and it was still daylight! Your father leaves school at six; and at six, at this time of year, it's dark! You can't make a trip like that every day, in pitch darkness!'

'But with a lamp? I'd be holding the lamp, and——'

'Now, really!' my father said. 'You can see the sort of weather we're having! It'll be raining more and more often. And it's hardly worth the trouble of covering so many miles, only to be cooped up by the fire once you get here.'

He suddenly adopted a stern tone:

'And anyway there's no need to give you so many explanations. The holidays are over, you've got to go back to school, and we're leaving tomorrow.'

218

He began to nail down the lid of the wooden crate; I could see he was nailing the coffin of our holidays, and that nothing could be done to change things.

With an air of indifference I strolled over to the window and pressed my face against the pane. The raindrops were slowly trickling down the glass, and down my face, the tears were slowly trickling. . . .

There was a long silence, then my mother said:

'Your coffee-and-milk is getting cold.'

I answered without turning round:

'I'm not hungry.'

'You didn't eat anything last night,' she insisted. 'Come and sit down.'

I didn't answer. As she began to come towards me, my father —in a *gendarme's* voice—rapped out:

'Leave him alone. If he's not hungry, food might make him sick. We mustn't take on such a responsibility. The boa constrictor, after all, only eats once a month.'

And in the ensuing silence he drove in four nails: war had been declared.

I remained where I was, in front of the window, without looking at them.

I heard such phrases as:

'They've been gr-rand holidays, all considered, but one's glad to be going home, too!'

And this, pronounced by my father himself:

'It may be I'm vicious, of course, but the fact is I'm already longing for my boys and my blackboard!'

And the *bartavelles*, did they mean nothing any more to this maniac?

As for Aunt Rose, she declared simply:

'What I miss here is the Gas. Frankly, I've been hankering to leave, because of the Gas!'

How could such a charming and—seemingly—sensible woman utter such extravagant rot, and prefer that hissing stench to the resinous breeze of the hills?

Uncle Jules, however, outdid her in ignominy by saying:

'What I've missed most are comfortable lavatories, without ants, spiders, scorpions, and *with* a flush!'

So that's what he was thinking, the great wine-bibber, with his fat rump! Amid the thyme, rosemary and lavender, the chirping of crickets and cicadas, under a bright blue sky across which the downy Provençal clouds floated, he had only thought of *that*! And he admitted it!

I was profoundly indignant, but noticed with pride that my mother alone was not uttering blasphemies against my beloved hills; on the contrary, there was a touch of such tender melancholy about her that I went over to her and furtively kissed her hand.

Then I crouched in a dark corner to think.

Mightn't it be possible to gain a week, or maybe two, by pretending to be gravely ill? After typhoid fever, parents are apt to send you into the country: it had happened to my friend Viguier, who had spent three months in the Lower Alps, with his aunt. What was the proper course of action to acquire typhoid fever, or at least to feign it credibly?

The invisible headache, the uncheckable sickness, an ailing air and heavy eyelids always produce a sure-fire effect. But if matters look really serious, the thermometer appears, and I had suffered several times already from its merciless denials. Happily, I knew it had been left behind in Marseilles, in the drawer of the bedside table. . . . But I realized at once that, at the least alarm, I should be moved in its direction, and probably the very same day.

And if I were to break my leg? Really break it, not just pretend to? Someone had shown me a wood-cutter who had cut off two of his fingers with an axe in order not to have to go into the army, and it had proved very successful. I did not intend to cut anything off myself, because that would bleed so frightfully, and wouldn't grow again. Whereas a broken bone heals perfectly and doesn't show at all. Cacinelli, at school, had had a leg broken by a kick from a horse's hoof: it didn't show in the least, and afterwards he ran just as fast as before! But this brainwave did not stand up to serious scrutiny: if I was unable to walk, I'd be carried in François' cart; I'd have to stay in a chaise-longue for a month and (Cacinelli had told me so) with my leg encased in plaster and 'a two hundred pound weight pulling at it day and night'.

No, no broken leg for me.

But what was I to do, then? Was I to resign myself to leaving my dear old Lili—for an eternity?

At that very moment he was coming up the small hill, shielded against the rain by a sack folded like a hood. I immediately felt imbued with fresh courage and opened the door wide before he had reached it.

CHAPTER TWELVE

LILI carefully scraped his shoes against the rough doorstep, to remove the mud, and politely greeted the company who answered him gaily while going on with their odious preparations. Then he came up to me, saying:

'We must go and fetch our snares. . . . If we wait till tomorrow, the chaps from Allauch may have pinched them!'

'You want to go out in this rain?' my mother asked in amazement. 'Do you want to catch pneumonia?'

This was, at that time, the most dreaded of illnesses. But I was only too happy to leave this room where I was not free to speak my mind.

So I stood out for it.

'Please, Mama, I'll put on my cape and hood, and Lili can take Paul's.'

'You know, madam,' Lili said, 'the rain is getting less, and the wind has dropped . . .'

My father broke in:

'It's their last day,' he said. 'Just dress them warmly, with newspapers on their chests. And stout shoes instead of rope-soles. They aren't made of sugar, after all, and the weather looks like brightening.'

'But if it starts all over again, like yesterday . . .' my mother argued, worried.

'We got home all right yesterday, in spite of the thick fog. And there isn't any today!'

She dressed us. Between my flannel vest and my shirt she

slipped several issues of the *Petit Provençal*, folded in four. She put some more down my back. I then had to put on two sweaters, one on top of the other, then the windbreaker, carefully buttoned, and the cloth cape over the lot. Finally, she crammed a beret down over my ears and pulled over it the sort of pointed hood that is worn by Snow-White's dwarfs and police constables.

Meanwhile, Aunt Rose was swaddling Lili in the same fashion. Paul's cape was rather on the short side but, at least, it protected his head and shoulders.

As we were leaving the house, the rain stopped and a ray of sunshine suddenly made the gleaming olive-trees sparkle.

'Let's walk fast!' I said. 'They may go out shooting and we'll have to act as retrievers again. I don't want to, today. As they are so set on leaving tomorrow, they can jolly well go shooting by themselves.'

We were soon safely away under the pine-trees. Two minutes later, we heard a long, appealing call: it was Uncle Jules' voice, but the echo was the only one to answer. . . .

Despite the bad weather, our snares had been most successful, and when we reached Font-Bréguette, our haversacks were crammed with whitetails and plumed larks. . . .

This success, which proved how cruel and absurd my imminent departure was, only deepened my grief.

As we reached the top shelf of the Taoumé, where our last snares were set, Lili said thoughtfully in an undertone:

'It's too bad, really. . . . When we have enough ants to last the whole winter. . . .'

Didn't I know that we had ants in plenty! I knew it, with bitterness. I did not answer.

He suddenly raced off towards the edge of the cliff, where a tall juniper stood, bent down and held up a bird at arm's length. It looked to me like a small pigeon.

'The first fieldfare!' he cried.

I stepped closer.

It was the big thrush of the Alps; my father had talked about it one day. Its head was bluish grey, and from its red throat a black-flecked waistcoat fanned out to its white underside. It was heavy in my hand. As I was sadly looking at it, Lili said:

'Listen. . . .'

I could hear a great many birds calling in the pine-trees around us. It sounded like the magpie's cry, but without its brash vulgarity, without that thieving bird's noisy impudence. On the contrary, this was a guttural, tender voice, a sad little voice like a song of autumn. . . . The fieldfares were coming to see me leave.

Lili said: 'Tomorrow I'll get Baptistin's thrush-snares ready, and I'll set them tomorrow night. And on Monday morning, I can promise you I'll need two sacks to carry them home.'

I said curtly:

'On Monday morning you'll be at school!'

'Oh no, I won't! When I tell my mother that the fieldfares have come and that I can catch fifteen or twenty francs' worth a day, she won't be crazy enough to send me to school! Till Friday—or perhaps till the Monday after—I needn't worry!'

I imagined him, all alone, on the sunny *garrigue*, beating the brushwood and the cades, while I would be sitting under the low ceiling of a classroom, facing a blackboard covered with squares and rhomboids. . . .

My throat tightened suddenly, and I shook with rage and despair.

I wept and screamed and stamped and sobbed, and rolled on the pebbles, while the *Petit Provençal* rustled on my chest and back.

'No! No! I won't go!' I shouted in a shrill voice. 'No! I don't want to leave! I won't! No, I won't!'

The flight of fieldfare plunged into the valley, and Lili, bowled over by my despair, gathered me in his arms, crumpling sixteen thicknesses of the *Petit Provençal* between two disconsolate hearts.

'Don't make yourself sick!' he said. 'You mustn't fret so! Listen to me, listen. . . .'

I listened, but there was nothing he could say, except murmur words of friendship.

Ashamed of my weakness, I suddenly made a great effort to pull myself together and said distinctly:

'If they want to force me to go back to town, I'll let myself starve to death. As a matter of fact, I've started already: I didn't eat anything this morning.'

This disclosure upset Lili.

'Nothing at all?'

'Nothing.'

'I've got some apples,' he said, rummaging in his sack.

'No, I don't want them. I don't want anything.'

It was such a fierce refusal that he did not insist.

After quite a long silence, I announced:

'I've made up my mind. If they want to go, nobody's stopping them. But *I'm* staying here.'

To stress the finality of my decision, I went and sat down on a big boulder, and folded my arms over my chest. Lili looked at me, perplexed.

'How are you going to do *that*?'

'Oho!' I said, 'it's easy. Tomorrow morning—or perhaps during the night—I'll pack my bundle and I'll go and hide in that small cave under the Taoumé.'

He opened his eyes wide.

'You'd do that?'

'You don't know me!'

'They'll search for you at once!'

'They won't find me!'

'Then they'll go and tell the *gendarmes* and the rural policeman at Allauch.'

'Since nobody knows that hideout—you said so yourself—they won't find me either. And first I'll write a note to my father and leave it on my bed. I'll tell him not to go and look for me, because I'll be *untraceable*, and that if he notifies the *gendarmes*, I'll throw myself from the top of the cliff. I know him. He'll understand, and he won't say a thing to anyone.'

'All the same, he'll worry himself sick, he will.'

'Not half as much as if he saw me pining to death at home.'

I was myself fully convinced by this argument, which clinched my decision irrevocably, but after some thought, Lili declared:

'I'd be awfully glad if you stayed. But how are you going to live up in the hills?'

'In the first place, I'll take some provisions with me. There is chocolate at home, and a whole box of biscuits. And I know you've heard of the hermit who stayed for twenty years down at the Passe-Temps well. Well, I'll do as he did: I'll look for asparagus, snails, mushrooms, and I'll plant chick-peas!'

'You don't know how to cook 'em!'

'I'll learn. And then I'll go to La Pondrane and swipe Roumieu's plums: he never gathers them, anyway . . . I'll dry figs, almonds, sorb-apples, I'll pick blackberries, sloes. . . .'

He did not look very convinced, and I was beginning to feel exasperated:

'It's obvious you've never read any books! But I've read scores of them. And I can tell you that there are lots of people who manage quite well in virgin forests . . . and those forests are full of poisonous spiders, so big a soup-tureen couldn't hold them, and they jump at your face, and then there are boa constrictors which hang from trees, and vampires which suck your blood while you're asleep, and fierce Red Indians who try to shrink your head. Whereas here there are no Indians, no wild beasts. . . .'

I hesitated a little, then suggested:

'Apart from wild boars, perhaps?'

'No,' said Lili, 'not in winter.'

'Why?'

'It's thirstiness that makes them come. In winter they have water, so they stay up in the mountains, over at Sainte-Victoire. . . .'

This was splendid, reassuring news, for the uncoiled guts of the wretched one-armed wood-cutter would sometimes sprawl across the paths of my dreams.

'What's going to be hard,' Lili said, 'is lying down at night.'

'I'll make myself a bed of *baouco* in a corner of the cave. It's as good as a mattress. . . . Besides, I may tell you one gets used to anything. Of course, you don't know Robinson Crusoe, but I know him very well. . . . He was a sailor. He could swim like a fish, but he was no good at all at running, because there isn't room for it on ships. . . . Well, when he was shipwrecked on a desert island, before three months were out, he could run so fast he could catch wild goats!'

'Ho! Ho!' Lili exclaimed forcefully, 'I don't know about him, but I do know goats! If he's the one who told you that, you can be sure he's a first-rate liar!'

'But I'm telling you it's in print! In a book that's given away as a prize at school!'

This brooked no reply: he had to give way, but did so without losing face:

'If they were nanny-goats in kid, it might be . . . but if you have a shot at catching my father's goats. . . .'

'Of course I shan't!' I said. 'I just meant it as an example to show one can get used to anything! If I catch one of your father's goats, some day, I'll just draw off a glass of milk and then let it go!'

'That's possible,' Lili said, 'nobody will be any the wiser.'

In this way, the conversation continued till noon.

He gradually let himself be persuaded as I was beginning to settle down to my new life under his very eyes.

He first declared that he would complete my store of provisions by stealing a sack of potatoes from his mother's cellar, and also at least two hard sausages. Then he promised to keep half his bread and his bar of chocolate for me every day. Finally, as he was of a practical turn of mind, his thoughts turned towards money.

'First of all,' he said, 'we'll catch dozens of thrushes! I'll only take home half the catch, and we'll go and sell the rest to the Pichauris' at the inn. One franc apiece for the thrushes, and two for the fieldfare! With that you can buy yourself bread at Aubagne!'

'And I'll sell snails in the market, too!'

'And what about fennel?' he cried. 'The herbalist at La Valentine buys it for three *sous* the kilogramme!'

'I'll tie it in little bundles, and you'll take them to him!'

'And with all the money we'll go and buy rabbit-snares!'

'And thin wire for making traps! If we catch a hare, it'll mean five francs at least!'

'And birdlime to catch thrushes alive! A live thrush is worth six francs!'

As I was getting up to go home, a huge flight of starlings banked steeply and swooped down on the pineland. Some hundreds of birds settled in the suddenly teeming tree-tops. I was amazed and delighted.

'Every year, they come and stay here for at least a fortnight,' Lili told me. 'And when they've chosen a tree, they come back to it every night. If we'd had fifty twigs, you realize what we would have caught today?'

'Uncle Jules told me they can be tamed. . . .'

'Of course,' Lili said. 'My brother had a tame one. And he talked too, but only in dialect!'

'Oh, but I'd teach them French,' I said.

'I'm not so sure they'd learn it,' Lili observed, 'because they're country birds, you see. . . .'

We walked downhill in great strides, making endless plans.

I could see myself roaming on the cliffs of the Taoumé, my hair blowing in the wind, my hands in my pockets, a faithful starling perched on my shoulders, at times tenderly nibbling my ear and making conversation.

The guns had gone to Pichauris, rather vexed that we had let them down. Lili stayed for lunch, with my aunt, my mother, my little sister and Paul.

He was grave, while I pretended to be noisily gay, which greatly pleased my dear Mama. I looked at her tenderly but was quite determined to leave her during the coming night.

*

I have often wondered how I could take such a decision without a shadow of remorse and without the least uneasiness. Only today can I understand it.

Until the dismal age of puberty, the child's world is not ours: he has the wonderful gift of ubiquity.

228

Every day, while I was having lunch at the family table, I was also running over the hillside and releasing a still warm blackbird from a snare.

The bush, the blackbird and the snare were as real to me as the oil-cloth, the coffee and milk, the portrait of President Fallières vaguely smiling down from the wall.

Whenever my father suddenly asked me: 'Where *are* you?' I would return to the dining-room, but without coming down from the clouds: the two worlds were on a level.

I would promptly reply: 'I'm here!' in a protesting tone of voice.

It was true, and for a moment or two I played at living with them; but the buzzing of a fly at once conjured up the ravine of Lancelot, where three small blue flies had been following me about for an awfully long time. And so powerful is a child's memory that I discovered, in this sudden recollection, a thousand fresh details which I didn't know I had noticed—as the ruminant ox, chewing his cud finds in it the flavour of seeds and flowers on which he has grazed without knowing it.

I was thus in the habit of leaving my beloved family, for I lived most of the time without them, and far away from them. My expedition would not be a scandalous novelty, and the only change from everyday life would be my bodily absence.

But what would *they* be doing during that time? That was something I only vaguely thought of, for I was not at all certain that they could exist in my absence; or if they persisted in living on, it must be an unreal and, therefore, painless life.

Moreover, I wasn't leaving for good; I intended to return some day and bring them back to life. I would thus be giving them so great and real a joy that it would instantly blot out the anxieties of their bad dream and, on balance, there would be a net profit of happiness.

★

After lunch Lili left us, saying that his mother was waiting for him to flail the chick-peas; in actual fact, he was going to inspect

229

the contents of the cellar and get my provisions ready, for he knew she was out in the fields.

I immediately went up to my room, making the excuse that I was going to collect the few personal effects that I wanted to take back to town—and I composed my farewell letter:

My dear Papa,
My dear Maman,
My dear Parents,

Now, above all, you mustn't wurry. It won't do any good. I have now found my vocation. It is: a hermitt.

I have taken with me all that I shall need.

As for my lessons, it's too late now, for I've Given them Up.

If it doesn't work out, I'll come back home. But happiness for me lies in Adventchure. There is no danger. I'm taking along two Aspirin tablets of the Rhône Factory brand. So don't frett.

Besides, I wont be all alone. A person (whom you don't know) will bring me bread and keep me company in stormy whether.

Don't search for me: I'm untraceable.

Look after Maman's health. I'll think of her every night.

You can be quite proud, on the contrary, because to become a hermitt takes Courage, and I have it. I'm proving it.

When I come back, you won't know who I am till I'll say: 'It's me.'

Paul will be a little jealous, but that can't be helped. Give him a big kiss from his Elder Brother.

I kiss you tenderly, and above all my dear Maman,

Your son,
MARCEL,
the Hermitt of the Hills.

I then fetched an old length of rope which I had noticed in the grass near the Boucan Well. It was not quite two yards long, and several strands had been frayed by wear and tear, as it scraped the rim of the well. However, it seemed to me that the hemp would still bear my weight and enable me to climb down from my bedroom window. I hid it under my mattress.

At last I prepared the all-important bundle: some underwear, a pair of shoes, the sharp-pointed knife, a hatchet, a fork, a spoon, a notebook, a pencil, a ball of string, a small saucepan, some nails and a few rejected old tools. I hid the lot under my bed, intending to bundle everything up in my blanket as soon as the whole house had gone to sleep.

The two haversacks had been laid to rest in a wardrobe. I filled them with various foodstuffs: dried almonds, prunes, some chocolate, which I had managed to extract from the parcels and packages that had been made ready for our return to town.

I was much excited by these clandestine preparations. As I was shamelessly rummaging in the luggage—even in Uncle Jules'— I compared myself to Robinson Crusoe foraging 'tween-decks on the stranded ship and discovering all sorts of treasures, such as a hammer, a ball of string or a grain of wheat.

When everything was ready, I decided to devote to my mother the last hours I was destined to spend with her.

I carefully peeled potatoes, shook out the salad, laid the table and, now and then, went to her and kissed her hand.

The last dinner was excellent and more plentiful than usual as if to celebrate a happy event.

Nobody uttered a word of regret. On the contrary, they all seemed rather glad to be returning to the ant-heap.

Uncle Jules talked of his office, my father confessed he was hopefully expecting to be awarded the *palmes académiques* at the end of the year, Aunt Rose once more mentioned Gas. . . . I could see that they had left already.

But I was staying.

CHAPTER THIRTEEN

A PEBBLE clinked against the iron fitting of the shutter. That was the agreed signal. I was fully dressed; I slowly opened the window. A whisper rose out of the darkness: 'Are you there?'

By way of reply, I lowered my bundle at the end of a string. Then I pinned my *Farewell Letter* to my pillow and stoutly fastened the rope to the window-catch. I blew a kiss to my mother through the partition and slid to the ground.

Lili was there, under an olive-tree. I could hardly make him out. He took a step forward and said in a whisper:

'Let's go.'

He picked up a rather heavy sack from the ground and swung it onto his shoulder with a jerk.

'It's potatoes, carrots and snares,' he said.

'And I've got bread, sugar, chocolate and two bananas. Come on, we'll talk later.'

In silence we climbed uphill until we reached Petit-Oeil.

I breathed in the cool night air with delight and thought, without the least concern, of the new life which was beginning.

Again we took the path that mounted towards the Taoumé.

The night was calm but overcast: no star in the sky. I felt cold.

The swarming holiday crowd of insects that had been humming happily all summer, had packed up their music and no longer quickened the sad silence of invisible autumn. But a tawny owl hooted in the distance, and a screech-owl sent out its flute-like calls, faithfully repeated by the sorrowful echo from Rapon.

We walked fast, as all fugitives should. The weight of our packs pulled our shoulders back, and we did not utter a word. The motionless pines by the wayside looked like silhouettes cut out of sheet-metal, and the dew had made everything smell wet.

After half an hour's walk, we reached Baptiste's Pen and sat down for a moment on its large stone threshold.

Lili was the first to speak.

'I almost didn't come and call you.'

'Were your parents keeping an eye on you?'

'Oh no. It wasn't that.'

'What was it then?'

He hesitated, then said:

'I thought you wouldn't do it.'

'Do what?'

'Take to the hills. I thought you'd just said it like that, but that in the end . . .'

I got up, my pride hurt:

'So you think I'm a girl who changes her mind all the time! Do you think I only talk hot air? Well, you'll find out that when I've decided on something, I always do it! And if you hadn't come, I'd have left on my own! And if you're scared, you can stay where you are: I know where I'm going!'

I strode on self-confidently. He rose, heaved his sack back onto his shoulder and hurried to catch up with me. He got ahead of me, stopped, looked at me for a second, and said with heart-felt conviction:

'You are terrific!'

I promptly assumed a terrific air, but did not reply.

Still gazing at me, he said:

'There's nobody like you!'

At last he turned his back on me and resumed walking. . . . Ten paces further on, however, he stopped again and said, without turning round this time:

'There's no denying it: you're terrific!'

This dumbfounded admiration which flattered my vanity suddenly seemed to me very disquieting, and I had to make an effort to keep on being terrific.

I was succeeding pretty well in this attempt when I thought I heard, far to our right, something slithering on the pebbles. I stopped and pricked up my ears. The sound started again.

'That's one of the noises of the night . . . one never knows where they come from. Mind you, they scare you at first, but they aren't dangerous: you'll soon get used to it.'

He started walking again and we arrived at the edge of the cliff which overhangs the plain of La Garette. On our left the thick pinewood of the Taoumé began to fan out. The mist of dawn was rising from the ground between the tree-trunks, and rolled in slow whorls over the scrub.

A kind of sharp, short bark, repeated three times, gave me a start.

'Is that someone out shooting?'

'No,' said Lili, 'it's a fox. When he does that, it means he's heading some animal back to his mate: so he warns her. . . .'

The savage little voice cried three times more, and I thought of my natural history textbook: the elephant *trumpets*, the stag *bells*, the fox *barks* or *yelps*.

So because I had a name for it, the cry lost its nocturnal power: this fox was *yelping*, there was nothing more to it. I had carried the word for his cry in my satchel a hundred times: I was completely reassured and was going to impart my comforting knowledge to Lili when, on my left, deep in the pine-wood, half-hidden by the mist, a rather tall shadow swiftly passed under the hanging branches.

'Lili,' I said in a low voice, 'I've just seen a shadow pass!'

'Where?'

'Over there.'

'You're dreaming,' he said. 'You can't see a shadow in the dark. . . .'

'I tell you I saw something pass!'

'It was the fox perhaps!'

'No . . . it was taller. . . . It wouldn't be your brother, after thrushes?'

'Oh no! It's too early. . . . There's at least another hour of darkness. . . .'

'Or else a poacher?'

'I'd be surprised. . . . Unless. . . .'

But he stopped and, in turn, looked towards the pine-wood in silence.

'What are you thinking about?'

He answered with another question.

'What was it like, this shadow?'

'A bit like a man's.'

'Tall?'

'Well, it was a long way off. . . . Yes, rather tall.'

'With a cloak? A long cloak?'

'I couldn't see it very well, you know. I saw something like a shadow moving and disappearing behind a pine, or a cade. Why do you ask? Are you thinking of someone who's got a cloak?'

'Might be,' he said pensively. 'I've never seen him. But my father has.'

'Who?'

'Big Felix.'

'Is he a shepherd?'

'Yes,' he said. 'He was, in the old days.'

'Why do you say in the old days?'

'Because it happened in the old days.'

'I don't understand.'

He came closer to me and explained in a low voice:

'He's been dead for at least fifty years. But it's better not to talk about it, because that may make him come!'

As I looked at him in amazement, he whispered into my ear:

'He's a ghost!'

This was such a disturbing revelation that, to reassure myself, I fell back on my well-tried sarcastic laughter and asked in a cuttingly ironic tone:

'Do you believe in ghosts?'

He looked frightened and muttered:

'Don't shout so loud! I tell you it may make him come!'

To please him, I lowered my voice.

'Well, let me tell you that my father, who is a learned man, and my uncle, who works at the Prefecture, both say it's bunkum! They laugh at ghosts. And me too, I laugh at them. That's what I do. Yes, LAUGH AT THEM!'

'Well, they don't make my father laugh, because he's seen the ghost, he has. He's seen it four times.'

'Your father's a good sort, but he can't even read!'

'I'm not saying he can read, I'm saying he's *seen* it!'

'Where?'

'One night, when he was sleeping at Baptiste's Pen, he heard someone walking about outside. And then a great sigh, like someone dying. So he peeped through a chink in the door and he saw a very tall shepherd, with a cloak, a stick and a huge hat. Quite grey from top to toe.'

I whispered—still to please him:

'Perhaps it was a real shepherd?'

'Oh no, it wasn't! And the proof that it was a ghost is that when he opened the door, there was nothing there any more. No shepherd, no ghost, NOTHING.'

It was a crushing proof.

'And what does the ghost come for? What does he want?'

'Well, it seems he was very rich, he had at least a thousand sheep. Bandits murdered him; they stabbed him with a big dagger between his shoulder-blades and they took a big bag of gold coins off him. So he comes back all the time to complain and look for his treasure.'

'He knows quite well we weren't the ones who took it.'

'That's what my father told him.'

'He spoke to him?'

'Of course. The fourth time he came, my father talked to him through the door. "Listen, Felix," he said, "I'm a shepherd, just like you. I don't know where your treasure is. So don't come and bother me, because I need sleep." The ghost didn't say a word, but he began whistling for at least ten minutes. So my father got angry and told him: "I respect the dead, but if you keep on like this, I shall come out and give you four signs of the cross and six kicks up the arse".'

'Did he really say that?'

'Yes, he did, and he would have done it too! But the other understood: he went away and he's never come back again.'

It was a preposterous story and I decided not to believe it. I therefore turned for support to some of my father's favourite words:

'Frankly,' I said, 'I think you're rather silly to have such prejudices, which are mere superstitions. Ghosts are in people's imagination. And signs of the cross are sheer obscu-curantisy!'

'Ho! Ho!' he exclaimed, 'the sign of the cross is a knock-out for ghosts! Now that's something no one can deny! Anybody can tell you it cuts them in two.'

I sneered—rather half-heartedly—and asked:

'And of course, you know all about making the sign of the cross?'

'Of course!' he answered.

'How do you perform this rigmarole?'

He solemnly crossed himself several times. I promptly imitated him, with a sneer. Whereupon something came buzzing out of the darkness and I received a light but sharp tap in the middle of my forehead. I could not suppress a faint cry. Lili bent down and picked something up.

'It's a capricorn beetle,' he said.

He crushed it under his heel and started walking again. I followed him, occasionally glancing over my shoulder.

CHAPTER FOURTEEN

W E were almost below the Taoumé, and I could clearly see the outline of the cliff which towered over the subterranean passage where I was going to embark upon my great adventure.

Lili suddenly stopped.

'There's something we've forgotten!'

His voice betrayed considerable alarm.

'What's that?'

But instead of answering me, he shook his head, dropped his sack on the lavender and started talking to himself.

'Think of forgetting that, it doesn't seem possible! I'm the one who should have thought of it. But you forgot all about it too. . . . And *now* what are we going to do?'

He sat down on a rock and, still shaking his head, folded his arms and fell silent.

This somewhat theatrical attitude irritated me, and I said sternly:

'What's come over you? Are you going mad? What have we forgotten?'

He pointed with his finger towards the cliff and pronounced this mysterious word:

'Thowl.'

'What do you mean?'

'Therbiggowl.'

'What?'

He lost his patience and said forcefully:

'The one that tried to pluck our eyes out! The grand duke! He lives up in the vaulting, he's sure to have his mate with him. . . . We've only seen one of 'em, but I bet you twelve traps that there are two!'

This was a terrifying piece of news. Terrific though you may be, there are moments when your destiny lets you down.

Two biggowls! I saw them circling round my head, their yellow beaks gaping over their black tongues, with glassy eyes, crooked claws, and rendered a thousand times more dangerous by the description I myself had given of them and which my nightmares had since corroborated. . . . I closed my eyes as hard as I could and took a deep breath.

No, no, it wasn't possible: I'd prefer any time Monsieur Besson's class, with its squares, rhomboids and its citizen's duties.

'There are sure to be two!' Lili repeated.

At this I became all the more terrific since I had decided to beat a retreat when the moment came.

'There are two of us, too!' I retorted coolly. 'You wouldn't be scared, by any chance?'

'Yes,' he said, 'yes, I'm scared. There's something you don't realize. When we saw that owl, it was daytime: that's why he didn't budge. . . . But at night he feels more at home: they'll come and pluck your eyes out while you're asleep. . . . A biggowl, at night, is worse than an eagle!'

I thought that if I overdid my bravery he would refuse to follow me, so I answered gravely:

'That's why we'll wait until daybreak, and then we'll go and attack them! With my sharp knife at the end of a stick, I'll make it my business to let those chickens know that the cave has changed its tenant! And now, there's been enough palaver. Let's get ready!'

I did not move, however. He gazed at me, then bounded to his feet.

'You're right!' he said ardently. 'They're only birds, after all! We'll cut two short cades, I'll whittle mine down to a fine point, and we'll spit the owls like a pair of chickens!'

He took four steps, opened his shepherd's knife, crouched down so that he could crawl into the thicket and got to work.

Sitting on the pebbles at the foot of a pine, I did some thinking.

'If they don't want to come out of their hole,' Lili said as he worked, 'I'll poke my stick in, and you'll hear them squeal!'

I saw he wasn't joking, and that he was quite determined to attack the 'biggowls'. He was the terrific one of us two, and I felt ashamed of my cowardice.

Then I summoned one of my favourite heroes to my rescue: Robinson Crusoe. . . . If he had found these two birds when settling down in his first cave, what would he have done? It wasn't hard to imagine: he would have strangled them promptly and plucked them, thanking Providence, before roasting them on a bamboo spit! If I fled before those birds, I'd never again gain admittance to an adventure story, and the characters in the illustrations, who had always looked me straight in the eye, would turn their heads away so as not to see 'a squaw heart'.

Besides, I was no longer up against 'grand dukes', those fierce and powerful birds whose very name emphasized their size and courage, but against 'biggowls' which seemed to me infinitely less formidable.

I gripped the pointed knife with a steady hand and proceeded to sharpen it on a stone.

There remained the ghost. I repeated to myself my father's powerful assertion: GHOSTS DO NOT EXIST. Whereupon I discreetly made the sign of the cross five or six times, to cut them in half.

Lili came out of the thicket. He was dragging two branches after him; they were longer than he was and perfectly straight. He gave me one of them.

I pulled a long piece of string from my pocket and tied the handle of the terrible knife to the thinner end of the cade-stick. Lili, at my side, was whittling down his weapon as carefully as if he were sharpening a pencil.

Around us, dawn was beginning to pierce the pale mist. In the diffused light, small wisps of fleecy cloud were caught up under the pine-tree branches and clung to the tops of the brushwood. It was cold.

My nerves, which had supported me all night, suddenly gave way, and I felt that my neck was now holding my head up only by an effort of will; I leaned my back and the nape of my neck against a tree-trunk for a moment, and my swollen eyelids warmed my gritty eyes. I would have dozed off, no doubt, but I heard a dry branch crack, down in the pine-wood. I called Lili under my breath.

'Did you hear?'

'It's a rabbit!' he said.

'Rabbits don't climb trees.'

'That's true. So perhaps it's a fox.'

He was still cutting away at his branch, and he added:

'You're terrific!'

I was going to tell him that this was a silly answer when, over there, between the black tree-trunks which were beginning to glow faintly, I saw a tall silhouette: under a large hat, draped in a long cape, the shepherd was slowly passing, in front of a flock of misty, roughly-cropped sheep, and straight between his shoulder-blades he bore, as a cross, the hilt of a dagger. . . .

I hastily directed four or five signs of the cross towards him with a trembling hand. But instead of falling to pieces, the ghost turned towards me, made the sign of the cross himself, defiantly raised his eyes heavenward and came towards us with a sneer. . . . I wanted to shout, but fear gripped my throat and I lost consciousness. . . .

I felt two hands holding me by the shoulders and was about to scream when I heard Lili's voice.

It was saying:

'Hi! Wake up! This isn't a time to sleep!'

He straightened me up, for I had fallen sideways.

I stammered:

'Did you see?'

'Yes, I did,' he said, 'I saw you falling. A good thing there was all that thyme: else you'd have scratched your face! Are you as sleepy as all that?'

'Oh no!' I said. 'That's over. You didn't see . . . the ghost?'

'I saw nothing, but I heard something again up there. . . . It may be Mond des Parpaillouns, after all. . . . We must be careful he doesn't see us. . . . Look at my pike!'

He had stripped the bark off the branch, and the wood was as polished as marble. He made me feel the tip, as sharp as my knife's. . . .

A few waning stars had just appeared at the edge of the sky, over by Sainte-Baume. He got up.

'We're ready,' he said. 'But it isn't light enough yet for the battle with the owls. We've got time to pass by the Bréguette Pool: we'll go and fill your bottles there.'

I followed him through the dew-drenched lavender.

CHAPTER FIFTEEN

THE Bréguette Pool was on the left of the Taoumé, under a small cliff: a square hole, no bigger than a mortar-trough, and about a foot deep. Some goat-herd had dug it out of the rock in the old days, at the bottom of a moss-grown crack, and it was always half-full of ice-cold water.

Lili placed an empty bottle lengthwise under water: the gurgle cooed like a wood-pigeon.

'This is where you'll come and drink,' he said. 'It never dries up and it yields at least ten litres a day!'

I had a brainwave—for some time now I had been cudgelling my brain for one. Looking greatly perturbed, I said:

'Ten litres? Are you sure?'

'Oh yes! Perhaps even fifteen!'

'You must be joking?' I exclaimed, amazed and indignant.

'Not at all!' he said. 'If I say fifteen, you can rely on it.'

'And what on earth am I to do with a wretched fifteen litres?' I cried.

'You aren't proposing to drink all that, are you?'

'No. But what about washing?'

'Oh, you only need a drop of water for washing!'

I sneered:

'*You* may only need a drop, perhaps! But I've got to soap myself from head to foot!'

'Why? Are you ill?'

'Of course not. But don't forget I am from the city, and so I'm covered in microbes! You've got to be awfully careful with microbes!'

'What are they?'

'A kind of lice, but so small you can't see them. And so, if I don't soap myself every day, they'll nibble me away little by little until, one fine morning, you'll find me dead in the cave, so you can just fetch a shovel and bury me.'

This appalling prospect dismayed my good Lili.

'That would be silly!' he said.

I promptly moved in to attack, with shameless bad faith:

'And it's all your fault, too! If you hadn't promised that there was all the water for the asking at the Bréguette Pool . . .'

He looked desperate.

'But I didn't know! I haven't got any microps. I don't even know what you call 'em in *patois*! I only wash on Sunday, same as everybody! And even Baptistin says washing isn't natural and makes for illnesses! And Mond de Parpaillouns, he's never washed himself in his life, he's over seventy, and look how fit he is!'

'Come on, come on, don't make excuses. . . . It's a flop, a complete wash-out. . . . A real catastrophe, but after all you didn't do it on purpose. . . . It's fate. . . . It was written. . . .'

Leaning on my lance, I said solemnly:

'Farewell. I'm defeated. I'm going home.'

I climbed back towards the plateau: sunrise was edging the distant cliffs of the Holy Ghost with rose.

When I had walked twenty yards and found that Lili wasn't following me, I stopped for I was afraid he might lose sight of me in the dim light of dawn. I dug the shaft of my lance into the gravel of the *garrigue*, grasped it in both hands, and let my forehead drop forwards on my arms, in the attitude of a warrior overcome with grief.

This stratagem was immediately effective: he came running to catch me up and put his arms round me.

'Don't cry,' he said, 'don't cry. . . .'

'I? Cry?' I sneered. 'No, I don't feel in the least like crying. I feel more like biting! Never mind, let's say no more about it.'

'Give me your parcels,' he said. 'As it's all my fault, I'll carry them.'

'What about your sack?'

'I left it down there. I'll come back for it during the day. Now let's walk fast, before they see your letter. . . . I'm sure they're still in bed. . . .'

He trotted in front of me; I followed him without saying a word but giving an occasional loud, heart-rending sigh.

From a distance the house seemed dark and dead. But as we came closer, my heart sank: the shutters of my father's bedroom were edged with light.

'I bet you he's dressing!' I said.

'Then he hasn't seen it yet. Climb up quickly!'

He gave me a leg up so that I could reach the rope which was to have revealed my departure and now assured my return. Then he passed up my bundle.

High above the last layers of mist a lark suddenly sang out: the sun was rising on my defeat.

'I'm going back to fetch my sack,' he said. 'Then I'll come back again.'

My farewell letter was still in its place. I pulled out the pin, tore the note into a hundred little pieces and flung them, hand-ful by handful, out of the window which I noiselessly closed again.

Then in the silence I heard a low murmur coming from my father's bedroom.

He was talking very fast, and his voice sounded gay: it seemed to me that I could even distinguish a soft chuckle. . . .

Oh yes, he was laughing because the holidays had come to an end. . . . Hardly awake, he was laughing already at the thought of going back to his desk with his dreary pencils, his ink, his chalks. . . .

I hid my bundles under my bed: if somebody found them, I would say that I had wanted to carry some of my mother's parcels.

I crept into bed, ashamed and freezing. . . . I had been frightened, I was only a coward, a 'squaw heart'. I had lied to my parents, I had lied to my friend, I had lied to myself.

I tried in vain to find excuses: I felt I was going to cry. . . . I pulled the heavy blanket over my tremulous chin and took refuge in slumber. . . .

CHAPTER SIXTEEN

WHEN I woke up, daylight was filling the 'moon hole' in the shutter, and Paul was no longer in his bed. I opened the window: it was pouring with rain. Not a fine, ringing, purple cloudburst, but a teeming, patient drizzle that came steadily down in silence.

I suddenly heard the creak of wheels, and saw, emerging round the corner of the house, François walking ahead of his mule, followed by a cart surmounted by an open umbrella. Aunt Rose, wrapped in a blanket, was sheltering beneath it. She was surrounded by luggage, and on her left arm my little cousin was perched, and on her right my little sister. I deduced from this that my mother and Paul must have refused to take their places in the vehicle which was, in fact, crammed full.

Uncle Jules walked behind it, under another umbrella; he was pushing his bicycle, and I watched them moving away on the sad road back to town.

I found my family sitting round the table: they were breakfasting heartily, and Lili was with them.

My arrival was greeted with a small ovation. My father had a funny look on his face.

'Grief doesn't seem to have kept you awake on your last night here,' he said laughing.

'He snored!' Paul cried. 'I tried pulling his hair to wake him up, but he didn't even feel it!'

'He's overtired!' my father said. 'Now, come and eat, because it's nine o'clock and we won't be home before one, even with the help of the Sunday bus!'

I devoured my slices of bread and butter. I was ashamed of my fiasco in front of Lili and only ventured sidelong glances at him.

As I didn't know what to say, I asked:

'Why have the others gone already?'

'Because François had to take his vegetables to the market before ten o'clock,' my mother replied. 'Aunt Rose will wait for us at Durbec's, at the bus stop.'

We left in the downpour, wearing our capes. Lili, carrying his sack, insisted on accompanying us. Small rivulets were flowing in the furrows, all sounds were muffled, we did not meet a soul.

At the end of the village, in front of the green gate, the omnibus was waiting.

Aunt Rose had already settled herself in it with the babies, in the middle of a crowd of peasants wearing their Sunday best.

It was a long, green coach, and from its roof hung short canvas curtains with a fringe of string. The two horses were pawing the ground, and the coachman, in his grey cape and oilskin hat, was sounding the horn to call the stragglers.

We said good-bye to Lili watched by our fellow-passengers.

My mother kissed him, which made him blush once more, then it was Paul's turn. As I was shaking his hand in a manly way, I saw there were tears in his eyes, and his mouth was twitching. My father stepped forward:

'Come on,' he said, 'you're not going to cry like a baby in front of all these people!'

But Lili dropped his head under his sack-cloth hood and scraped the ground with the toe of his shoe. I felt like crying too.

'You children must understand,' my father said, 'that there can't only be fun in life. I would like to stay here too and live in the hills. Even in a cave! Even all alone, like a hermit! But one can't always do as one likes!'

I was struck by the allusion to a hermit: but I assumed it was a natural idea to come to anyone, since it had come to me. He went on:

'Next June, Marcel is going to sit for a very important exam, and there's a lot of work he has to do this year, especially on

248

spelling. He writes "worried" with a "u" and I bet he wouldn't know how to spell "hermit".'

I felt myself blushing, but my alarm lasted no more than a second: he couldn't have read my letter, since I had found it in its place. And besides, if he had read it, there would have been no end of a to-do about it on my return! Moreover, he was going on in a perfectly natural tone of voice:

'So he needs to put in some hard work. If he's serious about it and makes good progress, we'll come back at Christmas, on Shrove Tuesday and at Easter. So stop sniffling in front of all these people, shake hands like the two hunters that you are! . . . Goodbye, young Lili. Don't forget that you're slowly getting near your school certificate, and that one educated peasant is worth as much as two or three illiterate ones!'

He would probably have continued his lay sermon, had not the coachman blown his horn peremptorily and cracked his whip twice. So we hurriedly got into the bus.

The last row of seats, which had their backs to the horses, was empty. As my mother and Paul had fits of giddiness when travelling backwards, the family sat down among the peasants, while I went to sit at the back, all alone.

The coachman released the brake, and we set off at a light trot. It was still raining.

With my head ducked between my shoulders, as if I were withdrawing into myself, I nibbled a sprig of mint; my hand in my pocket was clutching a snare which had lost its murderous quality, but had become a sacred object, a relic, a promise. . . . The blue mass of the beloved Taoumé was towering, eternal, in the distance, commanding the ring of hills in the shroud of rain. I was thinking of the gnarled service-tree below the cliff of Baume-Sourne, of the tinkling water of Bréguette Pool, of the three tremulous little flies in the Précatori valley. . . . I was thinking of the thyme that carpeted La Pondrane, of the bird-filled terebinths, of the musical rock, of the sweet lavender among the gravel of the *garrigue*. . . .

On each side of the narrow road, two bare stone-walls, on which rain-sodden creepers were trailing, stretched endlessly before us in the drizzle.

The high rattle-trap was creaking, the iron rims crushed the gravel, the horses' hooves rang on the cobble-stones, the whiplash gave a dull crack, like a damp squib. . . .

I was being carried away from my homeland, and the soft rain-drops on my face were weeping for me. . . . I was not setting out towards a destination, sticking my chin and my chest out: lonely and desperate beyond words, I was sinking backwards into the future to the rhythmical beat of the hooves, like Queen Brunhild being dragged over the stones, her fair hair plaited to a horse's tail.

CHAPTER SEVENTEEN

I EXPERIENCED no joy at seeing the big school-house again: the plane-trees in the courtyard were beginning to lose their yellow leaves, and the caretaker would burn them every morning, in small heaps at the foot of the high, grey wall. . . . Through the class-room window I could see, instead of the pine-woods, the drab rows of lavatory doors. . . .

I had entered the fourth year at the primary school, Monsieur Besson's class. He was young, tall, lean, and already going bald, and he couldn't straighten the forefinger of his right hand.

He gave me a great welcome, but upset me thoroughly by telling me that my whole life would depend on my studies during that year, and that he would be obliged to crack down on me because I was his 'candidate' for the scholarship competition for the *lycée*. In this redoubtable tournament, 'primary' school would be vying with 'secondary' school.

I felt full of self-confidence in the early stages, for to my mind 'secondary' stood for 'second-rate' and, consequently, for 'easy'.

I soon realized that my father and his colleagues did not share this opinion, and that the honour of the entire school was bound up in my candidature.

This G.H.Q. took the business in hand, after the fashion of a C.I.D. squad, whose inspectors take over, in turn, the questioning of a suspect.

Monsieur Besson, who taught me for six hours a day, was in charge of the investigation and pooled the intelligence.

I had to attend school, even on THURSDAY MORNINGS, at nine a.m.

Monsieur Suzanne, the revered master of the Upper Form, whose pedagogy was infallible, would await me in the empty class-room, in order to tease me with additional problems: trains would be catching up with one another, cyclists would meet, and a father, who was seven times older than his son, would see his advantage melt away with each passing year. At about eleven, Monsieur Bonafé would check my 'logical analyses' and present me with fresh ones which I should certainly be unable to solve today. During week-days, Monsieur Arnaud (who had at one time been toying with the idea of entering the postal service) forced me to take a stroll with him during the breaks, while chanting the litany of the sub-prefectures (where I have never set foot and of which my memory has happily rid itself).

In addition, Monsieur Mortier, who sported a handsome fair beard and a gold ring on his little finger, occasionally entrusted his pupils to my father during evening studies, and then took me along with him to his empty class-room, where he fired at me a thousand questions about the history of France. This science interested me as long as it proved romantic: 'Bow your head, proud Sicambrian!', Rollon's amusing pranks, the iron cage of Cardinal de la Balue, the crow soup on the retreat from Russia, and the all-too-important gaiter-button, the lack of which made us lose the war of 1870.

My father had reserved the supervision of my spelling for himself and every morning, before breakfast, he dosed me with dictation, each phrase of which was as studded with mines as a landing beach.

'*The soldiers passed through the village. The day is past. The knight rode along the road all night. The farmer sowed good seeds while the farmer's wife sewed a dress. . . .*'

I worked with spirit, but often the knights and soldiers passed in vain, for I would hear the crickets chirp and, instead of the bare branches of the plane-trees in the school-yard, I would see a blood-red sunset over Tête-Rouge: my good Lili would be clambering down the steep path from La Badauque, whistling, his hands in his pockets, with a garland of ortolans round his neck and a belt strung with thrushes. . . .

In the class-room, while Monsieur Besson would follow with the tip of a long ruler the meanderings of some futile river on the wall-map, the big fig-tree of Baptiste's Pen would slowly appear on the wall; above its mass of shiny leaves a tall dead branch would rear and, on the end of it, at the very top, a black-and-white magpie.

Then a very sweet pain would swell my childish heart and, while the distant voice reeled off the names of tributaries, I would try to measure the eternity that lay between me and Christmas. I would count the days, then the hours, then I'd subtract the hours of sleep, and through the window and the light mist of the winter morning I'd watch the school-clock: its big hand advanced by jerks, and I could see the little minutes drop like beheaded ants.

At night, by lamp-light, I would do my homework without speaking a word. There wasn't much time left to attend to Paul. And yet he was beginning to be quite interesting, for he had a class-mate who was a fountain of knowledge: almost every evening he brought home some scatological joke or some meaningless pun that would make him choke with laughter. We had scarcely any time to talk, except during the familiar operation that we had charge of twice a day, which was called laying the table.

My dear *maman* was appalled to see me bent over my home-work for so many long hours, and the Thursday morning session seemed to her a barbaric invention: she tended me as if I were a convalescent, and cooked the daintiest dishes for me which, unfortunately, were preceded by a big spoonful of cod-liver oil.

Taking all in all, I was 'making the grade', and the progress I made gave such pleasure to my father that it lost some of its painfulness for me.

CHAPTER EIGHTEEN

O NE day, when I came home from school for lunch, after an extra lesson in parsing, young Paul was leaning over the banister and shouting down the ringing well of the staircase:

'Someone's sent you a letter through the post! There's a stamp on it!'

I raced up the steps two at a time, and the vibrating banister twanged like a bronze harp.

On the table next to my plate was a yellow envelope, with my name scrawled on it in uneven letters with a pronounced slope.

'I bet this brings you news from your friend Lili!' my father said.

I could not manage to open the envelope, though I tore all four corners one after another; my father took it and, with the tip of a knife, slit open the edge as deftly as a surgeon.

Out of it fell, first a sage-leaf, then a dried violet.

On three sheets of a schoolboy's notebook, Lili talked to me in large handwriting, whose wavy lines circumvented the inkstains.

O colleague!

I tak up my Pen to tell you that the thrushs did not come this year. nothing, juss nothing. even the darnagas hav left. like You. I didnt katch two. no partritches neither. I dont go up there enymor it aint wurth the truble. it is much better to Work at School to lerne Spelling wot else cann you do? Nuthing. their arnt even any wingdants. they are so littul the burds wont eet em. Its too Badd, youre lucky your not here its a Dizaster. Im longing for you come. then the Burds too, and the partritches—and the Trush for crismis. And then theyve pinchd twelv of my snaires and at least Fifty Trushes. I no hoo did it. The Best Snaire of all. Its the bloke from Allo, the lame un. Be shure I'll rememmber it. and then its cold and the mistrall bloing. evry day out hunting Ive feat like ise. Im glad I hav the Skarf. but Im longing for you. batistin is pleezed: he ketches thirty thrush aday. with Lime. Day for yestrday ten ortollans, and Satterday twelve gavotte fieldfairs. with Lime. day for yestrday i wennt below tête-Rouge, i wanted to lissen to the Ston. It froze me eer. it jess wont sing enymor, it jess weaps. thets all the niews. Lov to Evryboddy. I send you a leef of saige for you and a viollet for your muther. yor friend for life Lili.

my Adress. Les Bellons Par Lavalantine France.

Ive bin writting you fer three days becos I continnu every nite. my Mother is pleezed. Shee thinks I'm duing my Homwurk. In my Copibook. Afterwuds I taire out the paje. the thundre has krackblasted the big Pine of Lagarète. Only the Trunk is lefft, and a poynt sharp as a wissle. Adessias.* Im longing for yu. My Adresse: les Bélons parlavalantine. France. The postmans nam is Fernan, evryboddy nose him, he cant mak a mistak. He nose me very Well. and I himm.

Your friend for life. Lili.

It wasn't easy to decipher his writing which the spelling did little to render more intelligible. But my father, a great expert on the subject, managed it after some initial groping. Afterwards he said:

'A good thing he's still got three years to prepare his school certificate!'

Then he added, looking at my mother:

'That child has a warm heart and real delicacy of feeling.'

At last he turned to me.

'Keep the letter. You'll understand it later.'

I took it, folded it, put it into my pocket, and did not answer: I had understood long before he had.

* Provençal for *Adieu.*

CHAPTER NINETEEN

NEXT day, after leaving school, I went into a tobacconist's and bought a beautiful sheet of notepaper. It was edged with lacework, its top left-hand corner was adorned with a swallow stamped in relief, which was holding a telegram in its beak. The thick, glazed envelope was bordered with forget-me-nots.

On my free Thursday afternoon I spent a long time drafting my reply. I don't remember the exact words, but I recollect its general import.

I first commiserated with him on the disappearance of the thrushes and asked him to congratulate Baptistin on catching them with lime in their absence. I then talked to him of my school work, the careful attention that was bestowed on me, and my teachers' satisfaction. After this not over-modest paragraph, I informed him that Christmas lay thirty-two days ahead but that we would still be young enough at that time to roam the hills and I promised him a massacre of thrushes and ortolans. At last, after giving him news of my family—who seemed to be flourishing—I asked him to convey my condolences to the 'crackblasted' pine at La Garette and to give my consoling love to the Disconsolate Stone. I ended with words of fervent friendship which I would never have dared to express to his face.

I read my prose through twice over and made some minor corrections; then, armed with a fresh nib, I copied it out, with blotting-paper under my hand, and my tongue between my teeth.

My handwriting was painstaking and my spelling perfect, for

I checked some doubtful words in the *Petit Larousse*. In the evening, I showed my father my handiwork: he made me add a few s's and cross out an unnecessary t, but he congratulated me and declared that it was a beautiful letter, which filled my dear little Paul with pride.

At night, in bed, I read Lili's message again, and his spelling struck me as so funny that I could not help laughing out loud. . . . But I suddenly realized that so many errors and so much clumsiness were the outcome of long hours of hard work and of a great effort of friendship. I got up noiselessly, went on my bare feet to light the paraffin-lamp, and carried my own letter, my copybook and my ink-well to the table in the kitchen. The whole family was asleep: the only sound to be heard was the little music made by the trickle of water that dribbled into the metal basin above the sink.

I first tore out, with a jerk, three pages of my copybook, thus obtaining the jagged edge I wanted. Then, with an old nib, I re-copied my over-beautiful letter, suppressing the witty phrase which made fun of his loving white lie. I also deleted in passing the paternal s's, I added a few spelling mistakes which I chose among his own: the ortollans, the partritches, batistin, the snaires and the dizaster. Finally I took care to embellish my text with un-expected capitals. This delicate labour took me two hours and I felt sleep overcoming me. . . . However, I read his letter again, then mine. It seemed all right but something was still missing: so with the end of my pen-holder I fished out a big drop of ink and, on my elegant signature, dropped this black tear: it burst like a sun.

CHAPTER TWENTY

T H E last thirty-two days of the term, drawn out by rain and autumn winds, seemed interminable to me, but the patient clock eventually got the better of them.

One December evening, after leaving school—where Monsieur Mortier had kept me in for an extra fifteen minutes among the Merovingian kings—my heart missed a beat as I walked into our dining-room.

My mother was piling woollens into a cardboard box.

On the table, brilliantly lit by the hanging lamp, the separate parts of my father's shotgun were spread out around a saucer full of oil.

I knew that we were to leave in six days, but in an attempt to keep calm I had always tried not to imagine this departure. The sight of these preparations, of all this activity that seemed already part of the holidays, produced such violent emotion in me that tears came to my eyes. I dropped my satchel on a chair and ran to the lavatory, where I locked myself in so that I could cry and laugh as much as I liked.

I emerged from it five minutes later, a little calmer but with a bursting heart. My father was refitting the locks of his gun, and my mother was trying a hand-knitted Balaclava helmet on Paul's head.

'Shall we go even if it rains?' I asked in a strangled voice.

'We have nine days' holiday!' my father said. 'And even if it pours, we're going.'

'What if there's a thunderstorm?' asked Paul.

'There aren't any in winter.'

'Why not?'

'Because.' My father replied categorically. 'But of course, if it rains too hard, we'll wait until the day after.'

'And if it rains just ordinarily?'

'Then we'll make ourselves as thin as we can,' said my father, 'we'll walk fast, with our eyes shut, and dodge between the raindrops!'

★

On Thursday afternoon, my mother took us to Aunt Rose's to find out what she had decided. A great disappointment was in store: she declared that she could not 'go up to the villa' on account of cousin Pierre, who was assuming an altogether unwarranted importance. This insatiable bottle-drainer was beginning to utter formless gurgles, to which Aunt Rose replied with real words to make us believe that he had said something intelligible. It was a painful spectacle.

Moreover, in front of my marvelling mother, she forced open the little beast's jaws and, pointing to a grain of rice on its gum, asserted that it was a tooth, and because of this tooth she feared what the cold, the wind, the rain and the damp might do to him, as well as, last but not least, the absence of Gas.

We tried to coax her, but without success. We had to resign ourselves: there was no Aunt Rose any more.

There were still, however, some traces of the sportsman in Uncle Jules: he declared that every morning he would come on his bicycle to shoot thrushes and go back to town before nightfall. He spoke jovially enough but I could see that he would have preferred to stay with us. I then realized for the first time that grown-ups never do as they like and that they are foolish.

As we were going down the stairs in the semi-darkness, Paul, drawing a conclusion from this disaster, said in a level voice:

'When I have children, I'll give them away!'

259

CHAPTER TWENTY-ONE

O N Friday morning, my father went to take his last 'supervision' at school, where the few remaining pupils were marking time in the court-yard which suddenly looked much bigger. It had been bitterly cold for the last few days: in the kitchen cupboard the bottle of olive-oil looked as if it were filled with cottonwool, which gave me an opportunity of explaining to Paul that at the North Pole 'it looked like that every morning'.

But my mother had forestalled the winter's sudden aggression. She enveloped us in successive layers of knickers, vests, combinations, shirts and smocks and, under the ear-flaps of our 'Balaclava helmets', we looked like seal-hunters.

The beauty of this outfit delighted me; but I was later to discover its inconvenience. There were so many buttons, hooks and eyes and safety-pins that to relieve yourself properly became a major problem, which Paul, for one, never managed to solve.

In place of our little sister, all we could see was a small red nose poking out of a sort of walking eiderdown. My mother, wearing a fur toque, collar and muff (all made of rabbit-skin, of course), looked very much like the lovely Canadian skaters who glided across the post office calendars, and as the cold brought out her colour, she looked prettier than ever.

At eleven, Joseph arrived. He had already donned—for his colleagues' admiration—a brand-new sports jacket. It was simpler than Uncle Jules' for it had fewer pockets, but was handsomer, being a bluish grey, which made the brass buttons, embossed with a dog's head, shine more brightly.

After a token lunch, everyone got his 'parcels' ready.

My mother had foreseen that, once the summer was over, the 'baker - cum - tobacconist - cum - grocer - cum - haberdasher - cum general food shop' in the village would not be able to supply us with anything but bread, flour, mustard, salt and chick-peas: these last were a real vegetable buck-shot which had to be softened by three days' soaking before being cooked in ash-filled water.

For this reason we were taking rather substantial supplies with us.

These riches (which included a de luxe sausage, since it was un-cut and girt with a golden belt) were enclosed in square pieces of cloth, with the four ends tied together. There were three of them, all rather heavy: I had contrived a fourth, crammed with cotton-wool, empty boxes and crumpled balls of paper, to give little Paul something to carry proudly.

But this wasn't all: as the family fortunes had never enabled us to acquire two specimens of any household utensil, none were available at the Bastide Neuve. My father had therefore crammed the indispensable hardware items into a capacious rucksack: saucepans, a sieve, a frying-pan, a chestnut-roaster, a funnel, the cheese-grater, the coffee-pot and the mill, a stew-pan, several tumblers, some spoons and forks. All these were immersed in a torrent of chestnuts, intended to fill the gaps and ensure the silence of the ironmongery.

This load was lashed to my father's back, and off we went to the 'Eastern Station'.

This 'station' was nothing more than the underground terminus of the tram-line, and its very name was a typical piece of bragga-docio. The East, in the context, was neither China nor Asia Minor, nor even Toulon: it was Aubagne where, under very Occidental plane-trees the Oriental rails came to a modest halt.

The station nevertheless impressed me greatly, on account of the tunnel which began there. This tunnel plunged into the night, which was still pitch-black from the ancient smoke of a steam-driven tram which, with its funnel-shaped chimney, had once—like most things—been the very last word in Progress. But

Progress has never uttered its last word and yet another had since been spoken: the 'electric tram'.

We waited for it, corralled between barriers of iron tubing, in the middle of a long queue which new arrivals did not lengthen but simply compressed.

Even today I can see Joseph, with his chin thrust forward, his shoulders pulled back by the Tyrolean straps, leaning like a bishop on a broom with bristles pointing upwards. . . .

*

Heralded by the rattling of its wheels on the bends, the twinkling tram eventually emerged from the darkness and stopped right in front of us.

An employee in a peaked cap opened the turnstile, and the stampede carried us forward.

My mother, swept along between two overpowering housewives, found herself comfortably seated without having done anything about it: we three men remained standing on the platform at the back, because of our voluminous parcels. My father wedged the knapsack against the partition, and right from the beginning of the journey the funnel and the frying-pan, regardless of the muffling chestnuts, indiscreetly clanked together in a sort of angelus.

The tunnel, feebly lit by dim lights placed in recesses, did nothing but twist and turn: so much so that after fifteen minutes of creaking and jolting we emerged from the bowels of the earth at the beginning of the Boulevard Chave, hardly three hundred yards from our point of departure. . . . My father explained to us that this curious construction had been started at opposite ends, but that the two teams of workmen, after meandering underground for a long time, had met only quite by chance.

The open-air ride was pleasant and passed quickly, and I was quite surprised when I saw my father preparing to get off: I had not recognized La Barasse.

In the centre of the city, the only signs of winter were the roaring of the stove, the woollen scarf, the cape, and the lamplighter who passed at teatime, pressing his pear-shaped bulb; but in the outskirts, which now looked like a drawing in pen and ink, I could see the true face of the season.

Under a small winter sun, pale and cropped like a monk's skull, we walked again along our holiday road. It had grown a good deal wider: December, that night-working road-mender, had burnt the stray grass and cleared the foot of the walls. The powdery summer dust, which a single well-aimed kick could send up in lovely clouds of mineral flour, now lay petrified, and the sharp ridges of the hardened ruts broke and crumbled under our feet. Over the top of the walls the emaciated fig-trees stuck out their skeletal branches, and the clematis dangled like loops of black string. No cicadas, no grasshoppers, no lizards. Not a sound, not a movement. Only the olive-trees had kept all their holiday leaves, but I could see they were shivering and were not in a talkative mood.

Yet we did not feel cold, thanks to our outfits and to the weight of our parcels, and we firmly strode along this unfamiliar road. We hungrily devoured our afternoon snack as we walked, and it shortened our journey. But just as I was beginning to distinguish, high up, the big cone of Tête-Rouge, the sun suddenly disappeared. It did not decline in triumphant glory, between layers of purple and scarlet light, but seemed to slither furtively, almost involuntarily behind grey and shapeless sheets of cloud. The light faded, the fleecy sky seemed to sink down and settle like a lid on the hill-tops, which were already forming a big bay around us.

I was thinking of my dear Lili as I walked along. Where was he? We wouldn't be at the villa before nightfall. Perhaps we would find him at the Bastide Neuve, sitting on the stony doorstep, with a haversack full of thrushes beside him. Or perhaps he was on his way to meet us?

I hardly dared to hope so, because it was so late and so cold. In the violet dusk a fine shower of icy rain had begun to fall slowly. Just then I saw, gleaming through the drizzle, the small flame of the first paraffin-lit lamp-post. It stood at the foot of the hill and heralded the village.

In the pool of yellow light which flickered on the wet road I could make out a shadow under a hood. . . .

I ran towards him, he ran towards me. I stopped two steps from him. . . . He stopped too and, like a man, held out his hand. I shook it in a manly way, without saying a word.

He was flushed with pleasure and emotion. My face must have been even redder.

'Have you been waiting for us?'

'No, I'd come to see Durbec,' he said.

He pointed towards the green gate.

'What for?'

'He promised me some winged ants. He's got lots of them in a willow, on the edge of his field.'

'Did he give you any?'

'No. He wasn't at home. . . . so I waited about a bit in case he came back. . . . I suppose he must have gone to Camoins.'

But at that moment the gate opened, and a little mule came trotting out of it. It was drawing a cart with lighted lanterns, and holding the reins was Durbec.

He called out: 'Hello there! Good-day to you all!'

Lili flushed scarlet and abruptly ran towards my mother, to relieve her of her parcels.

I did not ask any more questions. I was happy because I knew he had lied: yes, he had come to wait for me in the grey Christmas dusk, in the cold drizzle whose glistening drops still clung to his long eyelashes. He had come down from Les Bellons, my little brother from the hills. . . . He had been there for hours, he would have stayed on till dead of night in the hope of seeing at last, around the bend of the gleaming road, his friend's pointed hood.

*

Our first day—Christmas Eve—was not a real hunting day. I had to help my mother put the house in order, nail draught-excluders round the windows (through which an icy music whistled) and bring back a big load of dry branches from the neighbouring pine wood. However, despite all these occupations, we found time to set a few snares at the foot of the olive-trees in the frosty *baouco* studded with black olives.

Lili had managed to preserve some winged ants in a small box where they fed on blotting paper: served amid the surrounding olives, they tempted a dozen thrushes which, tumbling straight from branch to spit, completed the Christmas dinner. This took place that very night, for we had our great supper with its traditional 'thirteen kinds of desserts' in front of a crackling fire.

Lili—our guest of honour—observed all my gestures and tried to imitate the gentleman whom he believed me to be.

In a corner of the dining-room there was a small pine-tree, turned into a Christmas-tree for the occasion: from its branches hung a dozen brand-new snares, a hunting-knife, a powder-flask, a clockwork train, binding wire for making snares, lollipops, a pop-gun, and all sorts of treasures. Lili opened his eyes wide and did not say a word: if he had been a moth one could have caught him under a hat.

It was a memorable evening: I had never stayed up for such a long one. I stuffed myself with dates, crystallized fruit and whipped cream; I was so stoutly backed up by Lili that towards midnight I noticed that his breath was coming in jerks and that he kept his mouth open for minutes on end. Three times my mother suggested we should go to bed. Three times we refused, for there were still some raisins left which we munched not because we really enjoyed them but because of the luxury they stood for.

At one in the morning my father declared that 'those children were going to burst', and got up.

But at that very moment I thought I heard in the distance the mouse-like squeak of Uncle Jules' bicycle: yet it was one a.m. and freezing hard! His arrival seemed to me most improbable and I thought I must have been dreaming when my mother pricked up her ears and said in a surprised voice:

'Joseph, it's Jules! Can anything have happened?'

My father listened in turn: the crunching noise was drawing closer.

'It's him,' he said. 'But don't be alarmed: if anything had happened, he wouldn't have come up here!'

He got up and opened the door wide: we could distinguish the outline of an enormous bear undoing the straps of the luggage-rack. Uncle Jules made his entrance wearing a long-haired fur overcoat, topped by a scarf wound four times round his neck. He put a big parcel on the table, saying: 'Merry Christmas!' and began to unwind his scarf.

I promptly opened the parcel: more toys, more snares, a big bag of *marrons glacés*, a bottle of liqueur.

My father frowned: then he inspected the label which was resplendently multi-coloured, and cheered up.

'This is an honest liqueur!' he declared. 'It's wine, but boiled wine; that is to say, it has had the spirits boiled out of it!'

He poured out two thimblefuls for each of us and the feast continued, while my mother carried away the sleeping Paul.

'We are delighted to see you,' my father said, 'but we weren't expecting you. . . . So you've deserted Rose and the baby?'

'My dear Joseph,' Uncle Jules replied, 'I couldn't very well take them to midnight mass which I have never once missed since my childhood. On the other hand, it wouldn't have been sensible to come home at one in the morning: I might have woken them up. So I chose to attend Christmas mass at the church at La Treille and come up here to celebrate our Saviour's birth with you.'

I thought his idea was an excellent one, for I was already tucking into the *marrons glacés*, watched by Lili who had never seen them before.

'It was a very beautiful mass,' my uncle went on. 'There was an enormous crib, the church was carpeted with flowering rose-mary, and the children sang lovely fourteenth-century Provençal carols. A pity you didn't come.'

'If I had gone, I should merely have been a sightseer,' my father replied, 'and I hold that people who go into churches just for the spectacle and the music don't show respect for other people's faith.'

'That's a fine sentiment,' Uncle Jules admitted. 'Anyhow, whether you came or not, you were there all the same tonight.'

And he gleefully rubbed his hands.

'And how was I there?' my father enquired somewhat ironically.

'You were there with your whole family, because I spent a long
time praying for you all!'

My father did not know how to reply to this unexpected
announcement. But my mother gave Uncle Jules a lovely, warm
smile, while he rubbed his hands faster and faster.

'And what favour did you ask of the Almighty?' Joseph asked
at last.

'The finest of all: I implored Him not to deprive you any longer
of His Presence and to give you Faith.'

My uncle spoke with great fervour and his eyes were sparkling
with tenderness.

My father, who was munching three or four chestnuts at once
with obvious pleasure, took some time to finish his mouthful,
gulped it down in one go, and said in a slightly coated voice:

'You know, I don't believe the Creator of the Universe conde-
scends to busy himself with microbes like us, but your prayer is a
fine and kindly token of your friendship for us, and I thank you
for it.'

He then got up to shake his hand. Uncle Jules got up, too: they
looked at each other smilingly, and my uncle said:

'Happy Christmas, dear Joseph!'

He gripped Joseph's shoulder with his big hand and kissed him
on both cheeks.

Children hardly ever know real friendship. They only have
'chums' or accomplices, and they change friends as they change
schools or classes or even school-benches. That night, on that
Christmas Eve, I felt a new emotion: the firelight flickered and I
saw a golden-headed blue bird fly upwards in a wisp of smoke.

★

When at last we had to go to bed, I no longer felt sleepy. It
was too late. I intended to chat with Lili, for whom my mother
had put down a straw mattress in my room. But he had rather

overdone his dose of cooked wine, about the strength of which my father knew little, and fell asleep without even being able to undress.

Lying on my back, my hands clasped behind my head and my eyes wide open in the darkness, I was re-living the scenes of this beautiful Christmas Eve, lit up by Uncle Jules' goodness, when I was suddenly overcome by alarm: there flashed through my mind the story of the soldier Trinquette Edouard, which my father had told us one day at table.

This fellow Trinquette, who was Monsieur Besson's cousin, was in those days doing his military service at Tarascon. Trinquette senior, who was a widower, doted on his only son, and worried very much about him. To his joy, he discovered one day that the colonel of his son's regiment was none other than his closest childhood friend. . . . He promptly grasped his finest pen and wrote him a long letter, reminding him of moving memories from their common past and recommending to his friend's care his beloved son—an exceptional boy and the only consolation of his old age.

The Colonel—a faithful friend—immediately sent for Trinquette Edouard to assure him of his benevolent interest: but the sergeant-major in charge that week came and informed him, standing to attention, that the exceptional boy had been granted a week's compassionate leave to attend his old father's funeral, comfort his disconsolate mother and settle certain difficult questions arising from the will with his four brothers and sisters.

The colonel nearly died of apoplexy and the constabulary was sent out to look for the jester.

As Tarascon is a small town where people are not slow to talk, he was discovered that very night at the Hôtel of the Three Emperors, where he became the Fourth, for he lived in hiding in the room of a red-haired servant-girl who fed him at the expense of the hotel-kitchen. The *gendarmes* arrived when he was less than halfway through a thrush-pie, and the soldier Trinquette Edouard was taken back to barracks, loaded with chains, to be jailed by the Colonel in a rat-infested cell for three weeks.

That's what can happen to people whom you commend to someone, when no favours have been asked for.

Of course, I knew very well that God didn't exist, but I wasn't absolutely sure of it. There were lots of people who went to mass—even quite serious-minded people. Uncle Jules himself talked to God frequently, and yet he wasn't mad.

After much thought, I arrived at the—not very rational—conclusion that God, though he didn't exist for us, certainly existed for others: like the King of England, who exists only for the English.

But in that case, my uncle had been very imprudent to attract his attention to us: this God would probably—if he examined our case, which perhaps he was doing at that very moment—fly into a terrible temper, as the Colonel had done: and instead of sending us Faith, I was afraid he might despatch three or four thunderbolts in our direction, thus bringing the house down over our heads. However, as I could hear Uncle Jules' peaceful and trusting snores through the partition, I set my mind at rest with the reflection that the God he worshipped would surely not play him such a dirty trick, and that I could therefore go to sleep in peace, at least for that night: which I promptly did.

CHAPTER TWENTY-TWO

THE next day's shooting was a flop as far as we were concerned, for the guns left without us. We were woken up at noon and lunched off an '*aïgo boulido*', that is to say some cloves of garlic boiled in water, and spent a somewhat woebegone afternoon at the fireside, while little Paul, who had been preserved by hypersomnia from our excesses, nibbled the last *marrons glacés* and made fun of us, calling us '*galavards*'—guzzlers. But the second night repaired the disaster, and the winter shoot started in earnest.

*

This Christmas week passed as quickly as a dream. But nothing was at all like the long holidays: we might have been in a different country.

At six in the morning it was still dark. I got up, shivering, and went down to light the big log-fire; then I made the coffee which I had ground the night before, so as not to wake my mother. Meantime, my father was shaving. In a little while we would hear the distant creak of Uncle Jules' bicycle, which was as punctual as a suburban train. His nose was as red as a strawberry, tiny icicles hung from his moustache, and he would rub his hands together vigorously, like someone who is very pleased with himself.

We breakfasted in front of the fire and talked very softly.

Then we would hear Lili's running feet echoing on the hardened road.

I'd pour out a big cup of coffee which he would decline at first, saying: 'I've already had some'—which wasn't true. Then all four of us would set out before daybreak.

In a purple velvet sky, innumerable stars were glistening. They were not the gentle stars of summer. Hard, bright and cold they gleamed, congealed by the night frost. . . . Over Tête-Rouge, invisible in the darkness, a big planet was hanging like a lantern, so close that you imagined you could see the empty space behind it. Not a sound, not a murmur, and in the icy silence our steps rang out on the hard winter stones.

The partridges had become wary and the echo, with its new-found sensitiveness, protected them against our approach. The guns nevertheless bagged four hares, a few wood-cock and quite a number of rabbits. As for our snares, they gave us such a regular supply of thrushes and larks that our daily success began to lose the charm of unexpectedness.

We came home from our shoot at nightfall; sprawling, flat on our stomachs, before a big, resinous log-fire, we played draughts, dominoes, snakes-and-ladders, while my father played the flute— and sometimes the whole family joined in a game of lotto.

From half past six onwards, the spit began to turn, and the reddish fat of the melting thrushes would soften up thick slices of home-made bread. . . .

Those were marvellous, full days, which seemed endless to me in the morning, but so short when it was time to leave!

On the last evening, as we were finishing our packing, my mother, seeing me downcast, said:

'Joseph, we must come up here every Saturday.'

'That might be possible once we have the tram service,' my father replied. 'But for the time being. . . .'

'By the time we have trams, the children will have moustaches! Look at them: they've never looked so well, and I've never had such a good appetite.'

'I quite see your point,' my father said thoughtfully, 'but the journey takes four hours! . . . We'd get here at eight on Saturday night, and we'd have to leave again on Sunday afternoon.'

'Why not Monday morning?'

'Because I've got to be at school at eight o'clock sharp, as you very well know.'

'I've got an idea,' my mother said.

'And what might that be?'

'You'll see.'

My father was surprised. After some reflection, he said:

'I know what you have in mind.'

'Oh no,' said my mother, 'you don't! But don't ask me any more questions. It's my secret. And you won't hear any more about it unless I succeed.'

'All right,' my father agreed. 'We'll wait and see.'

CHAPTER TWENTY-THREE

ER idea wasn't a bad one.

She would often meet the headmaster's wife at the market: she was a big, handsome woman, who wore a gold chain round her neck, and a gold watch hanging from her pleated silk belt.

My mother, small and shy, would greet her discreetly from a distance. But as she was capable of doing anything for her children, she began to make her greeting more noticeable, drew nearer and nearer by degrees and eventually brushed the hand of *Madame la Directrice* in a sack of potatoes. The headmaster's wife, a kind-hearted woman, advised against the purchase of those particular tubers which she declared were frostbitten, and led my mother to another stall. Two days later they were doing their shopping together, and the following week *Madame la Directrice* invited her to come and try an English herb concoction which was called tea.

Joseph was completely unaware of this conquest, and his surprise was complete when he read a decision of the headmaster's on the duty roster: the omnipotent Head, swayed by a sudden fancy, had decreed that my father would henceforward take charge of the Thursday morning supervision, while the gym master and the music teacher would, in exchange, take over his pupils on Monday mornings, which left us free till half past one.

As men don't understand a thing about feminine wire-pulling, he would never have known the truth of the matter if Monsieur Arnaud, who always knew everything, being on very friendly terms with the headmaster's maid—had not put him wise to the situation one day during break.

After that he was faced with two problems: first, should he thank his superior? At dinner he declared he would not do it, because it would be tantamount to admitting that the headmaster had upset the whole public school time-table for one teacher's convenience.

'And yet,' he said, perplexed, 'I really ought to do something. . . .'

'Don't worry, I've thought about it,' my mother said, with a smile.

'What have you in mind?'

'I've sent a lovely bunch of roses to the headmaster's wife.'

'Ho! Ho!' my father exclaimed. 'I'm not at all sure this gesture won't seem too . . . familiar . . . or perhaps too pretentious. . . . She looks a pleasant enough woman, certainly, but . . . I wonder how she'll take it. . . .'

'She took it very well. She even told me I was a "darling".'

My father's eyes widened.

'You've spoken to her?'

'But of course!' my mother said, laughing. 'We go shopping together every day, and she calls me Augustine.'

My father took off his spectacles, polished them hard with the edge of the table-cloth, put them back on his nose and stared at her in amazement. That brought him his second problem. My mother had to tell him the whole story in detail, beginning with the sack of potatoes. . . . When she had finished, he silently shook his head several times. Then, in front of the whole family, he declared with scandalized admiration:

'She has a Genius for Intrigue!'

*

That's how we were able to 'go up into the hills' almost every Saturday after Shrove Tuesday.

The February slush splashed and squelched under our feet. Then, in April, long, green-leaved branches appeared above the top of the walls and, here and there, formed arched domes above our heads. It was a delightful walk but, no doubt about it, an awfully long one.

Carrying our normal load and stopping for a short rest in the shade now and then, the journey would take us four hours. When at last we arrived at the 'villa', we were exhausted. My mother particularly, sometimes carrying our little sister asleep in her arms, seemed at the end of her endurance. . . . It was her pallor and the rings under her eyes that made me frequently forgo those lovely Sundays on the *garrigue*. I would complain of a stitch in my side or a dreadful headache and suddenly go to bed. But when my eyes were shut, in the darkness of my little room, the beloved hills would come towards me and I would fall asleep under an olive-tree, engulfed by the fragrance of lost lavender. . . .

One fine Saturday in April, at about five o'clock, our caravan was tramping, tired but cheerful, between the two long walls of honey-coloured stone. Some thirty yards ahead of us, a small gate opened. A man came out and locked the door behind him with a key.

As we drew level with him, he suddenly caught sight of my father and cried:

'Monsieur Joseph!'

He was wearing a dark uniform with brass buttons, and a peaked cap like those worn by railway attendants. He had a small black moustache, and big brown eyes which were sparkling with pleasure.

My father stared back at him and began to laugh.

'Bouzigue!' he exclaimed. 'What are you doing here?'

'I? I'm doing my job, Monsieur Joseph. I'm a canal pricker, and I may say, all thanks to you! You *did* take such trouble to get me my school certificate! I've been a pricker for seven years now.'

'A pricker?' my father said. 'What do you prick?'

'Ha! Ha!' Bouzigue cried triumphantly, 'at last *I'm* going to teach *you* something! A pricker, that means that I watch over the canal. . . .'

'With a prick?' asked Paul.

275

'No!' said Bouzigue, with an inexplicable wink. 'With a big, T-shaped key' (he pointed to the one hanging from his belt) 'and this little black note-book. I open and shut the regulators, check the flow. . . . When I see a crack in the canal-bank, or a lot of mud and silt, or a foot-bridge that's getting rickety, I jot it down and at night I draw up my report. When I see a dead dog floating I fish it out, and when I catch people either throwing their dirty water into the canal or bathing in it, I take their name and address and report them.'

'I say!' my father said. 'You're an official sort of person!'

Bouzigue winked again and gave a smug little smile.

'And what's more,' my father said, 'it can't be a tiring job.'

'Oh no!' Bouzigue admitted. 'It's not exactly forced labour.'

His voice suddenly took on a wailing note, as if he were on the point of tears.

'Anyhow, why should anyone wish to send me to hard labour, I ask you, when I'm such a decent chap? I've never done anything wrong, except when it comes to spelling. . . . And you, Monsieur Joseph, I see your little family has increased in size: Madame Joseph hasn't spread much, but she's as charming as ever.'

Then, placing his hand on my head, he asked:

'But where are you off to, with all this load?'

'Well,' my father said, not without pride, 'we're on the way to our country-house to spend the week-end there.'

'Oho!' Bouzigue cried, delighted. 'Have you come into a fortune?'

'Not exactly,' my father said. 'Though it would be true to say that I'm now in the fourth grade and my emoluments have considerably increased.'

'That's fine!' said Bouzigue. 'Now, that really gives me pleasure. Pass me some of those parcels, I'll come with you!'

He took the sack out of my hands and the three kilogrammes of soap and relieved my brother of his pack which contained sugar and noodles.

'This is very kind of you, Bouzigue,' said my father. . . . 'But you don't realize what a long way we have to go.'

'All the way to Les Accates, I bet?'

'Further.'

'To Camoins, then?'

'Further still.'

Bouzigue opened his eyes as wide as saucers.

'You're not going to tell me you're going all the way to La Treille?'

'We pass through the village,' my father said, 'but we're going even further than that.'

'But there *is* nothing further, beyond La Treille!'

'There is,' my father replied. 'Les Bellons.'

'Well!' said Bouzigue, flabbergasted. 'The canal doesn't go up there and never will. Where d'you get your water from?'

'From a cistern and from the well.'

Bouzigue shoved his cap back the better to scratch his head, and stared at the four of us.

'And where d'you get out of the tram?'

'At La Barasse.'

'You poor things!'

He quickly did some mental arithmetic.

'That means at least eight kilometres on foot!'

'Nine,' said my mother.

'And do you do that often?'

'Almost every Saturday.'

'You poor things!' he repeated.

'Of course, it's a bit on the long side,' my father admitted. 'But once we get there, we don't regret the effort. . . .'

'Personally,' Bouzigue said solemnly, 'I *always* regret an effort. But I have an idea! You won't walk nine kilometres today. You're going to come with me, and we'll follow the bank of the canal which cuts straight through all these estates. In half an hour we'll be at the foot of La Treille!'

He pulled a gleaming key out of his pocket, took us back to the gate he had just locked, and reopened it.

'Follow me,' he said.

He walked through. But my father stopped on the threshold.

277

'Bouzigue, are you certain this is quite lawful?'

'What do you mean?'

'You're given this key because of your official position and you're entitled to walk through other people's property. But do you think we're entitled to go with you?'

'Who'll know?' asked Bouzigue.

'You see!' my father said. 'In hoping that nobody will see us, you're admitting you're at fault.'

'But what harm are we doing?' Bouzigue asked. 'I've met my old school-master and I'm proud to show him the place where I work.'

'You may have to pay for it. . . . If your superiors learnt about it. . . .'

Bouzigue winked two or three times mysteriously. Then he shrugged twice, shook his head with a mocking little laugh, and at last said:

'Seeing as you have to know, I'll tell you something good: if anything should go wrong, I take it upon myself to iron it out, because my sister is married—in a left-handed sort of way—to a councillor general!'*

This seemed to me, at first, a mysterious phrase; but I suddenly visualized this left-handed sister leaving the town-hall on the arm of a general in splendid uniform, who gave her invaluable counsels.

As my father still seemed to hesitate, Bouzigue added:

'And what's more, she was the one who got Bistagne appointed as assistant manager of the canal; and if Bistagne were to rap me over the knuckles, she'd put him to sleep with a bolster.'

I conceived then and there a great admiration for this brave woman who was able to lay low her brother's foes without so much as hurting them. My father must have shared my feelings, for we followed Bouzigue onto other people's property.

* Provincial councillor of a *département*.

278

CHAPTER TWENTY-FOUR

THE canal ran along the top of a low embankment, between two hedgerows of shrubs and bushes which sprang out of a tangle of rosemary, fennel, rock-rose and clematis. Bouzigue explained to us that this unkempt vegetation was infinitely valuable because it held back the soil of the embankment, and the people who owned the estates were not allowed to touch it.

The concrete bed was no more than three yards wide, and the transparent water mirrored the white clouds in the April sky.

Between the bank and the flowering hedgerow we walked in single file along a narrow tow-path.

'That's my canal,' said Bouzigue. 'What do you think of it?'

'It's rather pretty,' my father answered.

'Yes, it is pretty. But it's getting old. . . . Have a look at those embankments. . . . They're full of cracks. . . . We lose a lot of water that way; in some places it's a proper sieve.'

The word 'sieve' greatly struck my brother Paul, who repeated it several times.

As we were approaching a small foot-bridge, Bouzigue said proudly:

'Now this part was shored up again last year. I had it redone with underwater cement.'

My father inspected the embankment, which looked quite new.

'There's a fissure in it, though!' he said.

Bouzigue leaned over it with sudden alarm:

'Where?'

My father pointed to a very thin grey line and started scraping it with his finger-nail. Some gritty particles came loose; he broke them between his fingers and inspected them for a moment.

'This isn't underwater cement,' he said. 'It contains too large a proportion of sand.'

Bouzigue stared, round-eyed.

'What?' he said. 'Are you sure?'

'Absolutely. My father used to be a builder, and I know something about it.'

'Ho! Ho!' Bouzigue exclaimed. 'I'm going to put that into my report and the contractor who's responsible will have hell to pay!'

'If you don't fill in this crack, it'll be four fingers wide in a month's time.'

'It's a sieve!' Paul cried.

'I'll see to it,' said Bouzigue.

He removed a fragment of the cement rendering, wrapped it in a leaf of his notebook, and walked on.

We walked through four vast estates.

In the first of them there were flower-beds surrounding a turreted château, and around the flower-beds spread vineyards and orchards.

'This is a nobleman's castle,' Bouzigue said. 'He must be ill, for one never sees him.'

'If this aristocrat came across us on his property, he might dislike it,' said my father. 'I don't care much for noblemen.'

The lessons learnt at the *Ecole Normale* remained deeply ingrained in him. And yet, in the course of his reading, some aristocrats had found favour in his eyes: Du Guesclin, Bayard, La Tour d'Auvergne, the Chevalier d'Assas and, above all, Henri IV, because he used to canter about on all fours to amuse his grandchildren. But, generally speaking, he continued to view the 'nobles' as a cruel and insolent lot, which was proved by their eventually having had their heads cut off. Misfortunes never inspire confidence, and the horror of great massacres makes even their victims look ugly.

'He's a count,' Bouzigue said, 'and the people around here don't speak ill of him.'

'That may be so,' my father said, 'because they don't know him. But he probably has some hired ruffians at his bidding.'

'He has a tenant-farmer and a keeper. The farmer is a friendly old codger, and the keeper isn't young. A giant of a fellow. I have met him a few times, but he never talks to me. Good morning, good evening—that's all.'

We reached a second gate without incident. The canal passed under a low archway in the enclosing wall. Long creepers hung down from it and trailed in the current. Bouzigue unlocked the gate, and we saw a wilderness ahead of us.

'This is the castle of the Sleeping Beauty,' he announced. 'The shutters are always closed, I've never seen a soul here. You can make all the noise you like, there's no danger.'

A forest of arbutus and terebinth had invaded the abandoned grounds. A copse of century-old pine-trees sprawled around a huge square building; it looked unapproachable, because the needle-gorse was growing in serried ranks below the lofty trees. My brother Paul was bowled over by the thought that the Sleeping Beauty was slumbering behind those closed shutters and that we were the only ones—thanks to Bouzigue—to know about it.

We came upon another wall and another gate: we entered the grounds of a third château.

'This one belongs to a lawyer,' Bouzigue said. 'Look: it's always closed, except in August. There's only a peasant family here. I often come across the grandfather: he's the one who looks after those fine plum-trees. He's stone-deaf but nice enough. . . . He always chats away about the war of 1870 and he wants to get back Alsace-Lorraine.'

'He's a good Frenchman,' my father said.

'That he is,' Bouzigue agreed. 'Pity, though, that he's a bit cracked with age.'

We did not meet anyone, but we saw a long way off, through a hedge, the lower and posterior half of a farmer, busy hoeing his tomatoes.

Then Bouzigue opened yet another gate: this was set in a stone wall that rose at least twelve feet high: its top was decorated with broken glass all the way along, which gave a deplorable impression of the owner's generosity.

'Now this château,' Bouzigue said, 'is the biggest and the most beautiful of the lot. But the owner lives in Paris, and there's never anyone here except the keeper. . . . There, look!'

Through the hedgerow we could see two high towers flanking a façade at least ten stories high. All the windows were closed, except some of the dormer-windows under the slate roof.

'The keeper's apartment is up there,' Bouzigue explained. . . . 'That's so he can keep a look out for marauders who come and pillage the orchard. . . .'

'He may be watching us at this moment,' my father suggested.

'I don't think so. He's mostly watching the orchard, which is over on the other side.'

'Is he a friend of yours, too?'

'Not exactly. He's an ex-sergeant-major.'

'They aren't very easy-going, on the whole.'

'This one is like all the others. But he's always drunk as a lord, and he has a gammy leg. If he ever saw you—which would be most unlikely—you'd only have to move at the double and he'd be quite unable to catch you, even with his dog!'

'Has he a dog?' my mother enquired anxiously.

'Yes,' Bouzigue replied. 'A huge mastiff, but he's at least twenty years old. He's one-eyed and can hardly move: his master has to drag him along on a chain. I assure you there's no danger at all. But to set your mind completely at rest, I'll go and have a look. Stay behind this bush!'

There was a long gap in the protective hedgerow. Bouzigue stepped through it deliberately and halted in the middle of the danger area. His hands in his pockets, and his cap pushed to the back of his head, he gazed at the château for a while, then towards the orchard.

We were waiting, huddled together like sheep, in the shelter of the arbutus. My mother was pale and breathing hard. My brother Paul had stopped crunching lumps of sugar, stealthily filched from his parcel. My father was peering through the branches, his neck craning forward.

At last Bouzigue said:

'All clear. You can come out. But keep your heads down,' he added.

My father was the first to step forward, bent double, and with his packages brushing the ground.

My brother bent himself at a right angle, like a village ancient, and literally disappeared in the long grass. When my turn came, I slipped out, hugging the noodles to my horizontal heart. At last my mother, who was unaccustomed to gymnastic exercises, advanced clumsily, with lowered head and hunched shoulders, like a sleep-walker on the edge of a roof. Despite her petticoats and her whale-bone corset, she looked so thin. . . .

Twice more we had to repeat this manoeuvre. At last we reached the boundary wall. Bouzigue opened the small door, and we suddenly found ourselves looking at the café of the Four Seasons.

What a happy and wonderful surprise!

'It isn't possible!' my mother exclaimed, delighted.

'And yet it is so!' Bouzigue declared. 'We have cut right across the loop of the road!'

CHAPTER TWENTY-FIVE

M Y father pulled his silver watch out of his waistcoat
pocket.
'We have taken just twenty-four minutes to cover a
distance which usually takes us two and three-quarter hours!'

'I told you so!' cried Bouzigue. 'This key is faster than an auto-
mobile!'

I thought he was exaggerating a little, for I had just seen in a
newspaper the following fabulous caption under a photograph of
the Panhard: 'The car that covered a *kilometre* in *one minute.*'

'I told you so,' Bouzigue repeated. 'It's as easy as that! And
now,' he added, 'let's have a drink!'

He boldly advanced towards the small outdoor café where the
plane-trees were displaying their first leaves.

The café owner, a big, burly man with a thick red moustache,
made us sit round an iron table and brought a bottle of white
wine. What would my father do? Decline Bouzigue's generous
invitation, or drink the white wine before our amazed eyes?

'Have you some Vichy water, Monsieur?' he asked the inn-
keeper.

The man stared at him in perplexity for a moment, and said
at last:

'If you're really set on it, I have some in my cellar.'

'Oho!' cried Bouzigue, much upset, 'have you a bad liver?'

'No,' my father replied. 'But I prefer to mix white wine with
mineral water. It turns it into a kind of champagne that tastes very
pleasant.'

I marvelled at this stroke of genius, which enabled him to

reduce the dose of poison by adding to it health-giving water that could be bought at the chemist's. But Bouzigue, for his part, drank without any sign of alarm two big glasses of undiluted white wine, one after the other.

My mother, meanwhile, was still ecstatic about the shortness of our trip.

'Well, Madame Joseph,' Bouzigue said with a big smile, 'please allow me to give you a present.'

With a sly wink he extracted the silver key from his pocket.

'Take it, Madame Joseph. I'm giving it to you.'

'What for?' my father asked.

'So as to save you two hours every Saturday, and another two hours on Monday morning! Take it. I have another one.'

He showed us a second key.

But my father slowly shook his head, three times over.

'No,' he said. 'No, that's impossible.'

Why?' Bouzigue asked.

'Because I'm a civil servant too. I can just imagine the face *Monsieur l'Inspecteur de l'Académie* would make if someone came and told him that one of his school-teachers was trespassing on other people's property by means of a forged key!'

'But it isn't forged! It's a Government key!'

'All the more reason!' my father declared. 'You have no right to part with it.'

Bouzigue was beginning to lose patience.

'But nobody will ever say anything about it! You saw the way things went!'

'Nobody said anything because we didn't meet anybody. But you yourself said, as we walked through the grounds of the Sleeping Beauty: "There's no danger here!" Which means that elsewhere there *was*!'

'But, my saintly friend,' Bouzigue cried, 'when I said "danger", I didn't mean "catastrophe"! All I meant was that, by some un-lucky miracle, some old fuss-pot might perhaps go and complain to the Canal but it would go no further, because my sister's there! Don't forget my sister!'

I entirely shared his view. But my father said sternly:

'I do not doubt your sister's capacity or influence, although I'm distressed to learn that she is following a very sad profession. But I have principles.'

'Oya-ya-ee!' Bouzigue said. 'Principles! Oya-ya-ee!'

Then, in the tone of voice a grown-up adopts with a child:

'Now come, Monsieur Joseph! What principles?'

'I'd be ashamed to enter someone else's home surreptitiously, for strictly private purposes and in my own interest. It seems to me that it wouldn't be worthy of a schoolmaster who teaches children morals. . . . And what would this child' (he placed his hand on my shoulder), 'what would he think if he saw his father sneak through the undergrowth like a thief?'

'I'd think that it was quicker,' I said.

'And you are right,' Bouzigue agreed.

'Listen, papa,' my mother broke in, 'I know many a man who wouldn't hesitate. Two hours on Saturday evening and two on Monday morning, that makes four hours saved.'

'I prefer to walk for an extra four hours and keep my self-respect.'

'It's cruel, though,' Bouzigue said, distressed, 'to make those children march as if they were already in the Foreign Legion. With those heavy packs, too, and legs no thicker than spaghetti. . . . And Madame Joseph hasn't much fat on her either.'

'Walking is the healthiest sport of all,' my father declared.

'But also the most tiring one, perhaps,' my mother remarked, with a sigh.

'Listen,' said Bouzigue suddenly, 'I have another idea which will settle everything: I'll give you an official Canal cap. You walk ahead of the others, and if anyone sees you from a distance, you just raise your hand in greeting and nobody'll ask any questions!'

'There's no doubt,' my father said, scandalized, 'that you have the mentality of an old lag! A Canal cap on a schoolmaster's head! Don't you realize that we might end in the dock?'

'And what about my sister? You keep forgetting *her*!'

'You'd be well advised not to talk so much about her. I thank

286

you for your kind offer, it shows your gratitude and your friendship. But I'm obliged to refuse it: so please don't insist!'

'Too bad,' said Bouzique. 'It's a pity. ...'

He poured himself a generous measure of white wine and continued in a deeply regretful tone:

'It's a great pity for the kids and for Madame Joseph. ... And it's a great pity for me, because I thought I was doing you a service. But above all—*above all!*—it's a great pity for the Canal!'

'For the Canal? What do you mean?'

'Why!' Bouzigue cried. 'Do you mean you don't realize the importance of what you told me about the underwater cement?'

'That's true!' said my mother, suddenly adopting a very technical air. 'You don't realize, Joseph!'

'What you don't know,' Bouzigue resumed with warmth, 'is that that contractor who put in too much sand will be obliged to refund us at least two thousand francs, perhaps even two thousand five hundred! Because *I'm* going to send up a report and that crook will be caught. Thanks to whom? To you!'

'I just gave my opinion,' my father said. 'But I'm not absolutely sure. ...'

'But of course! Of course, you're sure! Besides, it'll be checked at the laboratory. And yet you only saw it once and you didn't examine it closely, because you were a little uneasy. But if you were to pass by twice a week. ... *Oh la la!*'

He repeated his '*Oh la la!*' with dreamy enthusiasm.

'In short,' my father said pensively, 'you think that my collaboration—*sub rosa* and free of charge—would, in some measure, pay for our passage?'

'Ten times, a hundred times, a thousand times it would!' Bouzigue declared. 'And if every Monday,' he added, 'you'd send me a little note, a short report, I'd copy it right away—adding a few spelling mistakes, of course—and submit it to my bosses! You realize the sort of build-up you'd give me? Between you and my sister, I'll be head of a department in a year!'

'Joseph,' said my mother, 'you should think it over before refusing.'

287

'That's what I'm doing.'

He drank a long draught of his white wine and Vichy water.

'It's a sieve!' Paul said.

'If we could get to the villa before seven at night,' my mother remarked, 'it would be absolutely wonderful. . . . And besides,' she added, turning to Bouzigue, 'what a saving on the children's shoe-leather!'

'Ah! shoes!' Bouzigue said. 'I have two boys myself, and I know what shoes cost. . . . '

There was a rather long silence.

'Of course,' my father said at last, 'if I can render the community some service—even if it's somewhat irregular . . . and if I can help you at the same time . . . '

'Help me!' Bouzigue cried. 'Why, it could change my entire career!'

'I'm not sure about it, but still I'll think it over.'

He picked up the key and gazed at it for a moment. At last he said:

'I don't know yet whether I'll make use of it. . . . We'll see about that next week. . . .'

But he put the key in his pocket.

CHAPTER TWENTY-SIX

ON Monday morning, when we went back to town, my
father refused to make use of the magic key, though he
looked at it for a moment, lying gleaming in the palm
of his hand. Then he put it back into his pocket, and said:

'For one thing, it's easier to go downhill than up, and for
another, we have no supplies to carry: it isn't worth running a
risk this morning.'

And so we made our way back by the ordinary road. But that
very evening, when school was over, he disappeared for half an
hour; when he came back, he was carrying three or four books
under his arm. I can't recall the exact number, for they were no
more than bundles of printed sheets, whose frayed, yellow edges
reminded me of the embroidery on my grandmother's drawers.

'We must brief ourselves on the subject,' he declared.

And, in fact, these books were odd volumes of works on
'Canals and Aqueducts', 'The Irrigation of Waste Lands' and
'Waterproof Revetments', as they were conceived in the days of
Monsieur de Vauban.*

'It's in old books that most common sense can be found,' he
told me, 'and also the tricks of the trade that have best stood the
test of time.'

He spread out those venerable relics and promptly set to work.

On the following Saturday, at five o'clock, we were facing the
first gate. My father opened it with a firm hand: he was at peace

* French marshal under Louis XIV and one of France's greatest military
engineers.

with his conscience, for he was crossing this forbidden threshold not to cut short an over-long road but to preserve the precious canal from rack and ruin, and to save Marseilles from drought, which would most certainly have been followed by cholera and the plague.

Even so, he feared the keepers. That's why, after relieving me of my parcels, he appointed me as a scout.

I walked ahead, hugging the hedgerow and keeping as much as I could in the shelter of the leafy bushes.

I covered some twenty yards, my eyes watchful and my ears pricked up. Then I stopped and listened to the silence. . . . After a moment, I motioned to my mother and brother, who were waiting in the shadow of the biggest bush. They came running and huddled behind me. At last my father appeared, notebook in hand. We always had to wait a little while for him, because he took notes with the greatest seriousness.

We didn't meet a soul, and the only incident in this uneasy journey was provided by my brother Paul.

My mother noticed that he was holding his right hand inside his mackintosh, like Napoleon.

'Have you hurt your hand?' she asked in an undertone.

He shook his head, without opening his mouth or looking at her.

'Take your hand out of there,' she said again.

He did as he was told, and we saw that his small fingers were clutched round the handle of a sharp knife which he had lifted from the kitchen-drawer.

'That's for the keeper,' he announced coolly. 'If he comes and strangles Papa, I shall come up from behind and stab him in the bottom.'

My mother complimented him on his bravery and added:

'You're still so little, you'd better give it to me.'

He handed over his weapon without demur, and added a judicious piece of advice:

'You're taller than me: stab him in the eye!'

This keeper who looked after the last château on our route

filled us with terror, and we covered his territory trembling. Fortunately he did not appear and, two hours later, when we were sitting round the table, Bouzigue's name was blessed a hundred times.

At dinner there was no mention of the keeper or the dog; but when we were in bed in our little room I had a long talk with Paul. We debated various ways of getting rid of the enemy: the lasso; a ditch studded with six well-sharpened knives, their tips pointing upwards; or steel-wire traps; or perhaps a cigar stuffed with gunpowder. Paul, who was beginning to read adventure stories, had the cruel idea of poisoning the tips of arrows by dipping them—through a crack—in the graves in the village churchyard. As I questioned the efficiency of this method, he invoked the Indian tribes of Brazil who keep the corpses of their grandfathers for months on end, in order to poison the tips of their weapons with the rank humours of their forebears.

I fell asleep while listening to him and, in a radiant dream, saw the keeper, disfigured by an exploded cigar, bristling with arrows like a porcupine, writhing horribly under the effect of poison, and finally falling into a deep ditch where he was impaled on six knives, while Paul, dancing like a madman, was chanting ferociously: 'It's a sieve!'

CHAPTER TWENTY-SEVEN

WE were now able to go 'up into the hills' every
Saturday without too much fatigue, and our life was
transformed.

My mother's cheeks became rosy again; Paul suddenly shot up
like a Jack-in-the-box, while I got deeper-chested, even if my
ribs still stuck out of my broadened thorax. I often measured my
biceps with a tape-measure, and my impressively bulging muscles
filled Paul with admiration.

As for my father, he would sing every morning as he shaved
himself with what looked like a sabre in front of the small broken
mirror which he fastened to the window-catch.

He would start in a falsetto tenor:

> 'Si j'étais un petit serpent,
> O félicité sans pareille . . . '*

Or, falling suddenly into a tremendous bass:

> 'Souviens-toi du passé, quand sous l'aile des anges,
> Abritant ton bonheur,
> Tu venais dans son temple en chantant ses louanges,
> Adorer le Seigneur . . . '†

He would hum on the staircase and, sometimes, even in the
street.

But this happy mood, which lasted throughout the week,

* Aria from 'Le Grand Mogol', an operetta by Audran.
† Aria from the Church scene in Gounod's 'Faust'.

collapsed before dawn on Saturday: for no sooner did he wake than he had to summon all his courage to step into unlawfulness.

*

Two events of major importance marked this period.

On a lovely Saturday in May, when the days are growing longer and the almond-trees seem to be laden with snow, we were—quite noiselessly—walking through the grounds of the 'nobleman'. As we were nearing the heart of the estate, our fears became thinner because the protective hedge was getting thicker and thicker. I was leading the way, light-footed despite the weight of the chloride water, washing-soda and a chair reduced to its component parts, all tied together with string.

The peaceful water of the canal was shimmering and flecked with sunshine. Paul, at my heels, was humming to himself. . . .

But suddenly I stopped transfixed, my heart pounding.

Twenty yards ahead of me a tall figure had stepped out of the hedge and, with a single stride, stood motionless in the middle of the path.

He watched us approach. He was very tall and had a white beard. He wore a musketeer's felt hat, a long, grey velvet jacket, and he was leaning on a cane.

I heard my father saying in a toneless voice: 'Don't be afraid! Go on!' I bravely walked on.

As I drew closer to the danger point, I could see the stranger's face.

A wide pink scar emerged from under his hat and ran down to his beard, touching in passing the corner of his right eye, which had a closed, flat eyelid.

This mask made such an impression on me that I stood stock-still. My father went ahead of me.

He was holding his hat in one hand, his 'expert's notebook' in the other.

'Good-day, sir,' he said.

'Good-day,' the stranger answered, in a deep, coppery voice. 'I've been expecting you.'

At this my mother uttered a sort of stifled cry. I followed her glance, and my consternation grew when I discerned a gold-buttoned keeper who had concealed himself behind the hedge.

He was even taller than his master, and his huge face was adorned with two pairs of reddish moustaches: one below his nose, the other above his eyes, which were blue and looked out between ginger lashes.

He was standing three paces away from Old Scarface and was watching us with a cruel-looking grin.

'I presume, sir,' said my father, 'that I have the honour of addressing the owner of this château?'

'Indeed you have,' the stranger said. 'And for several weeks I've watched your little stratagem every Saturday, in spite of all the precautions you take to hide yourselves.'

'The fact is . . .' my father began, 'one of my friends, the canal pricker . . .'

'I know,' the 'nobleman' said. 'If I didn't come and stop you before, it's because I've been tied to my chaise-longue by an attack of gout for three months. But I gave orders to have the dogs chained on Saturday afternoons and Monday mornings.'

I did not grasp this at once. My father gulped, my mother took a step forward.

'I sent for the canal pricker this morning. I believe he's called Boutique. . . .'

'Bouzigue,' my father said. 'He's a former pupil of mine. I'm a public school teacher, you see, and——'

'I know,' the old man interrupted him. 'This fellow Boutique told me everything. The cottage in the hills, the tram line that's too short, the road that's too long, the children, the luggage. . . . Incidentally,' he remarked, taking a step towards my mother, 'this little lady seems to be over-burdened.'

He bowed to her, as if he were asking for the honour of a dance, and added:

'Will you allow me?'

Whereupon, with lordly authority, he took from her hands two large bundles tied up in handkerchiefs. Then, turning towards his keeper, he said:

'Wladimir, take the children's parcels.'

In the twinkling of an eye, the giant had gathered in his enormous hands the bags, haversacks and the faggot that represented a chair. Then he turned his back to us and suddenly knelt down. 'Climb up!' he told Paul.

Paul, with intrepid boldness, took a running jump, leaped, and found himself perched on the neck of the soft-hearted scarecrow who promptly cantered off, neighing prodigiously.

My mother's eyes filled with tears, and my father couldn't get a word out of his mouth.

'Let's go,' the nobleman said, 'or you'll be late.'

'Sir,' my father finally brought out, 'I don't know how to thank you; I'm touched, really very touched. . . .'

'I can see you are,' the old man said brusquely, 'and I'm charmed by the natural nicety of your feelings. . . . Still, I'm not offering you much, after all. You're walking through my property quite modestly and without doing any mischief, and I raise no objection: there's nothing so marvellous about that, is there? What do you call this pretty little girl?'

He walked up to my little sister, whom my mother was holding in her arms: but she began to scream and hid her face in her hands.

'Come now,' my mother said, 'give the gentleman a little smile. . . .'

'No! No!' she cried. . . . 'He's too ugly! I don't want to!'

'She's right!' the old man said, laughing—and that made him look even uglier. 'I tend to forget this scar: it was the last stroke of a Uhlan's lance, in a hop-field in Alsace some thirty-five years ago. But she is still too young to appreciate military virtues. Walk ahead, madam, please, and tell her that I was scratched by a cat: it'll at least be a lesson in prudence for her!'

He accompanied us all the way, chatting with my father.

I was walking in front of them and could see little Paul's fair head in the distance: it was bobbing along above the hedgerow, and his golden curls were streaming in the sunshine.

When we reached the gate at the other end, we found him

sitting on our parcels; he was munching grey-green apples which the giant was peeling for him.

We had to take leave of our benefactors. The count shook my father's hand and gave him his card, saying:

'Whenever I'm away, this will serve as a pass with the caretaker. There'll be no further need to follow the embankment: please ring at the front-gate of the park and take the centre drive through the estate. It's shorter than the canal.'

Then, to my great surprise, he stopped two paces from my mother and bowed to her as if she were a queen. Finally he walked up to her and bending over with much grace and dignity, he kissed her hand.

She dropped a girlish curtsy in acknowledgement and then ran, blushing, to shelter behind my father, when a flash of gold streaked between them: it was Paul dashing towards the old gentleman and, seizing the big brown hand, he kissed it passionately.

That evening at dinner, after the soup had been served by the light of the hurricane lamp, my mother said:

'Joseph, show us the visiting card he gave you.'

He handed the card to her and she read aloud:

> Count Jean de X. . . .
> Colonel, of the First Cuirassiers

She was silent for a moment, as if troubled.

'But then . . .' she said.

'Yes,' my father answered her unspoken question, 'it's the regiment of Reichshoffen fame.'*

* Battle of the Franco-Prussian War, in which the French, though defeated, covered themselves with glory.

CHAPTER TWENTY-EIGHT

FROM that memorable day onwards, the journey through the grounds of the first château was our Saturday treat.

The caretaker—another old soldier—opened the gate wide for us; Wladimir would promptly appear and shoulder our loads. We would then go into the château to greet the colonel. He would give us liquorice drops and several times invited us to have tea. My father one day brought him a book (in tatters, of course) which he had found at the junk-dealer's: its pages contained a complete account, with maps and illustrations, of the battle of Reichshoffen. The colonel's name occupied an honourable place in it, and my father, who had thought of himself as an anti-militarist, had carefully sharpened three pencils to frame in red, white, and blue the pages in which the author celebrated the valour of the 'First Cuirassiers'.

The old soldier was all the more interested as he didn't approve of the historian's account by a long shot—'a civilian whose bottom never touched a saddle'—and he immediately began to draft a memoir to re-establish the truth.

Every Saturday, as he accompanied us through his gardens, he would pick in passing a bouquet of big red roses of a strain he had bred himself and which he had named 'the King's Roses'. He would clip the thorns with a small pair of silver scissors and, when leaving us, would present the flowers to my mother who could never prevent herself from blushing. She would not entrust them to anybody and took them back to town on Monday morning. During the whole week, they would glow on a side-table, leaning over the rim of a white pottery vase in a corner of the dining-room, and our republican house seemed practically ennobled by the King's Roses.

The castle of the 'Sleeping Beauty' had never frightened us. My father would say laughingly that he would not mind at all settling in it for the holidays. My mother, however, feared that it might be haunted.

Paul and I had tried several times to open a ground-floor shutter, in order to see the motionless lords around the Sleeping Beauty. But the oak planks were much too thick for my tin-bladed penknife.

However, by glueing one eye to a crack, Paul one day quite distinctly saw an enormous cook surrounded by eight scullions: they were all standing petrified in front of a boar on a spit. When it was my turn to peep in, I could not distinguish anything. But the picture he had described tallied so exactly with an illustration by Valvérane—a well-informed artist—that I thought I could suddenly sniff an ancient smell of roasting meat, and the strange scent of cold smoke perturbed me by its eeriness.

The third château, that of the lawyer, had another shock in store for us, and another surprise.

One day, as we were passing unhurriedly through a gap in the hedge, we were terror-stricken to hear a powerful and irate voice shouting:

'Hi, you there! Where are you going?'

We saw a farmer in his forties, running straight towards us, brandishing a pitch-fork. He had a thick, frizzy shock of hair, and a big black moustache which bristled like a cat's.

My father, rather frightened, pretended not to have seen him and began busily jotting something down in his protective note-book. But the man was in a murderous rage and came up at a gallop: my mother's hand trembled in mine, and Paul plunged, terror-stricken, into a bush.

The would-be murderer suddenly stopped four paces away

from us. Raising his pitch-fork, its prongs to the sky, as high as he could, he brought it down and jammed the handle into the ground. Then, with his arms widely flailing the air, he advanced on my father, jerkily shaking his head. Meanwhile, from his foaming mouth fell the following dulcet words:

'Don't worry. My bosses are watching us. They're at the first-floor window. I hope the old bastard will croak soon, but he's got another six months to go.'

Then, with both hands on his hips and his chest thrust forward, he began to talk right under my father's nose, as the latter recoiled, step by step.

'As long as you see those windows open, don't walk on top of the embankment. Go down below, on the other side of it, by the tomatoes. Give me your note-book, because he wants me to ask you for your papers and take down your name and address.'

He tore the note-book out of my father's hand. My father, a little alarmed, was saying: 'My name is. . . .'

'Your name's Esménard, Victor, eighty-two, Rue de la République. Now, make off and run for it, so it'll look good.'

With outstretched arm and pointing forefinger he showed us, with a fierce air, the road to freedom. While we scampered off at a quick trot, he cupped his mouth in his hands and yelled:

'And don't let me catch you at it again, because next time there'll be some shooting!'

As soon as we were in safety, on the other side of the wall, we stopped for a breather to congratulate ourselves and to have a good laugh. My father, who had removed his spectacles to wipe the perspiration from his brow, began to moralize:

'That's the people for you: their faults are the result of ignorance; but deep down they're good, as good as bread, and they're as big-hearted as children.'

Paul and I were dancing in the sunlight and singing with satanic glee:

'He'll croak! He'll croak!'

After that day the man with the pitch-fork, whose name was Dominique, gave us a great welcome whenever we passed that way.

We would always walk below the embankment, along the edge of the field, and we would find Dominique at work.

He would be digging around the vines, or hoeing potatoes, or tying up the tomato plants.

My father would say, with a conspiratorial wink: 'Here comes the Esménard family, and they wish you good-day.'

Dominique would wink back and have a good loud laugh at the weekly joke. Then he'd cry:

'Good-day to you, Esménard Victor!'

And my father would laugh back, and the whole family would shout with glee.

My mother would then give him a packet of pipe tobacco, a lethal gift which he accepted without fuss. Then Paul would ask:

'Has he croaked?'

'Not yet,' Dominique replied. 'But it's bound to come. He's in Vichy: he no longer drinks anything but mineral water!'

He added:

'Over there, underneath the fig-tree, there's a little basket of plums for you. . . . Mind you bring back the basket. . . .'

At other times, there were tomatoes or onions, and we would walk on, in Indian file, stepping on our shadows which the setting sun lengthened on the grass.

But there still remained the château kept by the drunkard and his ailing mastiff.

Whenever we reached that closed gate, we would stop talking.

Then my father would put his eye to the keyhole for a long time. Only after that would he pull out of his pocket the oil-can from our sewing-machine and inject a few drops of oil into the keyhole. Finally, he would insert the key quite noiselessly and slowly turn it round.

Then he would push the door open with a cautious hand, as if he were afraid of a possible explosion. When it was ajar, he would stick his head through the opening, listen, and sweep the forbidden territory with an exploratory glance. At last he would step through.

We would follow him in silence and he noiselessly closed the gate behind us. The hardest part was still to come.

In fact, we had never met a soul, but that sick dog haunted our minds.

I was thinking: 'He must be rabid, because there aren't any other dog-illnesses.' Paul would say: '*I'm* not afraid. Look!'

He showed me a handful of lump-sugar which he planned to fling at the monster in order to keep it busy while Papa strangled the keeper. He talked about it very confidently, but he walked on tiptoe. My mother stopped now and then, looking quite pale and pinched about the nostrils, with her hand over her heart. My father, who assumed a jaunty air to keep our courage up, would reason with her in an undertone:

'Augustine, you're being ridiculous! You're scared to death although you don't even know this man.'

'I know his reputation!'

'One doesn't always enjoy the reputation one deserves!'

'The colonel told us only the other day that he was a besotted old brute.'

'Besotted he certainly must be, as the poor wretch has given himself up to drink. But it's rare for an old toper to turn nasty. Besides, if you want my opinion, I'm sure he's already seen us many times and never said a word, because he doesn't care a hang. His employers are never there and we don't do any harm. Why should he bother to run after us, with his stiff leg and his sick dog?'

'I'm frightened,' my mother said. 'It may be silly, but I'm frightened.'

'All right!' my father said. 'If you persist in this childishness, I'll go right up to the château and simply ask for his permission.'

'No, don't, Joseph! I beg of you. . . . I'll get over it. . . .It's just nerves. I'll be better in a minute. . . .'

I would look at her, cowering white-faced against the wild rose-bushes, oblivious of their thorns. Then she would take a deep breath and say with a smile:

'There, I'm better. Let's go!'

We'd start off again and everything would go perfectly well.

CHAPTER TWENTY-NINE

JUNE that year was a month without Sundays: it seemed to me to be shut in by two high walls, and this long prison corridor was blocked at the far end by a thick iron door, the door of the Scholarships.

It was the month of 'general review'. I threw myself into the work with passion, not for love of knowledge, but supported by my vanity in being the champion who would defend the honour of the Chemin des Chartreux School.

My vanity very soon turned into histrionics. During the breaks I would stroll up and down, all by myself, along the wall of the courtyard. With a grave air, unseeing eyes and murmuring lips, I would 'review' under the gaze of my schoolfellows who did not dare to approach the Thinker—and whenever some foolhardy youngster was bold enough to speak to me, I would pretend to be dragged down from the lofty realm of Knowledge and lower my pained eyes to the importunate fellow, who was promptly rebuked by the champion's 'supporters'.

This comedy, which I played with an actor's sincerity, was not without its usefulness; by play-acting the hero, a ham may sometimes turn into a genuine one. The progress I made astounded my teachers, and when Examination Day came—with turn-down collar, carefully knotted tie, pale cheeks and flattened hair—I held my own quite creditably.

The Head—who had informers on the jury—was able to tell us that my essay had 'attracted much attention', that my dictation had been 'perfect', and my handwriting had received favourable comments.

Unfortunately, I had been unable to solve the second problem, which concerned alloys.

The terms of that problem had been worded with such subtlety that none of the two hundred examinees had understood them, except a certain Oliva, who thus passed First: I only passed Second.

Nobody scolded me, but it was a disappointment. And this found expression in a general uproar when the headmaster, standing in the yard surrounded by his teachers, read the fateful problem aloud. He declared—yes, right in front of me—that at first sight he couldn't make head or tail of it *himself*!

Monsieur Besson asserted that it was a problem for the Higher Certificate; Monsieur Suzanne was of the opinion that the person who had set the riddle had obviously never talked to children; and Monsieur Arnaud, who was young and vigorous, declared that it clearly showed the twisted craftiness and artful wiles of 'those secondaries'. He concluded that no one of sound mind could make any sense of it and he eventually congratulated me on not having understood the problem.

The general indignation subsided, however, when it was learnt that the boy called Oliva was not a traitor, since he too came from a primary school, the one in the Rue de Lodi, which was our sister school; the thought that the two Firsts came from 'our side' transformed my failure into a success.

I for my part was deeply disappointed, and basely tried to tarnish the triumph of the redoubtable Oliva by saying that a boy who was so much at home with alloys could only be the son of a counterfeiter.

This vengeful and romantic theory was accepted by Paul with brotherly delight and I planned to spread it throughout the school; and I would certainly have done so, if I hadn't forgotten all about it, for I suddenly became aware, as dazzled as if I had come out of a tunnel, that we were on the threshold of the long holidays!

Thereupon Oliva, the problem, the headmaster, those secondaries, all vanished without a trace: I began to laugh and daydream again, while—trembling with joy and impatience—I made ready for the GREAT DEPARTURE.

There lay, however, a faint shadow over the prospect: Uncle Jules and Aunt Rose would not be coming with us. That would leave a big empty space in the house, and I feared that our shooting party might come to grief in the absence of the moving spirit. This absence had very little justification, anyhow: a trip to the Roussillon country for the sole purpose of showing cousin Pierre to the wine-growing relations there who, allegedly, could not wait to see him.

'The child of old parents' had become a very fat baby, who laughed at everything, even bruises, and was beginning to talk intelligibly. As he had not yet decided how to pronounce his 'r's', I remarked to Aunt Rose that it was rather dangerous to take him to stay with foreigners who would foist upon him, without warning, the appalling accent of Perpignan.

She reassured me by a definite promise to come and join us before September 1st in our beloved Bastide Neuve.

CHAPTER THIRTY

AT last July 30th came, the solemn eve of the great event.
I made great efforts to go to sleep, but found it quite
impossible to sink into the slumber that so effectively
kills useless hours: I turned them to account, however, by living
in advance some episodes in the magnificent epic that would
start on the morrow. I felt sure it would be even more beautiful
than last year, because I was older and stronger and because I knew
the secrets of the hills; and a great tenderness filled me at the
thought that my dear Lili would not be sleeping either.

The next morning was devoted to putting the house in order,
since we would be leaving it for two months, and I was sent to
the chemist's to buy those mothballs that one always finds in one's
pockets on the first chilly day.

Then we put the finishing touches to our luggage which my
mother had been getting ready for several days, for it was almost
the same as removing. . . . She had declared several times that
it would be essential to have recourse to François' mule. But
my father, after not saying anything at first, eventually disclosed
the truth: our finances had suffered severely as a result of the
numerous purchases made to ensure our holiday comfort, and a
fresh expenditure of four francs might dangerously upset their
balance.

'Besides,' he said, 'there are four of us, since Paul is now strong
enough to carry at least three kilogrammes. . . .'

'Four!' shouted Paul, scarlet with pride.

'And I can carry at least ten!' I hastily put in.

'But, Joseph, look!' my mother groaned. 'Look at all those

parcels, bundles, suit-cases! Have you really looked at them? Can you see them?'

Whereupon my father, with half-closed eyes, and his arms reaching out as if towards an apparition, began to sing in a soulful voice:

> '*En fermant les yeux je vois là-bas*
> *Une maisonnette toute blanche*
> *Au fond des bois. . . .*'*

*

After a quick luncheon, the size and weight of our burdens were so skilfully spread that we managed to get away without leaving anything behind.

I was carrying two haversacks: one contained huge cakes of soap, the other cans of food and all sorts of sausages and cold meats.

I had a carefully tied bundle under each arm: they contained blankets, sheets, pillow-cases, towels. In the middle of this protective household linen my mother had slipped breakable objects: under my left arm, two lamp chimneys and a little plaster-cast dancer, stark naked and with her leg in the air. Under my right arm, an enormous Venetian glass salt-cellar (1.50 frs. at our friend the junk-dealer's) and an outsize alarm-clock (2.50 frs.) which was to sound a powerful Angelus for the sportsmen. As we had forgotten to stop it, I could hear its tinny tick-tock through the blankets.

And last of all, my pockets were stuffed with boxes of matches and paper bags containing pepper, nutmeg, cloves, thread, needles, buttons, shoe-laces and two ink-pots sealed with wax.

On to Paul's back was strapped an old satchel, full of packets of sugar and surmounted by a pillow rolled up in a scarf: from the back, his head was no longer visible.

In his left hand was a net shopping-bag which weighed little but could hold a lot: in this were the supplies of lime-blossom, verbena, camomile and St. John's wort. His right hand was left

* Aria from 'Manon' by Massenet.

free with a view to towing our baby sister, who was hugging a doll to her breast.

My mother intended to carry the two imitation leather cases herself. They contained our silverware (which was of tin-plate) and plates. All this was very heavy, and I decided to intervene. I slipped half the forks into my pockets, put the spoons into Paul's satchel, and six plates into my haversacks. She never noticed.

The rucksack, fantastically swollen and with all its pockets bulging, no doubt weighed more than I did.

We first hoisted it onto the table. Then my father took a step forward and turned his back to the table. His hips were already greatly enlarged by a belt hung with bags, from which protruded the handles of tools, bottlenecks and leek stalks. He knelt down in two stages.

We then tipped the load onto his shoulders. Little Paul stood open-mouthed, with clenched fists and his head sunk between his shoulders, as he watched the dreadful operation which he feared might make him lose his father. But Joseph was not crushed beneath his burden: we heard him buckling on the leather straps, and then the sack, very slowly at first, was lifted up. In the tense silence, one knee creaked, then the other, and Joseph stood up-right—an awe-inspiring sight.

He took a deep breath, drew back his shoulders a couple of times to settle the straps, and began to walk round the dining-room.

'It's perfect,' he said simply. Then, without the slightest hesitation, he went to pick up the two big suit-cases: they had been crammed so full that their sides had had to be reinforced with ropes encircling them three times. Their weight visibly stretched his arms which now seemed longer. Turning their tautness to account, he cleverly wedged his shot-gun (in its worn leatherette case) under one armpit and, under the other the naval spyglass, which must have suffered in hurricanes blowing round Cape Horn, for its lenses tinkled like jingle-bells.

*

It was rather difficult to get on to the back platform of the tram.

Nor was it easy to get off from it, and I can still see the tram-conductor with his hand impatiently on the leather thong of the bell while we laboriously got off.

Nevertheless, we were in a very happy mood, and our strength was redoubled at the sunny prospect of the seemingly endless Long Holidays before us. But from a distance, our procession looked so pathetic that passers-by offered us help: my father declined it, laughing, and broke into a little gallop to show that his strength far exceeded the weight of his burden. . . .

However, a genial carter, who was removing a whole houseful of furniture, stopped without a word, picked up my mother's two suit-cases and fastened them below his cart, where they swung rhythmically until we reached the colonel's front-gate.

Wladimir, who seemed to have been expecting us, first presented my mother with the ritual red roses, then told us that his master was obliged to keep to his room on account of a fresh attack of gout, but that he would soon pay us a surprise visit at the Bastide Neuve, which filled us with pleasure, pride and confusion. Then he took charge of all the packets and bundles which were not firmly fastened to whoever was carrying them, and walked ahead of us to Dominique's gate, beyond the 'Sleeping Beauty's Castle'.

The third property that we passed through seemed endless: Dominique wasn't there, and all the windows were closed.

We paused for a moment under the big fig-tree. My father, turning his back to the well, leaned his rucksack on its coping and, passing his hand under the straps, thoroughly massaged his shoulders. We set off again, refreshed.

At last we reached the black gate, the door of Fear and Freedom.

Once more we halted, in silence, to prepare ourselves for the ultimate effort.

'Joseph,' my mother said suddenly, and she was quite pale. 'I have a premonition!'

My father began to laugh:

'So have I!' he said. 'I have a premonition that we're going to have wonderful holidays! I have a premonition that we're going

308

to eat great spits laden with thrushes, *darnagas* and partridges! I have a premonition that the children will put on five pounds apiece! Come on, off we go! Nobody's said a word to us for the last six months. why should they say anything today?'

He injected the drop of oil, executed his usual manoeuvre, then opened the door wide and stooped to get his load through the doorway.

'Marcel,' he told me, 'give me your bags and go and scout ahead! We must take all possible precautions to reassure your mother. Walk quietly!'

I strode forward like a Sioux on the warpath, well covered by the hedgerow, to see how the land lay.

There was no sign of life. All the windows of the château were closed, even those in the keeper's apartment.

I summoned our party, who were waiting for my orders:

'Come quickly!' I whispered. 'The keeper's away!'

My father stepped forward, looked at the distant façade of the château, and said:

'Good Lord! So he is!'

'How do you know?' my mother remarked.

'It's natural enough, after all, for the man to leave the château now and then! He's all by himself: he's probably gone to do some shopping.'

'Well, I don't like the look of those closed windows. Perhaps he's hidden behind the shutters and is watching us through a hole.'

'Oh, come!' my father said. 'You have a morbid imagination. I bet you we could march along singing. But to spare your nerves, we'll play at Comanche Injuns "whose footsteps do not rouse so much as a rustle in the high prairie-grass".'

We walked with extreme caution and a wise stealthiness. My father, bowed down by the weight of his load, perspired dreadfully. Paul stopped to tie a handful of grass round the string of his parcel which was cutting his fingers. Our frightened little sister was as dumb as her doll.

From time to time, raising her tiny forefinger in front of her lips, she would utter a smiling 'Hu-u-ush!' with eyes like a scared rabbit. The wordless pallor of my mother cut me to the heart, but I could see in the distance, above the trees and beyond the walls, the blue peak of Tête-Rouge, where I would be setting my snares before nightfall, to the accompaniment of a solitary, chirping cicada; and I knew that at the foot of La Treille Lili was waiting for me with an air of indifference but bursting with news, plans and friendship.

CHAPTER THIRTY-ONE

THE long distance was covered without let or hindrance, if not without anguish, and at last we arrived at the ultimate door, the door that would open onto the summer holidays. My father turned to my mother, laughing:

'Well . . . what about your premonition?'

'Open it quickly, I beg of you. . . . Quickly . . . quickly. . . .'

'Don't be so nervous,' he said. 'You can see it's all over!'

He turned the key in the keyhole and pulled. The door resisted. He suddenly said in a toneless voice:

'Someone's put on a chain and a padlock!'

'I knew it!' my mother said. 'Can't you wrench it off?'

I had a look and saw that the chain went through two ring-bolts: one of them was screwed into the door, the other to the door-jamb, the wood of which, I thought, looked mouldy.

'Of course we can wrench it off!' I said.

But my father gripped my wrist and said in a low voice:

'Stop it! That would be trespassing with damage!'

'Trespassing!' a rasping voice suddenly shouted. 'Just so: trespass with damage! And that can mean three months in jail!'

From a tangle of bushes near the door, a man of medium height but enormous girth emerged. He was wearing a green uniform and a képi. From his belt hung a black leather holster from which protruded the grip of a regulation revolver. On a leash, at the end of a chain, he was holding a horrible dog, the very one that we had dreaded for so long.

It was a big, bovine beast with a bull-dog's head.

On his short hair, which was dirty yellow in colour, mange had left big pink blotches, which looked like maps. His left hind-leg, which twitched convulsively, was permanently off the ground; his thick chops drooped heavily and threads of slobber hanging from them made them seem even longer. On either side of his horrible snout two fangs stood out, ready to murder the innocent. Lastly, the monster had one dull glassy eye, while the other, abnormally dilated, glinted with yellow menace. A snorting, hissing breath issued at intervals from his dripping nostrils.

The man's face was just as terrifying. His nose was pitted with holes like a strawberry; his moustache, off-white at one end, was rusty-red at the other, and the lower rims of his eyes were studded with hairy little pimples.

My mother gave a moan of anguish, and hid her face in the trembling roses. My little sister began to cry. My father, his face drained of all colour, did not move: Paul hid behind his back, and I swallowed hard. . . .

The man was staring at us without a word; one could hear the mastiff snarling.

'Monsieur . . .,' my father said.

'What are you doing here?' the brute suddenly yelled. 'Who's allowed you to trespass on the Baron's land? Are you his guests, perhaps, or his relatives?'

He glared at each one of us in turn, with his popping, gleaming eyes.

Each time he spoke, his paunch shuddered, jerking the revolver upwards. He took a step towards my father.

'To begin with, what's your name?'

I quickly said: 'Esménard, Victor.'

'Be quiet,' said Joseph. 'This is no time for playing the fool.'

With great difficulty, laden as he was, he pulled out his wallet and handed over his card.

The brute looked at it, then turned to me:

'He's been well trained, that one has! He's got a false name pat on his tongue!'

He looked at the card again, and cried:

'A public school-teacher! That caps it! A schoolmaster who trespasses by stealth on other people's property! A schoolmaster! Anyway, that may not be true. If the children give a false name, the father may easily produce a false card!'

Joseph at last recovered his power of speech and began a long-winded plea. He spoke of the 'villa' (which he called a 'shack' for the occasion), of his children's health, the long walks which exhausted my mother, the School Inspector's sternness. . . . He was sincere and pathetic, but pitiful. My cheeks were burning, and I was seething with rage. He probably guessed my feelings for he said to me, in his dismay:

'Don't stay here. Go and play over there with your brother.'

'Play at what?' roared the keeper. 'At stealing my plums? Don't you move!' He turned towards me. 'Let this be a lesson to you!'

Then, turning towards my father:

'Now, what's this key? Did you *make* it?'

'No,' my father answered in a feeble voice.

The brute inspected the key, saw some mark or other on it, and cried:

'It's a government key! Have you stolen it?'

'Of course not.'

'Well?'

He looked at us with a sneer. My father hesitated, then said bravely:

'I found it.'

The other snickered even more openly:

'You found it lying in the road and you knew at once that it opened the lock of the canal gates. . . . Who gave it to you?'

'I can't tell you.'

'Aha! You refuse to answer! I'm making a note of it and it'll be in my report. The person who's lent you the key will probably have no more opportunities of coming through this estate.'

'No,' my father said hotly, 'no, that you mustn't do! You're not going to ruin the position of a man who, out of kindness, out of pure friendship . . .'

'He's an official with no sense of duty!' the keeper shouted. 'I've seen him stealing my figs a dozen times. . . .'

'You must be mistaken,' my father retorted. 'I have reason to believe that he is a perfectly honest man!'

'He's proved it,' the keeper sneered, 'by giving you a key that belongs to a public service!'

'There's something you don't know,' my father said. 'He's done it in the interest of the canal. I've some knowledge of cement and mortars, which enables me to contribute, to some extent, to the upkeep of this important work. Have a look at this note-book.'

The keeper took it and turned the pages.

'So you pretend you're here as a specialist?'

'In a way,' said my father.

'What about them?' said the brute, pointing to us. 'Are they specialists too? I've never yet seen specialists of that age! But what I can see, anyway, because it's written in this note-book, is that you've been fraudulently walking through this estate every Saturday for six months. An excellent piece of evidence!'

He put the note-book in his pocket.

'And now, open up all those parcels!'

'No,' said my father. 'They're my personal belongings.'

'You dare to refuse? Mind what you're doing. I'm a sworn keeper.'

My father pondered for a second, then put his rucksack down and opened it.

'If you'd persisted in your refusal, I'd have gone and fetched the *gendarmes*.'

We had to open the suit-cases, empty the haversacks, unroll the bundles, and this exhibition lasted almost a quarter of an hour. At last, all our poor treasures were spread out on the grassy slope, like the prizes of a fair-ground shooting-booth. . . . The salt-cellar glistened, the little dancer raised her leg, and the big alarm-clock, like the loyal recorder of the stars' course that it was, impartially announced it was ten past four even to the stupid brute who was distrustfully eyeing it.

It was a long and minute review.

The plentiful food aroused jealousy in his paunchy stomach.

'One would think that you'd burgled a grocery,' he said suspiciously.

He then inspected the bed-linen, the blankets, with the sternness of a Spanish customs official.

'And now the gun!' he said.

He had kept that as a special treat for the end: as he opened the tattered gun-case, he asked:

'Is it loaded?'

'No,' said my father.

'That's lucky for you.'

The keeper breeched the barrel and lifted it to his eyes like a telescope.

'It's clean,' he said. 'That's lucky for you too.'

He snapped the weapon shut with the click of a rat-trap, and added:

'With this kind of blunderbuss it's easy to miss a partridge, but quite possible to slug a keeper. An unsuspecting keeper. . . .'

He scowled at us sombrely, and I saw with horrid clearness a bottomless imbecility. When later, at college, I first came across Baudelaire's phrase about 'bull-browed stupidity', I thought of him. All he lacked was horns. But I hope, for the honour of womankind, that he was given them.

Suddenly assuming an engaging air, he asked:

'Where are the cartridges?'

'I haven't got them yet,' my father said. 'I only make them just before the start of the shooting season. I don't like to have loaded cartridges at home, because of the children.'

'Naturally,' said the keeper, glaring at me. 'When a child is capable of giving a false name and shows a disposition towards housebreaking, a loaded rifle is the last thing to leave lying about!'

I was rather proud of his estimate of me. For the last ten minutes I had been thinking of taking a jump at his belt, snatching his revolver and pleasurably killing him. Had it not been for that huge cur which would have made just one mouthful of me, I swear I would have had a try.

He returned the gun to my father and cast a roving glance over our scattered belongings.

'I didn't know there was so much money to be made in teaching!'

My father earned 150 francs a month. But he took advantage of this remark to say:

'That's why I'd like to remain in the profession.'

'If you're dismissed, you'll only have yourself to blame,' said the keeper. 'I can't do anything about it! And now collect your stuff and go back the way you came. I'll go and make my report while it's still fresh. Come on, Mastoc!'

He pulled at the leash and dragged the monster away; it turned its eyes towards us, snarling desperately, as if it was sorry not to have mauled us to death.

At that moment, the bell of the alarm-clock exploded like a display of fireworks: my mother uttered a feeble cry and sank down on the grass. I dashed forward; she fainted in my arms. The keeper, who had reached the bottom of the grassy slope, turned round and, seeing the scene, said with a merry laugh:

'Well played, but it doesn't bamboozle me!'

Then he shambled away unsteadily, tugging at the beast that so closely resembled him.

★

My mother soon came round. While Joseph was massaging her, the tears and kisses of her little boys worked as quickly as Epsom salts.

We then noticed that our baby sister had disappeared. She had hidden herself in the brambles like a terrified mouse; she didn't answer our calls and stayed motionless on her knees, with her hands over her eyes.

Afterwards we packed our parcels up again, stowing away at random the sausage, the cakes of soap, the dishes, and my father said quietly:

'You are so weak when you're in the wrong! This keeper is an unspeakable swine and a coward of the worst kind. But he had the law on his side, and I was bound and gagged by my imposture. Everything about me was tainted with guilt: my wife, my children, my key. . . . This hasn't been a good start to the holidays. What sort of an ending will they have, I wonder ?'

'Joseph,' my mother said, suddenly rallying, 'this isn't the end of the world, after all!'

Then my father uttered this sibylline sentence:

'As long as I'm a teacher, we are on holiday. But if I'm no longer one in a week's time, I'll be out of work. . . .'

And he tightened the straps of his rucksack on his shoulders.

CHAPTER THIRTY-TWO

IT was a lugubrious return. Our parcels had been fastened in a hurry, and various objects dropped out of them. As I was at the tail-end, I picked up from the grass a comb, a jar of mustard, a file, a skimming-ladle, a tooth-brush.

From time to time, my mother said softly:

'I knew it.'

'No, you didn't,' my father replied fractiously. 'You didn't know, but you feared it. And you had reason to fear it, although it could have happened at any other time. This has nothing to do with mysteries or premonitions, but merely with stupidity on my part, and cruelty on the part of that idiot.'

And he kept on repeating: 'You're so weak when you're in the wrong.'

Life has taught me that he was mistaken, and that you're weak when you are pure in heart.

We arrived in front of the first gate on our way back, and were faced with a new catastrophe: Joseph had, as usual, carefully locked all the doors behind us; but the key, the key to our holidays and to our misfortunes, was now in the pocket of the pitiless keeper....

Joseph put his parcels down and examined the wall. It was too high to be climbed, and all along its top the bits of broken bottles were sparkling cruelly....

For a moment we were in despair.

Then my father opened one of the pockets of his haversack and pulled a pair of wire-nippers from it. He looked gloomy but determined, and we watched him in silence, dimly aware that he was shouldering a grave responsibility.

And, indeed, he stepped down from the embankment, walked into the vineyard and, coolly and unhurriedly, cut off a length of wire that upheld the young shoots. He bent it into a kind of small hook. On his face there clearly showed the resolution and revolt of someone who has nothing more to lose and who is so dishonoured that nothing can add to his disgrace.

He went back to the door, inserted the hook into the keyhole, closed his eyes and bent forward to bring his ear closer to the guilty 'click' of his picklock. . . . It was the first time that I saw a burglar in action, and this criminal was my father!

At last, after some three dozen ineffective 'clicks' and just as Joseph was beginning to lose his nerve, there was a loud and happy 'clack!' and the forced door opened to let us pass.

We had rushed through before him.

'That isn't all!' he said. 'We must lock it again!'

He worked for a few more minutes, and then the lock clicked shut again.

Joseph now got up, and his puckered face broke into a smile at last, as if his guilt had been wiped out for good now that everything was back in its place.

Stoutheartedly, we marched towards the next gate. But as this opened on to Dominique's friendly domain, my father's hand did not tremble, and he picked the lock most elegantly. It even seemed to me that Joseph was quite proud of his burgling skill, for he winked at us gaily and aggravated it by a cynical grin. Then he said:

'I consider that we have acted in legitimate self-defence. The keeper had a right to indict us, but not to pass sentence on us. . . . Let's go and tell our story to Dominique: I think he may give us sound advice.'

We arrived at Dominique's place, impatient to tell him of our tragedy: the shutters of the lodge were still closed. He was probably in the village, having a game of bowls. But at the colonel's château we found Wladimir. He listened to my father's story—in a suitably abridged version—and said:

'Personally, I wouldn't mind going to see the fellow, but I've spoken to him three times in my life, and three times I've hit him. If I go, I'll hit him again, so it would be better to have a talk to my colonel. As bad luck would have it, he's at the clinic. Yes, he forbade me to tell you, but now I *am* telling you. They've performed an operation on him. Tomorrow morning I'm going to see him and, if he's well enough, I'll tell him. . . . But I don't know if he'll be able to do anything. . . .'

'But the other landlord is a nobleman too! He's a baron. . . .'

'No, that's just it!' Wladimir said. 'My colonel says it isn't true and that his name is Canasson.* It appears he is a big cattle-dealer. . . . One day, as he was coming out of mass, at La Valentine, the man came up and introduced himself, saying: "I am the Baron of Les Acates." And his lordship the Count replied: "I thought you were a Baron of Beef." And the man went away without a word.'

'Then I have no hope left,' Joseph said.

'Now, now,' said Wladimir, 'you mustn't take on so. Come and have a drink. No, no, I insist! It'll cheer you up!'

He forced my father and my mother to drink a small glass of brandy which they gulped down heroically like medicine, then he brought a cup of cocoa for Paul and me, while our little sister happily drank a glass of milk.

We set off again, physically restored, but in great distress of mind. My father, much warmed by the two sips of alcohol and conditioned by the rucksack, walked with a military gait, but his eyes gazed gloomily out of an impassive face.

My mother seemed to me to be as lightfooted as a bird. Paul and I were dragging our little sister along, her small, rather disjointed arms keeping us to the straight path. We had to take the enormous detour and, throughout the whole journey, nobody said a single word.

Lili had not been able, in his impatience, to stick to his post at the foot of La Treille. He had come to meet us, and we found him at La Croix.

* French for broken-down hack.

He clasped my hand, kissed Paul, then, blushing, took my mother's parcels. He seemed in a festive mood, but suddenly began to look perturbed and asked me under his breath:

'What's the matter?'

I motioned him to be quiet and slowed down to put some distance between us and my father who was walking as if in a dream.

Then, in an undertone, I told him of the tragedy. He did not seem to attach great importance to it, but when I came to the official report he grew pale and stopped in alarm:

'He took it all down in his note-book?'

'He said he would, and I'm sure he did.'

He whistled through his teeth for a while. To be reported by an official was, to the people of the village, tantamount to dishonour and ruin. A *gendarme* from Aubagne had been killed in the hills by a farmer—quite a decent, law-abiding fellow—for no other reason than that he was going to report him.

'Well!' Lili said, appalled. 'Well!'

He walked on again, with lowered head, and from time to time he turned a distressed face towards me.

As we passed the letter-box on our way through the village, he suddenly said:

'Supposing we talked to the postman about it? He must know that keeper. And besides, he wears a képi too!'

To his mind this was the symbol of power, and he imagined that things could be ironed out between képis. He added:

'I'll talk to to him tomorrow morning.'

We reached the *Bastide* at last: it was waiting for us in the twilight, under the big fig-tree which was alive with sparrows.

We helped my father to undo all the parcels. He was gloomy, and cleared his throat from time to time. My mother silently cooked the gruel for our little sister, while Lili lit the fire underneath the cooking-pot which hung from the chimney.

I went outside to look at the garden. Paul had already climbed into an olive-tree, and cicadas were chirping in all his pockets, but the beauty of the evening wrung my heart: nothing was left of all the delights I had promised myself.

Lili came to join me and said in a low voice: 'I must talk to my father about it.'

I saw him go off, with his hands in his pockets, through Orgnon's vineyard.

I went back into the house and lit the paraffin-lamp (the Matador burner), for nobody had thought of it. My father had sat down by the fireplace despite the warmth and was gazing into the dancing flames. Soon the soup began to simmer, and the omelette sizzled. Paul came to help me lay the table. We attended to this ritual operation with great care, to show our parents that all wasn't lost, but we only talked in whispers, as if there were a corpse in the house.

During dinner my father suddenly began to chat away gaily. He described the scene to us most amusingly, drew a funny portrait of the keeper, of our belongings strewn on the grass, and of the dog which had been dying to devour the sausage. Paul laughed immoderately, but I could very well see that my father was making an effort for us, and I felt like crying.

CHAPTER THIRTY-THREE

DINNER was soon over, and we went upstairs to bed. Our parents remained downstairs to finish storing away our provisions.

But I did not hear them move: only the murmur of muffled voices.

After a quarter of an hour I saw that Paul was asleep; I noiselessly walked down the stairs again barefoot and eavesdropped on their conversation.

'You're exaggerating, Joseph, you're being ridiculous. They're not going to chop your head off, after all.'

'Certainly not,' my father admitted. 'But you don't know the School Inspector. He'll forward the report to the *Recteur* and it may well end in a dismissal.'

'Oh come! There's nothing much *to* it!'

'Perhaps not, but certainly enough to get a teacher a reprimand. And a reprimand for me is tantamount to dismissal, for I'd resign. You don't remain in the teaching profession when you've got a reprimand hanging round your neck!'

'What?' cried my mother, amazed. 'You'd give up your pension?'

There had often been talk of the pension: rather as if it were a magic wand which transformed a schoolmaster into a *rentier*. The pension was a great word, a key-word. But that evening it made no impression, and my father sadly shrugged his shoulders.

'But what are you going to do, then?'

'I don't know, but I'll think about it.'

'You might become a private tutor. Monsieur Vernet lives quite comfortably by giving lessons.'

'Yes, but *he* hasn't incurred a reprimand. He took his proportional pension after a brilliant career. . . . It's not the same with me! If the parents of my new pupils learned of my reprimand, they'd give me the sack!'

I was appalled by this line of argument which seemed to me irrefutable. What *was* he going to do? He soon told my mother.

'I'll go and see Raspagnetto, who has a big trade in potatoes. We went to school together. He said to me one day: "You used to be good at figures. And my business is getting so big I could use a man like you." He's a fellow to whom I could explain matters, he wouldn't look down on me.'

I at once blessed the name of Raspagnetto. I didn't know him, but I could see him distinctly: a kind giant with a black moustache, completely stumped by multiplication-tables—as I was—and handing over to my father the key to a drawer filled with gold.

'You can't always count on friends,' my mother opined.

'I know. But Raspagnetto owes me a lot. I helped him with his maths in School Certificate. What's more, I want you to stop worrying. I've never told you but I have some railway debentures: seven hundred and eighty francs worth. They're in the Vidal-Lablache atlas.'

'It isn't possible!' my mother exclaimed. 'So you've been hiding things from me?'

'Well, yes. I put them away for a rainy day—an operation, an illness. . . . I did it with the best intentions: I wouldn't like you to think. . . .'

'Don't apologize,' she said, 'because I've done the same thing. But I only have two hundred and ten francs. It's all I was able to save on the five francs you've given me every morning.'

I immediately did some totting up: 780 plus 210, that made 990 francs. I thought I had seven francs in my money-box and I knew, despite Paul's secretiveness, that he had at least four francs. So the total came to one thousand and one francs.

I felt reassured at once, and had a strong urge to come forward and say that there was no need to look for a job when one owned more than A Thousand Francs.

But the sand-man had gone by and thrown a big handful in my direction. I climbed the stairs on all fours and immediately fell asleep.

CHAPTER THIRTY-FOUR

NEXT morning I did not see my father: he was in town. I supposed he had gone to see his potato friend, whose name I had forgotten. My mother was singing as she tidied up the house.

Lili arrived very late, not before nine.

He informed me that he had told his father everything, and that his father had said:

'I know that keeper. He's the one who denounced Mond des Parpaillouns to the Customs people, because Mond had hidden four thrushes in his bowler-hat. They made him pay four francs. If he ever ventures into our hills, he won't have to wait long for the gun-shot that's coming to him.'

This was comforting news, but the gun-shot would come too late.

'Have you talked to the postman?'

Lili seemed ill at ease.

'Yes,' he said. 'The fact is that he knew about it already, because he had seen the keeper this morning.'

'Where?'

'At the château. He went to deliver letters there.'

'And what did he tell him?'

'The lot.'

He made an effort to go on:

'He was busy writing his Official Report.'

This was dreadful news.

'So the postman told him not to do it, and the keeper said to him: "I won't deny myself the pleasure!" and so the postman asks him: "Why ?", and so the keeper says that schoolmasters are people who have holidays all the time, so the postman tells him that your father is the one who shot the *bartavelles*, and so the keeper says: "I don't care a damn" and then he went on with his report, and the postman says he could see he was thoroughly enjoying himself.'

This account filled me with dismay.

Lili then pulled two fine, rosy sausages from his bundle. This rather surprised me, but he at once explained:

'These are poisonous sausages. My father makes them to put round the chicken-run at night, because of the foxes. If you like, tonight we'll go and throw them over the wall of the château. . . .'

'Do you want to poison his dog ?'

'And him too, perhaps,' Lili suggested kindly. 'I've chosen the best so as to tempt him. If he takes just one bite, he'll fall down stiff as the law.'

This was a most attractive idea, and it made me laugh with pleasure. But the keeper's death, which could not be effective before the day after tomorrow (provided we had any luck and he hadn't), would not stop the report reaching its destination. Nevertheless we decided to hurl the avenging sausages over the wall that very night.

In the meantime, we went to set our snares in the Rapon valley, and then went picking green almonds and sorb-apples from the gnarled trees in a forgotten orchard till noon.

The first visit to our snares brought us six sandpipers and a big Corsican blackbird.

I emptied our two haversacks on the kitchen-table, spread out the birds, and said casually:

'What with game, almonds, sorb-apples, wild asparagus, and mushrooms, a poor family could live the whole year round.'

My mother smiled tenderly, came over and kissed my brow, while keeping her arms well away, because her hands were covered in lather.

'Don't worry, you big silly!' she said. 'We haven't come to that yet!'

*

Lili lunched with us and—supreme honour—was set in my father's place, since the latter was not due to come back before evening.

I talked of the farmer's life and declared that, if I were my father, I'd turn my hand to farming. Lili—who, to my mind, was very knowledgeable on the subject—extolled the chick-pea for its frugal and prolific habits, for it requires neither water nor manure, nor even earth, but feeds on air. He then praised the amazing rate at which early beans grow.

'You dig a small hole, you put the bean at the bottom, you cover it up, and then you run away: if you don't, it catches up with you.'

He cast a glance at my mother, and added:

'Of course, I'm exaggerating a little, but what I mean is that it's a fast grower.'

At two o'clock we left on our expedition once more, accompanied by Paul, who was a specialist in extracting the snails that hide in the holes of old walls or in the stumps of olive-trees. We worked without stopping for three hours, to pile up provisions so as to cope with our imminent ruin. About six we turned towards home, laden with almonds, snails, sloes, fine blue plums stolen from Master Etienne's, and a haversack full of almost ripe apricots, picked from a very old tree which had doggedly gone on flowering for the past fifty years among the lonely ruins of an abandoned farm.

I was looking forward to presenting all this booty to my mother, when I saw that she was not alone; she was sitting on the terrace, opposite my father, who was pouring a jet of water straight into his mouth from a porous earthenware crock which he held above his upturned face.

I ran towards him.

He seemed dead-tired, and his shoes were covered with dust. He kissed us tenderly, stroked Lili's cheek, and took my baby sister on his knee. Then he spoke to my mother, as if we weren't there.

'I went to see Bouzigue. He wasn't in. I left a note for him, telling him of the catastrophe. Then I went to the clinic, I met Wladimir there. The colonel has had his operation, no visitors are allowed. In four or five days one may talk to him. It'll be too late.'

'Did you see the School Inspector?'

'No,' my father said. 'But I saw his secretary.'

'You didn't tell her?'

'No. She thought I had come for news, and she informed me that I'd been promoted to third-grade.'

He gave a bitter laugh.

'That would have meant how much more?'

'Twenty-two francs per month.'

At the mention of this enormous figure, my mother made a little grimace as if she were on the point of crying.

'And what's more,' he added, 'what's more, she told me that I was going to get the *palmes*!'

'Look here, Joseph,' my mother cried, 'one surely can't dismiss a civil servant who's been awarded the *palmes académiques*!'

'One can always cancel the promotion of a civil servant who's been reprimanded. . . .' my father said.

He heaved a deep sigh, then went and slumped down on a chair, with lowered head, and his hands on his knees. Little Paul began to cry noisily.

At this moment, Lili whispered:

'Who's that coming over there?'

At the far end of the white road, above Le Collet, I could see a dark figure briskly striding towards us.

'It's Monsieur Bouzigue!' I cried.

I dashed to meet him. Lili raced after me.

CHAPTER THIRTY-FIVE

W E met the canal-pricker halfway, but I saw he was looking beyond us. My father and mother had followed on our heels. Bouzigue was grinning. He thrust his hand into his pocket and said:

'Here, that's for you!'

He held out to my father the black note-book which the keeper had confiscated. My mother uttered a gasp which was almost a cry.

'He gave it to you?' she asked.

'He didn't *give* it,' said Bouzigue. 'He bartered it for my official report on him.'

'What about *his* report?' my father asked, a little hoarsely.

'Confetti!' answered Bouzigue. 'He'd written five pages. I turned them into a handful of confetti and the canal carried them away. . . . At this moment,' he added pensively, and as if the matter were of some importance, 'they must be somewhere near Saint-Loup, or perhaps already as far as La Pomme. . . . And so,' he ended, 'let's have a drink!'

He winked once or twice, dug his fists into his hips, and burst out laughing. What a beautiful sight he made! . . . All at once I could hear two thousand cicadas and from the enchanted stubble-fields rose the sounds of the first holiday cricket filing down a silver rod.

We had no wine at home, and my mother did not want to

touch Uncle Jules' sacrosanct bottles; but in her bedroom cupboard she kept a bottle of *pernod* for alcoholic visitors.

Under the fig-tree, Bouzigue helped himself to a big tot and told us of his interview with the enemy.

'As soon as I'd read your note this morning, I went to fetch reinforcements: Binucci, who is a canal-pricker, same as me, and Fénestrelle, the turncock. Off we went to the château. When I tried to open the famous door—oh! Mother of God be praised!—I saw he hadn't removed the chain, nor the padlock! So we went round to the main gate, and I rang that damned bell like a sexton. After fully five minutes, he came stalking up, furious.

' "Are you mad to go pulling the bell like that? You, of all people!" he says as he opens the gate.

' "Why me?"

' "Because you've got something coming to you, and I'm going to have a few words with you."

' "Well," says I, "you'll talk after, because what I have to say to you is just two words. And maybe only one even, because there's a hyphen in the middle. And that word is: *procès-verbal*."

'So he opened his eyes as wide as saucers. Yes, even the other eye, the one that goes blinkety-blink.

' "Let's proceed to the premises first," says Fénestrelle. "We must verify the facts on the spot, obtain a confession, impound the chain and the padlock."

' "What?" cries the keeper, dumbfounded.

' "Don't shout!" I tell him. "You are scaring us!"

'And we walk in.

' "I'm the one who wants to talk to *you* about that padlock!" he says.

' "Did *you* put it there?"

' "Yes, I did. And d'you know why?"

' "No. Nor do I need to know to draw up my report on you."

' "Clause eighty-two of the Agreement," says Fénestrelle.

'He glanced at our three Peaked Caps, and he was begin-

331

ning to look scared. So Binucci says, in a conciliatory sort of way:

' "Don't get the wind up, though. It won't go up to the assizes. Just the police tribunal, that's all. It'll fetch a fine of two hundred francs or so."

'At that I said curtly:

' "Never mind what it'll fetch. The evidence is what *I'm* going to fetch!"

'And off I go towards the canal-gate. The others follow me, and the keeper hobbles behind.

'While I was wrenching off the chain, he was as red as a raspberry. I whip out my note-book and I says:

' "Your name, Christian name, place of birth."

'He says to me: "You aren't going to do that to me!"

' "And why," says Fénestrelle, "why are *you* obstructing our right of way?"

' "It wasn't meant for you," the keeper says.

'So I say: "Of course, it wasn't meant for those gentlemen, but for me! I know very well you can't stand the sight of me! Well, I can't stand the sight of you, and that's why I'm going through with this!"

' "Through with what?" he says.

' "You've tried to make me lose my job. Well, it's just too bad, but you're going to lose yours! When your boss receives the legal summons, when he has to go to the Law Courts, he'll realize perhaps that he'd be well-advised to change his keeper, and I only hope the next one will be more civilized!"

'He was as white as a sheet, my friends. So I go on:

' "Name, Christian names, place of birth."

' "But I swear it wasn't meant for you! I only did it to catch some people who come through the estate with a false key!"

'So I make a terrible face and I say:

' "Oho! A false key? Binucci, you hear that? A false key!"

' "Look here it is!"

'And with that he takes it out of his pocket. I grab it right away and I say to Fénestrelle:

' "Keep this, we'll investigate, because this is a matter that concerns the Canal. And did you catch these people?"

' "Of course," he says. "Here, that's the note-book I found on the culprit, here's my note to your Corporation, and here's my official report!"

'And he hands me your note-book and two reports several pages long, telling the whole story.

'I began to read his scribble, and all of a sudden I said:

' "You fool! You wretched fool! You've admitted in an official report that you affixed a chain and padlock! But don't you realize that, in the reign of our good King Louis XIV, you would've been sent to the galleys?"

'Binucci says:

' "T'aint exactly suicide but there's not much difference."

'The keeper was a sorry sight. He didn't look like a raspberry any more, he looked like a turnip. He says to me:

' "So what are you going to do?"

"I shake my head a few times, biting my lip. I consult Fénestrelle, then Binucci, then my conscience. He was waiting, with a wicked look, but scared. At last I say:

' "Now listen: this is the first time, but let it be the last. . . . Let's say no more about it. And above all, not a word to anybody if you prize your peaked cap!"

'Then I tore up his reports and I put the note-book in my pocket, with the chain and the padlock. I thought they were the kind of things that might come in handy in the country!'

And he placed his booty on the table.

We were all delirious with joy, and Bouzigue agreed to stay and dine with us.

As he unfolded his napkin, he declared:

'All this is dead and buried now. Still, it might be better not to go that way again in future.'

'It's out of the question!' my father said.

My mother, who was easing the small birds off the spit, said in a whisper:

'Even if we had permission, I'd never have the courage to set eyes on that place again. I think I'd faint.'

Lili took his leave and my mother kissed him: his ears turned as red as a cock's comb, and he ran quickly out of the dining-room: I had to run after him to tell him that I would be expecting him at daybreak next morning. He nodded a quick 'yes' and fled into the summer night.

CHAPTER THIRTY-SIX

I T was a very gay meal. When my mother apologized for not offering him any wine, Bouzigue declared:
'Never mind. I'll stick to *pernod.*'
My father ventured, with some diffidence:
'I wouldn't like you to think I'm begrudging you the spirits you mean to drink. But I don't know whether, for your health's sake. . . .'
'My health!' Bouzigue exclaimed. 'But my dear Monsieur Joseph, this is just what does it least harm! You're drinking water from the cistern here. Do you even know what's in it?'
'Rainwater,' my father said. 'Water distilled by the sun.'
'I bet you,' said Bouzigue, 'that I'd find in your cistern a dozen black spiders, two or three lizards, and at least two toads. . . . Cistern-water is concentrated toad-piss! Whereas *pernod* neutralizes the lot!'
My father gave up.
During dinner, he related our adventure in detail, and Bouzigue replied by going over his exploit once again. Then my father added fresh details to demonstrate the fierceness displayed by the keeper; this Bouzigue countered by stressing the scoundrel's fright and humility, as he stood in terror of the Three Képis. By the time they reached the fourth verson of their antiphony, my father disclosed that the keeper had only just failed to shoot us down on the spot, and Bouzigue described the monster crawling on his knees, with tears pouring down his face and whimpering for mercy in a childish quaver.

335

After the baked custard tart, 'floating islands' and biscuits, Bouzigue, as if inspired, began to tell the tale of his sister's exploits.

He started by comparing life to a mountain-torrent which you must ford by skipping from rock to rock after 'carefully calculating your leap'.

Félicienne, he told us, had first married a 'professional' *boules* player, who often left home to go and win competitions, and it was in this connection that I learnt the word '*cocu*'. From there she had skipped to the next boulder, in the shape of the superintendent of a tram depot, then to a stationer in the Rue de Rome, then to a florist in the Canebière, who was a municipal councillor, and thence, at last, to the councillor general. She was at that very moment contemplating a last leap which would carry her right to the other shore, into the arms of the Departmental Prefect.

My mother listened with interest to the account of this crossing, but she seemed a little surprised. She suddenly said:

'But are men really so stupid?'

'Ho! Ho!' Bouzigue exclaimed. 'They aren't stupid at all, only she knows her onions!'

He added that, anyway, 'brains wasn't everything', and that she 'had a hell of a balcony' which had to be seen to be believed! He pulled out his wallet to show us a photograph which he pronounced to be 'mighty juicy'.

Paul and I were goggle-eyed with expectancy: but at the very moment when he produced this interesting document, my mother took us by the hand and led us up to our room.

The abundance of the meal, the joy I felt at the keeper's inglorious defeat, and the mystery of that photograph troubled my sleep at first. I had a somewhat incoherent dream: a young woman, as naked as a statue, was leaping across the canal at a single bound and landed on top of a general, who looked like my father and exploded with a resounding 'pop'.

I woke up, rather bewildered, and heard my father's voice through the floor-boards. It was saying:

336

'It's most regrettable that vice is all too often rewarded in this world of ours, if you don't mind my saying so.'

Bouzigue's voice, which had assumed an odd nasal twang, answered him:

'Joseph, Joseph, you're shattering me heart. . . .'

CHAPTER THIRTY-SEVEN

TIME passes and turns the wheel of life, as water turns the mill-wheels.

Five years later, I was walking behind a black carriage, whose wheels were so high that I could see the horses' hooves. I was dressed in black, and young Paul's hand was gripping mine with all its strength. My mother was being borne away for ever.

I have no other memory of that dreadful day, as if the fifteen-year old that I was refused to admit a grief so overwhelming that it could have killed me. For years, in fact until we reached manhood, we never had the courage to speak of her.

Then little Paul grew very tall. He had outgrown me by a whole head and he wore a beard, a silky, burnished frill, but he had kept the bright blue eyes of childhood and its sunny smile. . . .

Along the hills of L'Etoile, which he couldn't bear to leave, he drove his herd of goats; and every night he would go to sleep on the pebbly ground of the *garrigues*, rolled in his woollen cloak, with the he-goat's rope tied to his foot. He would rise when day rose, and the weight of sleep would leave on his cheek the imprint of some juniper-seeds or the pattern of a spike of lavender: he was the last of Virgil's goat-herds.

I often went to see him in his kingdom, and a passing farmer would tell me:

'He'll be at Passe-Temps today, because the *mistral's* blowing, or perhaps over at Escaouprès.'

At other times, some poacher would have lunched with him among the ruins of Baptiste's Pen and seen him leave in the direction of Baume-Sourne. I would look for him on the plateaux, in the ravines or gorges, guided sometimes by the distant sound of his mouth-organ, more often, in Spring, by the smell of the billy-goat, and always by my brotherly affection—a surer guide than a dowsing-rod. . . .

I brought him things from the city: a leather belt, a water bottle, a pipe, a watch, a shepherd's knife. Then, by way of thanks, he would tell me the names of the plants, the springs, the stars, and challenge the echoes by name. . . .

But at the age of thirty he died in a clinic. On his bedside table lay his mouth-organ.

My dear Lili did not walk at my side as I accompanied him to the little graveyard at La Treille, for he had been waiting for him there for years, under a carpet of immortelles humming with bees; during the war of 1914, in a black northern forest, a bullet in the forehead cut short his young life, and he had sunk, under the falling rain, on a tangle of chilly plants whose names he did not even know. . . .

Such is the life of man. A few joys, quickly obliterated by unforgettable sorrows.

There is no need to tell the children so.

CHAPTER THIRTY-EIGHT

ANOTHER ten years, and I founded a film company in Marseilles. The venture was crowned with success, and I was ambitious to build a 'Film City' under the sky of Provence; an estate agent set to work, trying to find a 'domain' big enough to accommodate this grand project.

He found what I wanted while I was away in Paris, and informed me of his 'find' by telephone. But he also told me that the deal had to be closed in a matter of hours, because there were other prospective buyers.

He was most enthusiastic and as I knew him to be an honest fellow, I bought the property without having seen it.

A week later, a small caravan of cars set out from the Prado studios, carrying the sound engineers, cameramen and laboratory technicians. We were going to take possession of the promised land, and during the drive everyone talked at once.

We passed through a very tall gate, which stood wide open for us.

At the bottom of an avenue of ancient plane-trees, the procession stopped in front of a château. It wasn't an historical monument, but the vast residence of some great bourgeois of the Second Empire: he must have been pretty proud of the four octagonal turrets and the thirty carved stone balconies which adorned both façades. . . .

We immediately walked down towards the meadows, where I intended to build the studios.

There I found some men already busy unwinding surveyors' chains, others driving white-painted stakes into the ground, and I was watching, not without pride, the birth of a great enterprise when I saw in the distance, on top of an embankment, a hedgerow of shrubs. . . . My breath stopped, and without knowing why, I made a wild dash through the meadow and through time.

Yes, it was there. It *was* the canal of my childhood, with its hawthorn bushes, its clematis, its dog-roses laden with white blossoms, its brambles which hid their claws under big-grained blackberries. . . .

The water flowed soundlessly, eternally, all along the grassy path and the grasshoppers of my youth splashed like puddles all round my feet. I slowly walked again along our holiday road, and beloved shadows were walking at my side.

Only when I caught a glimpse of it through the hedge above the distant plane-trees, did I recognize the horrible château, the Castle of Fear, the castle that had so frightened my mother.

For a second or two I hoped that I might come across the keeper and the dog. But twenty years had gone by and consumed my vengeance: for villains too must die.

I followed the canal bank: it was still 'a sieve', but little Paul was no longer there to laugh about it, with his sparkling milk-teeth. . . .

A voice called me from a distance. I hid behind a hedge, and advanced slowly, soundlessly, as I had in the old days. . . .

At last I saw the boundary wall: beyond the broken glass along its crest, the sunny month of June was dancing on the blue hills; but at the foot of the wall, quite close to the canal, was the dreadful black door, the door that had refused to swing open on the holidays, the door that had humbled my father. . . .

In an upsurge of blind rage I picked up a big stone in both my hands and, first raising it high in the sky, I hurled it at the rotten planks, which came crashing down on the past.

It seemed to me that I was breathing more freely, that the evil spell was broken.

But in the shelter of the dog-rose bush under the cluster of white blooms, on the far bank of Time, a very young, dark-haired woman had been cowering for years, clutching the colonel's red roses to her fragile heart. She was listening to the keeper's shouts and the dog's hoarse wheezing. Pallid, trembling, and for ever inconsolable, she did not know she was at last safe at home, in her own castle, on the land of her son.